MOUNT LU REVISITED

MOUNT LU REVISITED

Buddhism in the Life and Writings of Su Shih

BEATA GRANT

HAWAI

UNIVERSITY OF HAWAII PRESS / HONOLULU

94 95 96 97 98 99   5 4 3 2 1

Library of Congress Cataloging-in-Publication Data
Grant, Beata, 1954–
Mount Lu revisited : Buddhism in the life and writings of Su Shih
/ Beata Grant.
p.   cm.
Includes bibliographical references and index.
ISBN 0-8248-1625-0
1.   Su, Shih, 1037–1101—Knowledge—Buddhism.   2.   Buddhism in
literature.   I.   Title.
PL2685.Z5G73   1994
895.1'142—dc20   94-9955
CIP

Designed by Kenneth Miyamoto

CONTENTS

ACKNOWLEDGMENTS

IT WOULD be difficult to mention by name all of the people to whom I owe heartfelt *gassho*s of gratitude. There are a few, however, whom I simply cannot let pass without more formal acknowledgment. I am particularly grateful to Hilda Chen-Apuy, who opened her home and her library of books on Asia to me so many years ago; to the late James J. Y. Liu, who carefully nourished my love of Chinese poetry; and to Chou Hsien-shen of Peking University, with whom I spent many happy and fruitful hours reading and discussing Su Shih's writings. I am also deeply grateful to Ronald Egan, who knows Su Shih even better than I do, and who has been extremely generous with both scholarly advice and moral encouragement. I am thankful for the suggestions and patient support tendered by my colleagues at Washington University, in particular Professors George Hatch, Robert Hegel, Robert Morrell, and James Shih. I have also benefited greatly from the expertise of Robert Gimello and Miriam Levering who steered me away from some of the more dangerous pitfalls that await a student of literature who dares venture into Buddhological terrain. Working with Sharon Yamamoto and Cheri Dunn of the University of Hawaii Press has been a pleasure, and, as someone who can edit everyone's work but her own, I am endlessly grateful for the editorial expertise of Susan Stone. My largest debt of gratitude, however, must surely go to my parents who, although they may not have fully comprehended why I lavished so much energy on such a seemingly obscure topic, have supported me from beginning to end. I dedicate this book to them.

1. Prologue

Su Shih (1037–1101) was unquestionably one of the most extraordinary men ever to grace the world of Chinese arts and letters. He was not only a great poet and writer but also a major political figure of the Northern Sung dynasty (960–1126) and, like many of his contemporaries, a painter and calligrapher of considerable merit. However, as a recent Su Shih scholar has rightly pointed out, Su's greatness lies not so much in his achievements as in his seemingly endless capacity for "responding critically and perceptively to the broadest range of institutions, ideas, and events in his time," a quality that enables his writings to illumine "the problems of Sung literati consciousness with a clarity few others cared to reveal."[1] It is not surprising, then, that students of Sung literature and intellectual history, both past and present, East and West, have returned again and again to Su's life and writings seeking insights if not answers to their changing questions. In fact, to few Chinese literary figures could be more aptly applied the old Indian parable of the blind men who, each feeling a different part of the elephant, come up with radically different descriptions of it. A similar analogy is one used by Su Shih himself in his famous description of scenic Mt. Lu in Chekiang province:

> Regarded from one side, an entire range;
> from another, a single peak.
> Far, near, high, low, all its parts
> different from the others.
> If the true face of Mount Lu
> cannot be known,
> It is because the one looking at it,
> is standing in its midst.[2]

Chinese scholars throughout the centuries have labored to compile biographical studies, commentaries, and annotated anthologies of Su Shih's voluminous body of writings. Japanese scholars, who seem to have a special feeling for Su Shih's poetry, have also been particularly thorough in this regard.[3] Recently, there have been a number of excellent studies in English as well, perhaps the most noteworthy being Michael Fuller's study of Su's poetry and poetics and Ronald Egan's rich and much-needed overview of the whole of Su Shih's life and art.[4] The existence of these studies relieves me of the need to provide certain background material that might otherwise be necessary and allows me to focus on a prospect of this Mt. Lu–like figure that has been noted but rarely explored in any depth: Buddhism in the life and writings of Su Shih.[5]

In large part, this neglect reflects the fact that, until recently, Sung intellectual historians have for the most part concerned themselves with the rise of Neo-Confucianism, the single major intellectual "event" of this period. The assumption has been that Buddhism as a force was so diminished as to be considered almost negligible. This assumption in itself reflects the traditional tendency of Chinese Confucian literary and intellectual historians to underestimate if not completely ignore the importance of Chinese Buddhism in general. This tendency has in turn been emulated by Western scholarship, which, as Norman Girardot has pointed out,

> has on the whole remained a philologically oriented exegetical tradition based on the classical texts. The mesmerizing quality of this is shown by the fact that even after Western scholarship had recognized the less than objective basis for this approach, the "great tradition" of Confucianism continued to consume most of the efforts of the Chinese specialists. The "little traditions" of Taoism and Buddhism were simply ignored or, as an afterthought, fitted into the preexisting scheme established as the "great tradition."[6]

However, as recent studies by Robert Gimello, Miriam Levering, T. Griffith Foulk, and others have convincingly shown—and the present study will further confirm—Buddhism played an extremely vital role in the literary, cultural, and religious life of the Sung dynasty.[7] We can see this clearly in the life and writings of Su Shih, which demonstrate a sustained, if constantly changing, engagement with Buddhist ideas, imagery, and personalities. Moreover, Su's

Buddhist-related writings have played a significant role in the lives not only of his contemporaries, but of literati and lay people down through the centuries. The poet and critic Yeh Meng-te (1077–1148), "one of the greatest scholars [of] things present and past,"[8] comments on the fact that Su delved into Buddhist ideas and literature despite the disapproval of his mentor Ou-yang Hsiu, noting: "He was able to go in and out of all the sutras of the Mahāyāna tradition, and there was nothing he could not grasp. It was truly marvelous."[9]

Many, although by no means all, of Su's Buddhist-related writings can be found in a collection titled the *Tung-p'o Ch'an-hsi chi* [Tung-p'o's joys of Ch'an collection], compiled in 1590 by Hsü Chang-ju (dates unknown). This collection was printed with the backing of the Han-lin scholar-official T'ang Wen-hsien (*chin-shih* degree, 1586) and contains prefatory inscriptions by the high-ranking official Lu Shu-sheng (1509–1605) and by Ch'en Chi-ju (1558–1639), a well-known scholar, writer, calligrapher, and painter who in 1587, just two years before the printing of that book, burned his Confucian official robes and retired to a life of reclusion. Another inscription to this collection was written by the eminent Ch'an monk Ta-kuan Chen-k'o (1542–1603), who, judging from his comments, was an avid admirer of Su's Buddhist writings. In the spring of 1603, the eminent official, scholar, and prose writer Feng Meng-chen (1546–1605) paid a visit to the home of his friend Ling Meng-ch'u (1580–1644), the famous writer of fiction and drama. There he found a copy of the *Tung-p'o Ch'an-hsi chi,* and the two men spent many hours reading and commenting on its contents. Almost two decades later, in 1621, Ling Meng-ch'u printed this text again, along with Feng's and his hand-written comments in vermilion ink as well as those of men such as Ch'en Chi-ju. In short, Su's Buddhist writings have been read and appreciated by monks, lay persons, and literati in his own time and down to the present day: Hsü's 1590 edition has been reprinted in Taiwan three times just since 1982.[10]

Su Shih's Buddhism has also been held in great regard by many Japanese readers, both lay and monastic. The great Buddhist master Dōgen Zenji (1200–1253), for instance, devotes an entire chapter of his *Shōbōgenzō* to a discussion of the enlightenment poem Su is said to have penned on Mt. Lu after hearing a dharma talk by

Ch'an Master Tung-lin Ch'ang-ts'ung (1025–1091). Later this poem was imitated and commented on by countless Zen monk-poets who, although perhaps only seeking to justify their love of his poetry, clearly regarded Su as a "real" Buddhist.[11] In particular, the highly literary-minded monks of the Gozan, or Five Mountains, Zen establishment considered Su Tung-p'o and his literary disciple Huang T'ing-chien (1045–1105) to be the greatest of all Chinese poets. The Gozan monk Ishō Tokugan (1360–1437) was acknowledged in his own time to be the greatest Japanese expert on Su's poetry, and another Gozan monk, Banri Shūkyū (1428–1502), compiled a voluminous annotated edition of Su Shih's works. Many other Japanese poet-monks wrote poetry in the style of Su and Huang, including Ishō and Kōzei Ryūha (1375–1446), who were considered the Su and Huang of their day. A fifteenth-century annotator of the famous Chinese collection of Ch'an poetry *Chiang-hu feng-yüeh* comments, however, that in his opinion, Ishō and Kōzei were "mere Confucians," whereas the poets Su and Huang were "real Zen Masters."[12]

This view was not shared by some of Su's more outspoken Chinese critics. "Buddhism was merely a tool to facilitate his social relationships with Buddhist monks," one recent Su Shih scholar emphatically states. "It did not become Su Shih's religious belief, nor did it determine Su Shih's attitude toward life, much less influence his creative [work]."[13] Equally emphatic in his dismissal of what he considered to be Su's desultory but dangerous interest in Buddhism was the great Neo-Confucian thinker Chu Hsi (1130–1200), who lamented the fact that "in the world there are but a few great men, and they've all been drawn into Buddhism—how detrimental!"[14] To understand this discrepancy of views, it is necessary to look, if only very briefly, at the intellectual milieu of Su Shih's time.

The Northern Sung dynasty was by all accounts one of the most intellectually and culturally vital periods in Chinese history.[15] Its artists produced the wonderfully evocative landscape paintings and the delicate crimson, purple, and cream porcelains well known by Chinese art lovers. Its inventors perfected the art of woodblock printing, thus making possible the wider circulation of texts. Its poets and writers—the greatest of whom was Su Shih—produced some of the finest poetry and prose in Chinese literature. And, perhaps most important, its thinkers began to tackle questions of significance with an urgency and a creativity that had not been seen since the time of Confucius.

As is so often the case, this intellectual and cultural flowering sprang from uncertain and insecure soil. In the late eighth century, the nomad tribes living along China's northern borders had begun to consolidate their power under new leadership. In 928 one of these tribes, the Khitans, invaded China proper. Eight years later the Chinese were forced to surrender parts of the north, including what is today Peking. Thus the first Sung emperor faced considerable problems when he ascended the throne in 960. The Sung was unsuccessful in its repeated attempts to recover the territory lost in 936, and in 1004 it was forced to negotiate a peace that involved, among other things, the annual payment of 200,000 bolts of silk and 100,000 taels of silver. Shortly afterward the security won by this humiliating concession was threatened by the growing power of yet another tribe, the Tanguts, who established the Hsi-hsia state. Eventually open warfare erupted. Although there were those who advocated a more aggressive approach, the Sung government adopted a cautious and defensive policy whereby the enemy would be not so much defeated as worn down. This policy, advocated by the great statesman and scholar Fan Chung-yen (989–1052), although initially disastrous, finally paid off when the Hsi-hsia signed a peace treaty with the Sung in 1044. Again, however, the Sung was forced to provide the Hsi-hsia with an annual subsidy consisting of a vast amount of silver, silk, and tea, a tremendous drain on the resources of the state.

In the face of this weakness on the part of the central government and fueled by a growing sense of urgency, the intellectuals of the Northern Sung began to debate the value of their state institutions and the philosophies behind those institutions. In the mid–eleventh century, the focus of these debates was the sociopolitical order and the need to change it. Inevitably, there were differing views regarding what these changes should be and how they should be implemented. These differences of opinion eventually crystallized around the two major political and philosophical factions of this period, the New or Reform faction and the Old or Conservative faction. Su Shih belonged to the latter.

Very generally speaking, the New faction believed that the institutions themselves were flawed and in need of a fundamental restructuring. Under the leadership of Wang An-shih (1021–1086) they pressed for often radical socioeconomic reforms.[16] The Old faction, headed by Ssu-ma Kuang (1018–1086), a highly respected Sung scholar, historian, poet, and statesman, believed that the institutions were basically sound and that the problem lay rather in the people who ran them. These two factions (largely informal and centered on personalities as much as on principles) continued their dispute throughout the Northern Sung; depending on the inclinations of the current emperor, their followers found themselves alternately occupying positions of power or languishing in exile.

More important, however, these urgent concerns sparked a revived interest in China's philosophical past, in particular Confucianism, to which these literati turned for support and inspiration. It is precisely their differing reinterpretations of this past and of the Confucian concept of the Way that define the intellectual climate of the Northern Sung. This interest in identifying the true Confucian Way, which could serve as an infallible guide for both governments and individuals, would eventually culminate in the thought of the great philosopher Chu Hsi, whose particular synthesis of Neo-Confucian ideas became the state orthodoxy until the early part of our own century.

The first generation of Northern Sung literati (especially Wang An-shih and Ssu-ma Kuang) were primarily interested in the question of how the Way should be implemented in the governance of the state. Under Wang An-shih a number of far-reaching reforms were actually implemented, but often with disastrous results. The controversies generated by these reforms led those who opposed them to seek ways to distance themselves from the court and the capital; some like Su Shih were actually sent into exile. This difficult political climate may partly explain why the second generation of Northern Sung intellectuals, to which Su Shih belonged, although still very much concerned with social and political issues, were often "more interested in how individuals might experience the Way in their own lives."[17]

This growing emphasis on the inner life and self-cultivation would become an important component of the emergent Neo-Confucianism. Previously, this spiritual and metaphysical need had been filled largely by Buddhism, which, particularly during the

T'ang, had enjoyed widespread popularity in China. The Buddhism brought from India around the start of the first millennium had over the centuries been slowly but surely adapted to Chinese tastes. However, for all of these accommodations, Buddhism, with its primary emphasis on final liberation from the cycle of life and death, was always vulnerable to charges of being life-denying, pessimistic, and selfish, especially when compared to the largely optimistic, world-affirming, and social Confucian worldview. Moreover, the fundamental metaphysical premise on which Mahāyāna Buddhism rested—the concept of *śūnyatā* (often, if misleadingly, translated as emptiness)—continued to be antithetical to the Chinese conviction of the essential realness of the world and the self. With the resurgence of Confucian ideals in the Northern Sung, this inherent tension resurfaced. Not only did Confucianism become the dominant value system, the elite for the most part regarded it, in the words of Sung historian James T. C. Liu, "as an inviolate body of secular truth [and] revered it with an attitude approaching religious faith."[18] This zealous faith meant that many of the important forerunners of Neo-Confucianism—men like Chang Tsai (1020–1077), Ch'eng Hao (1032–1085), and his brother Ch'eng I (1033–1107)—felt that it was necessary to refute Buddhism. Although they studied and even practiced Buddhism, and they often used Buddhist concepts and terminology in their philosophical formulations, in the end they believed, in the words of Ira Kasoff, "that Buddhist philosophy was wrong: there was only one Way, the Way described in the Classics. Despite the presence of so much diversity in the world, they believed that everything could be strung on the one thread of the Way."[19]

These men worried that many Buddhist ideas were quite similar to those of Confucianism. Chang Tsai, for example, who worried that "the words [of the Buddhists] . . . resemble the correct [Way],"[20] studied Buddhism for nearly ten years, only to come to the conclusion that "the origin and the key points are different from those of our Confucian [Way]. If this is correct, that is incorrect; if that is correct, I am incorrect."[21] This concern for the "correctness" of the Confucian Way was shared by the other important forerunners of Neo-Confucian thought.[22] Ch'eng I went so far as to warn his students against the study of Buddhist texts. "You must set [Buddhism] aside without discussing it," he told them. "Do not

say, 'We must see what it is like,' for if you see what it is like you
will yourselves be changed into Buddhists. The essential thing is to
decisively reject its arts."[23] To reinforce his point, he adds: "If you
make a complete investigation of Buddhist doctrines sorting out
the good from the bad, before you have finished you will certainly
have changed into a Buddhist. Only judge them by their practice;
their practical teaching being what it is, what can their ideas be
worth?"[24]

Su Shih's refusal to reject Buddhist teachings was considered by
many to be dangerous not only to himself but to those who admired
him. Chu Hsi writes:

> There are those who say that the Su brothers used their writings to
> praise the teachings of Buddhism. However, they didn't really
> grasp the meaning of these teachings. Many of their commenta-
> ries, such as those on the *Transmission of the Lamp (Ching-te
> ch'uan-teng lu)* contain egregious errors. What sickens me [how-
> ever] is not that they flounder in the meaning of words and fail to
> understand Buddhism fully, but that in their study of Confucian-
> ism they stray into heresy.[25]

In many ways, Chu Hsi's opinion was justified: Su's understanding of Buddhist ideas and principles was not particularly rigorous
or scholarly. However, the influence of Buddhism on his creative
writings, in particular his poetry, was far more pervasive and far
deeper than many orthodox Neo-Confucian contemporaries or
present-day scholars and critics acknowledge. In his personal life,
Su was never primarily interested in Buddhist scholarship; he was
more interested in practice than in theory. This, however, is not a
reason to dismiss his ideas, because, as Masao Abe puts it, Buddhism is in general more concerned with orthopraxy than with
orthodoxy.[26] Liu Nai-ch'ang, a contemporary Su scholar from
China comments that:

> [Su Shih] studied the profound discussions and marvelous princi-
> ples of Buddhism and Taoism with an independent mind and a rel-
> atively practical approach; for this reason he was able to pick and
> choose [what appealed to him] and formulate a philosophy that,
> while solidly rooted in Confucianism, was uniquely his own. In
> this he differed greatly from other members of the literary reform
> movement of the Northern Sung, and it is something that could
> not help but have had a great influence on his literary thought
> and art.[27]

This study, then, represents an attempt to fill an important gap in our understanding not only of Su Shih but of Northern Sung literary and intellectual life. The opening chapter offers a general discussion of the Buddhism of eleventh-century Sung China, a Buddhism that was struggling to recover from the blows dealt it by the devastating persecutions of the late T'ang and remaking itself in the process. What follows might be called a spiritual/literary biography of Su Shih. This chronological and biographical approach, although not particularly original and certainly not without problems, nevertheless provides a solid framework within which to trace Su's changing relationship and responses to Buddhism.[28] Su Shih is known for the creative and perceptive manner in which he responded to his world, a responsiveness that extended as well to the Buddhism of his time. A biographical approach makes it possible to trace the ways in which Su's response to Buddhism was influenced, inspired, and shaped by the monks he met, the Buddhist temples he visited, and the Buddhist texts he read as well as by his own constantly changing life circumstances. Thus we can see that his earliest years are marked by exposure to the Buddhism of his parents: his mother introduced him to Pure Land piety and devotion, and his father introduced him to Ch'an monks who were as well known for their intellectual, literary, and moral qualities as for their purely spiritual attainments. During Su's first years in office in Feng-hsiang, we find the young Su Shih thinking in aesthetic as much as religious terms about the ideas and images suggested by the many Buddhist-related paintings and sculptures he saw during this time. Nearly a decade later, when he is assigned to beautiful and cosmopolitan Hang-chou, with its proliferation of Buddhist temples and teachers, the inspiration comes not so much from paintings as from the personalities of the many Buddhist monks he meets. He also finds that the tranquil settings of the mountain temples provide him with a much-needed psychological release from the restrictions and pettiness of official life. Su's subsequent period in the relative wasteland of Mi-chou, in Shantung province, where there were far fewer such places in which to take refuge, represents a gradual turning inward to the workings of his own mind in an attempt to find a creative (and spiritual) accommodation with a life that was becoming increasingly unpredictable and unsatisfactory. This inward-looking tendency comes to a climax during Su's first exile in Huang-chou in 1080, when for a time he desists from writ-

ing and immerses himself in Buddhist texts and meditation. This
period of exile also marks a significant spiritual turning point in
Su's life. He could not refrain completely from writing, and when
he took up the pen again, he did so with a new creative vitality and
force. This new vitality is paralleled and even inspired by his personal struggle to find a modus vivendi between the inner and the
outer, the transcendent and the immanent—between samsara and
nirvana. For even as he is attracted to accounts of total spiritual
transcendence painted in glowing terms in Buddhist texts like the
apocryphal *Śūraṃgama Sūtra* (Ch. *Leng-yen ching*), so he is also
reluctant, as a Confucian and perhaps even more strongly as a poet
and artist, to abandon the physical world that is potentially the
source of so much delight. This tension finds its most creative
expression during the Huang-chou exile, and in many ways it is
the most outstanding characteristic of Su's Buddhist spirituality.
Finally, Su's exiles during the final decade of the century to Hui-
chou and later Hai-nan in the far south of China represent a slow
and gradual release of this creative tension, as hopes of political
success recede ever farther into the distance and Su turns increasingly toward more externally religious and even ritualistic aspects
of Buddhism. However, despite this gradual waning of creative and
spiritual intensity, to the very end Su continues to try to reconcile, if
not resolve, the apparent (and Su is quite aware that ultimately it is
only apparent) tension between what he sees as the two extremes of
samsara and nirvana, living in the world and leaving the world.

In this study I am not primarily concerned with disentangling
and comparing the various threads of Buddhist, Taoist, and Confucian ideas or influences in order to determine which had the most
important place in the rich tapestry of Su's life, thought, and art.[29]
That approach, even if it were fully possible, does little justice to
the complexity, variety, and syncretic richness so characteristic of
Su Shih. Moreover, although I have tried to choose examples of
Buddhist-related writings that reflect recurrent intellectual or spiritual concerns, I do not venture to state definitively which of Su's
Buddhist-related poems are purely "conventional" and which are
not. That I leave to the reader to decide. My aim is rather to explore
the many different levels—intellectual, aesthetic, and existential—
at which Su engaged the Buddhism of his time. What emerges is a
portrait of a great poet's struggle to achieve a personal resolution to

the classic tension between the social idealism represented by Confucianism and the promise of personal liberation offered by Buddhism. This personal struggle in some ways was unique to Su Shih;
in others it reflects the larger struggle taking place in the Northern
Sung, as Confucians sought to add a metaphysical dimension to
their traditionally humanistic agenda and Buddhists tried not only
to make their teachings more accessible to the average lay person,
but also to make tangible contributions to society as a whole. The
portrait painted here shows a man who eloquently expresses a relatively open-minded and pluralistic view of religions, a view that
would gain considerable momentum in China during later centuries
and that has much to offer to our own times as well.

2. Buddhism in Eleventh-Century China

NORTHERN SUNG BUDDHISM is a complex and rich topic that, until fairly recently, has been relatively neglected by scholars of Chinese religion and history. However, there are now a number of excellent studies that reveal the limitations of the traditionally accepted characterization of Sung Buddhism as a decadent and demoralized faith.[1] The brief overview that follows will draw from many of these studies. Its primary aim is to present, at the risk of simplification and overgeneralization, some of the major Chinese Buddhist personalities, doctrines, and texts of the eleventh century and thus to set the stage for a discussion of the Buddhism in Su Shih's writings. In this way, we can better appreciate Su's personal response to his spiritual environment as well as more clearly understand the extent to which he shared this response with contemporaries.

An account of early Sung Buddhism is largely a story of revival and recovery from the shock inflicted by the violent anti-Buddhist persecutions of 845, when, according to contemporary accounts, over 260,000 monks and nuns were defrocked and more than 4,600 temples and 40,000 shrines systematically destroyed.[2] The revival began almost immediately. Two months after the first Sung emperor, T'ai-tsu, ascended the throne in 960, the court sponsored the ordination of 8,000 young monks. The ordinations were continued by his successor, and by 1021 there were nearly 400,000 monks and over 61,000 nuns, more than twice the number that had been secularized under Emperor Wu-tsung of the T'ang.[3] In addition, the court supported the establishment of temples and monasteries, which sprang up in great numbers throughout China: between 1004 and 1007, for example, there were 25,000 Buddhist temples in China, but by 1077 there were 40,613.[4] Sung T'ai-tsu also sponsored large-scale translation projects. In 966 he sent 157 monks to

India to learn Sanskrit. By 982 the translation of Indian Buddhist texts had begun in earnest, and it would continue at full pace for over seventy years. As it turns out, however, many of the texts brought from India were Tantric in nature and, conflicting with the pervading Confucian values, they were as often as not banned as soon as they were translated.[5] As a result, the real impetus to the development of Sung Buddhism came not from translation but from the use of the newly developed printing technology to print and circulate texts already in existence. In 971, for example, the five-thousand-volume Buddhist canon was for the first time officially printed in Ch'eng-tu, Szechuan.

The lessons of the T'ang were not lost on the Sung rulers. It was largely the overwhelming economic power of the Buddhist institutions that had precipitated the backlash against Buddhism during the late T'ang. Thus, the Sung emperors were careful to balance patronage with control: no new monastery was to be built without government permission, and the leadership and internal affairs of newly approved monasteries were supervised by secular officials. One important means of control was the policy of official ordination, whereby the court issued monk certificates to those who applied successfully to enter religious life. The application process included an examination on Buddhist texts conducted by government officials rather than monks. During the Sung, especially after 1068, a person could also purchase ordination certificates from the government: when he was magistrate of Hang-chou, Su Shih sold a large number of these certificates to raise revenue.[6]

Thanks in large part to this imperial patronage, Chinese Buddhism began to recover some of its past greatness. However, there were inevitably some casualties. Of the many different schools and forms of Buddhism that developed in China subsequent to its arrival from India, only a few survived and flourished into the early Sung. Of all of these, Ch'an Buddhism fared the best by far, but the T'ien-t'ai, Hua-yen, and Vinaya schools also experienced significant revivals. In addition, Pure Land Buddhism, although more a set of practices and attitudes than a school per se, enjoyed a growing popularity among both the monastic and lay communities.

In the minds of many, Su Shih is most closely associated with the Ch'an school of Buddhism, which, subsequent to the persecutions of the ninth century, emerged as one of the strongest and most vital

schools of Chinese Buddhism. During the late T'ang and Five
Dynasties periods, there were five schools or houses of Ch'an Buddhism: the Lin-chi school, founded by I-hsüan (d. 866 or 877); the
Ts'ao-tung school, founded by Liang-chieh (807–869); the Kuei-
yang school, founded by Kuei-shan Ling-yü (771–853); and the
Yün-men and Fa-yen schools, both of which trace their original
lineage to Hsüeh-feng I-ts'un (822–908). By the early Sung, however, the Kuei-yang and Fa-yen lines had virtually disappeared, and
the Ts'ao-tung line had temporarily receded into obscurity (it
would emerge again later, during the Southern Sung). Thus, the
Northern Sung was dominated largely by the Lin-chi (and in particular the Huang-lung branch founded by Huang-lung Hui-nan,
1002–1069) and Yün-men schools of Ch'an Buddhism, and it is
with these two schools that Su Shih had the greatest personal and
philosophical contact. In fact, Su Shih is formally listed under the
lineage of a Huang-lung Ch'an master born in Szechuan, Ch'ang-
ts'ung (b. 1025).

It is, however, the Yün-men school that had the most significant
impact on Northern Sung life and culture. Its founder, Yün-men
Wen-yen (864–949) studied with the famous Buddhist master Mu-
chou Ch'en-tsun-su (ca. 780–877), whose methods of teaching were
eccentric, rigorous, and even violent—Wen-yen was enlightened
when, after he requested instruction for a third time, Mu-chou
slammed the door on his leg, breaking it in the process. Wen-yen
then went to study with Hsüeh-feng I-tsun. It is said that when
Wen-yen arrived at Hsüeh-feng's door and asked the master,
"What is the Buddha?" Hsüeh-feng's reply was, "Vast Heaven,
vast Heaven." These short, pithy replies were to become characteristic of Wen-yen's teaching style as well. Although Wen-yen, like
most of the great T'ang masters, emphasized an immediate, nonin-
tellectual insight into reality, he was by no means opposed to the
study of religious texts and, according to Henrik H. Sorenson, was,
together with his teacher Hsüeh-feng, "among the pioneers in using
the examples of former masters in his public discourses, [a] practice
[that] developed into the *kung-an* system which became prominent
in the Lin-chi School during the Sung Dynasty."[7] Sorenson also
notes that Wen-yen was on relatively close terms with the literati of
the time, including numerous high officials. In 923 he received the
permission of the king of Southern Han (Liu Yen, 917–942) to build

his monastery on Mt. Yün-men in northern Kuangtung, and when it was completed the king wrote out the plaque bearing the monastery's name.[8] Wen-yen was an example of a Buddhist monk whose life, unlike those of many of his contemporaries, was not only a "dedicated struggle for spiritual clarification and preservation of the Ch'an tradition, but also one of an ongoing relationship with the secular world."[9] Undoubtedly this willingness to work with the secular world (as well as with the scriptural tradition) contributed greatly to the fact that by the early eleventh century the Yün-men school had become one of the most influential in all of China.[10] It also presages the changing character of Buddhism in general during the Northern Sung, a period when, as Robert Gimello puts it, "Buddhism, true to the implications of Mahāyāna's distinctive acceptance of the secular world, and emboldened by its previous accomplishment of considerable feats of sinicization, could venture outside the monastery and take its public place in the larger world."[11]

Yün-men Wen-yen left behind a great number of disciples, and it is their students in turn whose names appear in Su Shih's poetry and other writings. These include, to name just a few, Ta-chüeh Huai-lien (1009–1090), Yüan-t'ung Chu-no (1010–1071), Hui-lin Tsung-pen (1020–1099), Fa-yün Fa-hsiu (1027–1090), Ming-chiao Ch'i-sung (1007–1072), and Fo-yin Liao-yüan (1032–1098).

THE CH'AN SCHOOL

The biographies of these monks, and indeed of many non-Ch'an Buddhists of the Northern Sung, show them studying a wide variety of Buddhist texts with a wide range of Buddhist teachers, a practice that actually begins in the Late T'ang and is an expression of the increasingly open syncretism of Chinese Buddhism. Often they move from teacher to teacher and school to school, from Vinaya to Hua-yen to T'ien-t'ai, for example, before finally settling into Ch'an Buddhism. And even afterward, many continue to cull ideas from these other schools in their teaching and writing. Master Chu-no, for example, received full ordination from a Vinaya master at the age of seventeen, then went on to study with a Hua-yen teacher, finally becoming a formal disciple of an eminent Yün-men Ch'an master.

An important characteristic of Northern Sung Buddhism in general is the avid interest on the part of the monks in communicating with the literati lay world on its own terms. Su Shih's father, Su Hsün, once lamented that some Buddhists were shamelessly eager to abandon their masters and their faith and even went so far as to take up drinking alcohol and eating meat in order to curry favor with the Confucian literati. He writes:

> Since the T'ang, the literati of the world have all vied to articulate [their belief] that Buddhism and Taoism should be rejected. Therefore, those followers [of Buddhism and Taoism] who seek recognition from us literati often turn against their own masters in order to find accommodation among us. Moreover, we literati are delighted at their coming and receive them graciously. [They] drink wine and eat meat in order to cut themselves off [definitively] from their faith. Alas![12]

Su Hsün goes on to praise a monk from Szechuan by the name of Pao-tsung, who, although clearly desirous of the friendship of the famous literatus, had not rejected either his master or his faith. Here Su Hsün's criticism is directed mainly at those fellow literati who considered it enough that a Buddhist "imbibe alcohol and eat meat" to be accepted as a good Confucian "convert." For Su Hsün, such values as loyalty, integrity, and devotion to duty transcended purely ideological or sectarian differences, and his son would express similar views. Su Shih later gives the following description of Fan Chen (also known as Fan Ching-jen, 1007–1089):

> Fan Ching-jen throughout his life had little love for Buddhism. In his later years [however] he was pure and circumspect; in fact he really was a Buddhist. Although when he came to die, he made no use of Buddhist rites, someone commented that although Ching-jen did not study Buddhism, he had understood its most basic principles, and although he slandered and even cursed the Buddha, it did no harm![13]

Most Buddhists moved to approach the Confucian literati on their own terms in order to better defend their faith. Many of these monks had thorough Confucian educations before entering the monastery, and they made use of this common background to make contact with the literati: perhaps the most outstanding example is the great Buddhist defender of the faith Ch'i-sung. Others sought to build bridges not only between Buddhism and Confucianism, but between the various sects and schools of Buddhism. Chu-no, for example, was known for his highly eclectic thinking; he is described as one who "wandered in and out of the hundred schools even though he was fully committed to Buddhism."[14]

A related characteristic of eleventh-century Ch'an is its relatively conservative and literary character. This character is perhaps most vividly exemplified by a story Su's friend Fo-yin Liao-yüan liked to tell about the monk from Szechuan named Hsiang-lin Ch'eng-yüan (908–987), who wore a paper robe to one of Yün-men Wen-yen's lectures so that he could secretly note down the master's words— something the master had expressly forbidden.[15] Wen-yen himself often made use of the sayings of previous masters in his public sermons. In fact, although Ch'an Buddhism has traditionally emphasized the personal and experiential nature of spiritual practice and characterized itself as a special transmission outside the scriptures, it has produced more texts than any other single school of Buddhism. In eleventh- and twelfth-century Ch'an in particular there appears a renewed interest in scriptural study, rigorous monastic discipline, and Buddhist history and lineage, evidenced by the tremendous proliferation of chronicles, discourse records *(yü-lu)*, *kung-an* anthologies, and hagiographical compendia. Su was very familiar with collections of Ch'an sectarian "histories" and biographies, in particular the *Ching-te ch'uan-teng lu* [Record on Transmission of the Lamp Compiled during the Reign of Ching-te], first compiled by the Ch'an monk Tao-yüan around 1004. This text contains the stories and dialogues of over a thousand Buddhist teachers, beginning with the Buddha, over a span of fifty-four generations. With his fascination with personalities and his highly developed dramatic sense, Su delighted in this treasure house of material, returning to it again and again for inspiration in his own writing. In fact, Su was greatly admired by his contemporaries for his wide-ranging knowledge of the Ch'an stories and legends to be found in such collections.

The term that embodies this growing trend to bridge the gap between the letter and the spirit is *wen-tzu Ch'an,* which can be translated either "literary Ch'an" or, in Gimello's more affirmative translation, "lettered Ch'an." In part, *wen-tzu Ch'an* can be seen as a conservative reaction to some Ch'an followers' complacent reliance on their tradition's image of iconoclasm. Whether T'ang Ch'an Buddhism was, in fact, as iconoclastic as some describe it as being is another question altogether. It would appear, however, that, as Gimello notes, the Northern Sung was one of those periods in Ch'an history in which "committed Ch'an practitioners—some recoiling from real or perceived spasms of Ch'an antinomianism, others moved by impatience with the recurrent stagnation of Ch'an quietism, still others distressed by attacks on Ch'an from non-Buddhist quarters—have reasserted the claim that Ch'an, for all its singularity, is nonetheless Buddhist."[16]

The T'ang masters had urged their students to put away their texts and seek an unmediated insight into the Buddha mind. Some even went so far as to do away with the idea of meditation. As Carl Bielefeldt notes, despite the emphasis in early Ch'an on "sudden practice that leads directly to enlightenment," it still recognized the distinction between theory and practice, and allowed for the practice of meditation. With the rise of the Sudden Enlightenment school of Buddhism, however, sometimes even meditation was considered superfluous: "The 'sudden' practice was to be precisely that which sees through the unreal and abandons all *upāya*—that which is without attributes *(wu-hsiang)*, without intentionality *(wu-wei)*, without artifice *(wu-tso)*, and so on. Since it was without characteristics, this practice could not be described; since it was without artifice, nothing could be done about it."[17]

There were periodic attempts to check these radical tendencies. Kuei-feng Tsung-mi (780–841), for instance, advocated a coming together of Ch'an and the more doctrinal schools of Buddhism *(chiao)* that stressed discipline, merit making and the study of Buddhist texts. He also drew on T'ien-t'ai ideas to redefine "sudden enlightenment" as the prerequisite awakening that could then be followed by gradual cultivation. However, the problem continued into the Northern Sung. The Buddhist monk Chüeh-fan Hui-hung (1071–1128), for example, spent much of his life decrying the moral and spiritual laxity of those so-called Ch'an teachers and followers who took their job to be eating their fill and getting a good sleep. Su Shih added his voice to these criticisms. In his preface to an edition of the *Laṅkāvatāra Sūtra,* for example, he writes

> In recent years, students [of the sutras] create sects around their particular teachers, serving and following that which is most sim-

ple and convenient. When they figure out a single line or a single *gāthā,* they declare themselves enlightened. Even women and children playfully vie to discuss Ch'an; the best among [the teachers] are motivated by [the desire for] fame, [while the] lowest among them are looking for profit. And so the empty froth spreads into every single corner, and Buddhism is diminished.[18]

In a piece written in 1072, Su praises a monk in Hang-chou who, after more than thirty years of great hardship and self-deprivation, was finally able to fulfill a vow to complete an immense (approximately seventy-two feet high) statue of Kuan-shih-yin as well as a four-story building in which to house it. He contrasts this monk with those Buddhists who

> believe that purifying body and mind and maintaining [spiritual] discipline is not as good as [simply seeking the state of] "no-mind" *(wu-hsin),* [that] reciting and [seeking fully to] understand the [Buddhist] sutras is not as good as "no-speech" *(wu-yen),* [and that] revering and adorning stupas and temples is not as good as "nonaction" *(wu-wei).* Within them there is no-mind, in their mouths there is no-speech, in their body there is no-action, so they do nothing but eat their fill and enjoy themselves. Such monks use Buddhism fraudulently *(ch'i Fo).*[19]

Interestingly enough, Su Shih in this piece also criticizes those among his contemporaries who would indiscriminately abandon [Confucian] learning and traditional rites and customs—referring to Wang An-shih and others who proposed "New Learning," the study of a small, carefully selected range of Confucian classic texts that pointedly did not include poetry. He then draws a parallel between these new scholars and those antinomian Ch'an Buddhist monks who rejected traditional Buddhist discipline and sutra study in favor of "no-mind." Elsewhere Su writes, "In the past, when literati were chosen on the basis of rhyme schemes, literati learned variously but were not committed to the Way. Today, when literati are chosen on the basis of knowledge of the classics, literati know how to seek *tao* but do not apply themselves to learning."[20]

Gimello makes a comparison between the two primary factions of Northern Sung Confucian thought, *Tao-hsüeh* (study of the Way) and *wen-hsüeh* (study of culture or literature), and the two primary factions of Ch'an, the radical one and the more conservative *wen-tzu Ch'an.* The *Tao-hsüeh* faction was represented by men

like the Ch'eng brothers, Chang Tsai, and Chou Tun-i (1017–1073)
who "were convinced that the Tao could be truly apprehended by
means of a restricted field of learning, and then "only directly,
immediately, and introspectively."[21] The *wen-hsüeh* faction was
represented by culturally conservative figures such as Su Shih, who
believed that "access to the Tao is possible only through the diverse
and cumulative mediation of culture."[22] Gimello links the oppo-
nents of *wen-tzu Ch'an* with the former and the advocates of *wen-
tzu Ch'an* with the latter. In other words, Su Shih believed that just
as the Confucian Tao could be achieved only through varied forms
of cultural "skillful means" so the Ch'an ideal of (sudden) spontaneity could not be achieved without prior cultivation of one kind or
another. Su often criticized the *Tao-hsüeh* faction for being too
"sudden" in its approach to understanding. In the essay quoted
above, he uses the analogy of people who live by the sea and so
begin at an early age to accustom themselves to the water, and then
begin to wade, and finally to swim. Plunging into the water without
having learned how to swim would be disastrous, as would be, he
implies, a sudden and untrained apprehension of the Tao.

Gimello notes the irony of the fact that Su Shih criticizes the
"sudden" learning of the *Tao-hsüeh* faction for being too much like
"the Buddhists and Taoists."[23] There are two possible reasons for
Su's remark. The first is that the piece in which these comments
appear is a relatively early one, written before Su had really delved
into Buddhist texts. The second is that Su is comparing the *Tao-
hsüeh* advocates not to all Buddhists (and Taoists), but only to
those Buddhists who persisted in maintaining their radical stance.
Thus Su ends the 1072 piece quoted above by saying that he has
written this account to persuade those who would disparage Buddhism that there were single-minded and highly disciplined practitioners yet to be found among its adherents. In other words, his
criticism of certain Buddhist trends reflects not a blanket condem-
nation, but rather a concern for the antinomian implications of
some of the more radical of the Ch'an teachings of "sudden"
enlightenment.

Su wrote the following encomium for a calligraphic copy of the
Heart Sūtra done in small seal characters by a calligrapher named
Li K'ang-nien. Here it is clear Su Shih believed that artistic sponta-
neity can come only after much practice, just as true Ch'an realiza-

tion, contrary to the claims of adherents of the Sudden Enlightenment school, requires gradual cultivation.

> The grass and *li* styles [of calligraphy] have been used for over a
> thousand years now. [Because] I have practiced them since child-
> hood, my hand is comfortable with them. When the tongue has no
> need to choose its words, it can engage in conversation all day
> long without any problem. [But] if suddenly I am asked to write
> something in large and small seal characters, it is like trying to
> walk straight along the edge of a wall. After repeated practice, I
> get a rough grasp of it, and I try to manage a naturalness in the
> way I manipulate my brush. [But] I am like a parrot who has
> learned to speak human language: if it is something it has learned,
> then it can say it; if not, then it remains silent. The state of the
> mind is reflected in the dots and strokes. When will I have the time
> to go back and seek out the meaning beyond the words? Men of
> the world do not leave the world without first seeking to learn the
> methods for doing so. [Although] their actions and thoughts are
> worldly and defiled, yet in a second they [think they can become
> followers] of Ch'an or Vinaya. . . . Excellent are the small seal
> characters of Master Li. In them there is no sign of either the seal
> or the *li* styles. The mind forgets the hand, the hand forgets the
> brush, the brush naturally lowers onto the page, without the ego
> exerting any effort. It is truly done quickly and without a
> moment's pause. Fast and fleeting, a hundred thousand [strokes]
> emerge without a single difficulty. I bow to this *Heart Sūtra:*
> please observe, where does it not [manifest] *prajñā?*[24]

Yet another aspect of *wen-tzu Ch'an* has to do with the relationship between the spiritual life and the writing of poetry. During the
Sung, the connection (and possible conflict) between the writing of
poetry and the practice of Ch'an was of particular concern to both
literati and Buddhist monks. It was a problem that arose because,
as William LaFleur puts it, "the writing of poetry and involvement
in the world of lyrical exchange and competition constantly threatened to deflect the energies of those who had chosen a religious
vocation."[25] LaFleur is speaking here of the world of Saigyō, a
twelfth-century Japanese monk and poet, but his point applies to
China as well. In fact, both Chinese and Japanese Buddhist poets
looked back to the T'ang poet Po Chü-i (772–946), who, although a
layman, had found a way to resolve the potential conflict between
his Buddhism and his love of poetry. Thus, although Po called his

poems *k'uang-yen i-yü* (floating phrases and fictive utterances), he wrote anyway, hoping that his lines would benefit the Buddhist dharma in some way.[26] Su Shih, who was a great admirer of Po's poetry, makes much the same decision. However, he still finds it necessary to seek support for this decision from his Buddhist friends, and he often expresses his admiration of those who are able to give up the writing of poetry altogether and completely "forget words" *(wang-yen)*. This may be a purely conventional gesture, but it does suggest that the reconciliation of the religious and the aesthetic was still a dilemma for some Buddhist followers.

Prior to the late T'ang and Five Dynasties periods, religious poetry had been largely limited to five- or seven-character-per-line *gāthā*s. During this time, however, there was a growing concern for the aesthetic qualities of religious verse. This tendency is exemplified by Ch'an Master Fa-yen Wen-i (885–958), who criticized the crudeness of much religious verse and advocated a more refined, poetic style. It can be seen as well in the poetic innovations of the Yün-men master Hsüeh-tou Chung-hsien (980–1052), who used different poetic forms, from regulated verse quatrains to *yüeh-fu* or old-style ballads, to convey his Ch'an message. Inevitably, this concern for language often resulted in the production of rather secular poetry: many Buddhist monks even went so far as to write lyric poetry *(tz'u),* usually considered off limits to men of the robe. A number of Su's Buddhist friends were famous for their ability to write romantic, even erotic, lyric verse.

If the writings of the Buddhists were being poeticized and secularized, the writings of the literati increasingly made use of Buddhist, in particular Ch'an, language and concepts. Su Shih is one of the best examples, as is his poetic disciple Huang T'ing-chien. Using Buddhist ideas in the writing of poetry was not new—Po Chü-i and Wang Wei (701–761) of the T'ang dynasty are well-known examples of "Buddhist poets." However, Buddhist ideas were used in new ways. Very generally speaking, the ideal Buddhist poetry of the T'ang was characterized by the profound stillness best exemplified by Wang Wei's famous four-line quatrains. Although the Southern school of Ch'an Buddhism, with its emphasis on "sudden enlightenment," had made its mark during Wang Wei's time, there was still a strong influence of the Northern school, with its emphasis on *ning-hsin ju-ting,* "settling the mind and entering tranquility." During the late T'ang and Five Dynasties, however, there was a growing emphasis on the use of the *kung-an* and other verbal techniques to spur the enlightenment seeker into a dynamic experience of nonduality. This development together with the rise of *wen-tzu Ch'an* and the popularity of the recorded dialogues *(yü-lu)* of the great Ch'an masters resulted in an intense interest not so much in conveying stillness with a minimum of words as in provoking motion with a playfulness of words. If the emphasis in the T'ang was on the emptiness that gives rise to form, in the Sung, perhaps, the emphasis was more on the forms that arise from the emptiness or, rather, on the dynamic interrelationship between the two. As the Ch'ing scholar Liu Hsi-tsai (1813–1881) writes of Su Shih: "[He] excels at emptying out that which contains form; he also excels at giving birth to form from emptiness: this technique must surely emerge from Ch'an realization."[27]

This emphasis on dynamism rather than quiescence would appear to characterize the Sung literati conception of Ch'an and poetry.[28] A good example is the popularity of verbal techniques designed to spur the seeker into an intuitive insight into truth, the *kung-an* and the *chi-feng*. Su Shih was endlessly admiring of Buddhist monks like Fo-yin, whose peerless *chi-feng* and koans poured from his lips "like water." Su himself was known for his use of a technique known as *chieh-fa* (rapid method). Although there were those who came to Su Shih for instruction in this method, it was really a nonmethod that lacked a prescribed form and, rather than seeking to create anything new or original, emerged from "no-mind" like a floating cloud, like a stream of water flowing downhill.[29] Whether or not he always achieved this in his own writings, it is clear that this was his highest poetic ideal: language that would flow like water, adjusting to all that it encountered, so that in the end there would be "no obstacles between form *(shih)* and principle *(li)*."[30] This last concept derives not so much from Ch'an Buddhism as from T'ien-ta'i and Hua-yen.

THE T'IEN-T'AI SCHOOL

Many of Su's closest Buddhist friends belonged to the T'ien-t'ai school of Buddhism. The man who completed the systematizing of the doctrines of the T'ien-t'ai school and is thus regarded as its founder was Chih-i (538–597), who spent most of his teaching life on Mt. T'ien-t'ai in what is today Chekiang province. Although he did more teaching than writing, his lectures were recorded and compiled by his disciple Kuan-ting (561–632), and it is around these texts—the most famous of which is the *Mo-ho chih-kuan* [The great stilling and insight]—that the T'ien-tai school is built. Chih-i's most important contribution to Chinese Buddhism was the systematic arrangement of the vast number of Buddhist sutras that had flooded into China during the previous six hundred years. Chih-i arranged the Buddhist canon according to a theory of gradual revelation. He claimed that Buddha preached his sermons in five periods corresponding to the various and changing capacities of his hearers and that the *Lotus Sūtra* represented the final and most complete teachings of the Buddha. The metaphysical heart of the T'ien-t'ai doctrine is the Threefold Truth, which holds that (1) although all things lack inherent existence or self-nature, (2) they do have a temporary or relative existence, and (3) this absolute emptiness and relative substance are both aspects of a single reality. In other words, Nāgārjuna's negative formulation of the Middle Path as being neither emptiness nor form, neither ultimate truth nor relative truth has been transformed into an affirmation of both emptiness and form, both ultimate truth and relative truth. Even more significant: "When this is applied to the religious life, it means that phenomenal life is not denied but affirmed absolutely. The everyday life of the layman is part of the life of the Buddha."[31] This idea naturally appealed to laymen such as Su Shih. In fact, during the Northern Sung some of these fundamental ideas came to be questioned, causing a deep rift in the T'ien-t'ai school.

During the chaos and confusion of the late T'ang and Five Dynasties periods, many of the important texts of the various Buddhist sects were either lost or destroyed. During the early Sung, there was a concerted effort on the part of both clergy and laity to reassemble these texts, in many cases involving trips to Japan and Korea. Among these recovered texts were a large number of texts by Chih-i, Kuan-ting, and other T'ien-t'ai teachers, and these texts contributed much to the revival of the school in the Sung. They also contributed to a major split in the T'ien-t'ai school precipitated by a debate over the authenticity of some of these texts (and thus the question of which teaching could be considered orthodox) but also involving a major doctrinal point. The debate, which began around

1000 and continued for nearly forty years, revolved around a two-chapter commentary on the *Suvarṇaprabhāsottama-sūtra* (Ch. *Chin-kuang-ming ching*) attributed to Chih-i. There was no problem with the first chapter, a general discussion about meditation and visualization. However, some T'ien-t'ai teachers refused to accept the authenticity of the second chapter, which described the stages or levels of meditation. The implications were considerable, since rejection of the second chapter implied a rejection of the fundamental T'ien-t'ai doctrine of the ten-step path to enlightenment, a process of spiritual cultivation that began with meditation on the ordinary or defiled mind *(wang-hsin)* and then moved gradually to ultimate enlightenment. The *shan-wai* faction argued that this gradual approach was unnecessary and that one could meditate directly on the ultimate, or "true mind" *(chen-hsin),* which theoretically contained all else within it. The result of this dispute, which continued for many decades, was a split between the self-styled orthodox, or *shan-chia* (Mountain) school headed by Chih-li (960–1028) and the *shan-wai* (Outside of the Mountain) school headed by Wu-en (912–986), Chih-yüan (976–1022), and others. Chih-li argued eloquently against the *shan-wai* stand, claiming that, with the exception of men like the great T'ien-t'ai patriarch Chih-i himself, it was impossible for most people to meditate on the ultimate "true mind" without beginning with a meditation on "ordinary mind." Here is yet another expression of the ongoing discussion about gradual and sudden enlightenment—not surprisingly Chih-li criticizes many Ch'an teachers for their disregard of the skillful means of various meditation practices.

However, at an even deeper level, Chih-li was defending the famous Threefold Truth doctrine of T'ien-t'ai—the belief that ultimately there is no duality between the ordinary mind and the enlightened one, between the phenomenon *(shih)* and the noumenon *(li),* and ultimately between the transcendent and the immanent, between nirvana and samsara. He severely criticizes the *shan-wai* monks for *ch'un-t'an li-kuan,* or "speaking solely of meditation on the absolute *(li),*" thus privileging it over *shih* and creating a nonexistent duality.[32] The contrast here is between the Mādhyamika nondualism on which the Threefold Truth doctrine of T'ien-t'ai was originally based and a potentially dualistic metaphysics based largely on the theory of the *tathāgata-garbha,* or inherent

Buddhahood, as expressed in such texts as the *Laṅkāvatāra Sūtra,*
the *Ta-sheng ch'i-hsin lun* [The awakening of faith], the *Yuan-
chüeh ching* [Sutra of original enlightenment], and the *Śūraṃgama
Sūtra.* In all of these texts, there is the basic assumption that, as
Peter Gregory puts it,

> the Buddha's enlightenment consisted in his realization that all
> sentient beings already fully possess the enlightened wisdom of the
> Buddha and are therefore fundamentally identical with all Bud-
> dhas. The defilements that appear to obscure this wisdom are
> merely adventitious. Buddhist practice should thus be directed
> toward uncovering the original enlightenment that is the funda-
> mental nature of all beings. Enlightenment is a matter of becom-
> ing aware of that which has always been present from the very
> beginning.[33]

Although Chih-li is generally considered to have won the debate
and thus preserved the integrity of the T'ien-t'ai teachings, the
school had faded into relative obscurity by the end of the Sung.
Moreover, the ideas espoused by the *shan-wai* school came to represent an important trend of Chinese Buddhist thought during the
Sung and afterward. It is a trend that can be seen in the popularity
of texts like the *Yüan-chüeh ching* and the *Śūraṃgama Sūtra,* both
of which were favorites of Su Shih.

The *Yüan-chüeh ching,* generally considered to be of Chinese origin, was composed sometime around the end of the seventh or the
beginning of the eighth century. It was first popularized by Kuei-
feng Tsung-mi (780–841), traditionally known as the fifth patriarch
of the Hua-yen school of Chinese Buddhism, and was later adopted
by various T'ien-ta'i and Ch'an masters. In this sutra, Mañjuśrī,
Samantabhadra, and the ten great bodhisattvas expound upon the
nature of Supreme Enlightenment and the means through which
one can reach this state. In general it teaches that all beings contain
an unchangeable essence, a completely awakened *(yüan-chüeh)*
state that is hidden only by our defiled thoughts. It then prescribes
the means by which one can clear away those defiled thoughts and
attain enlightenment. Although it begins by advocating "sudden
faith and understanding," the bulk of the text deals with "gradual
cultivation and realization." In other words, although one must
first understand the perfectly enlightened mind (through sud-

den enlightenment), this understanding must then be cultivated gradually.

The problems seem to arise in the emphasis on the mind over all else. In his study of this sutra, Tomoaki Tsuchida quotes a Japanese commentator by the name of Hotan (1657–1738) who criticizes Tsung-mi because he

> took the one mind *(i-hsin)* as primary and relegated sentient beings *(sheng)* and Buddha *(Fo)* to a secondary [position], thus failing to understand that there is no difference between the three. This is why [he] clings to the divinely luminous true mind, saying that this is the perfect ultimate. This doctrine pervaded the [*shan-wai*] group of the T'ien-t'ai school in the Northern Sung period. This is why Chih-li always accuses Tsung-mi of using the phrase "divinely knowing the true mind" in this way.[34]

Again there is a tendency toward dualism, a reaching toward the absolute that can result in a summary rejection of the relative. This tendency is even more evident in the *Śūraṃgama Sūtra,* an apocryphal text closely linked with the *Yüan-chüeh ching* that was particularly popular during the Sung period.[35] It was used during the debates by monks of the *shan-wai* school such as Chih-yüan and Chin-chüeh Jen-yüeh (992–1064), a student of Chih-li who later turned against his teacher. It was also widely studied by Buddhists from the Ch'an and Hua-yen schools: there are commentaries on the *Śūraṃgama Sūtra* by Ch'an Master Yung-meng Yen-shou (904–975) and later by Hui-hung as well as by the Hua-yen teacher Chang-shui Huai-yüan following the tradition of Tsung-mi. Su's close friend Fo-yin is said to have been so taken by this sutra when he read it that he abandoned his Confucian studies to become a Buddhist monk. It was also very popular among the literati: Wang An-shih and Chang Shang-yin (1043–1121) both wrote commentaries on it, and Su Shih refers to it constantly in his poetry and other writings. In fact, the *Śūraṃgama Sūtra* may well be, as Tsuchida says, the Buddhist text that best "captures the spirit of the age."[36]

The first part of the *Śūraṃgama Sūtra* consists primarily of an exploration of the various ways (possibly Tantric in origin) of becoming aware of the mind by meditating on the six sense objects, the six sense organs, the six types of consciousness, and the seven elements. The Buddha demonstrates to his disciple Ananda the falseness of his ordinary perceptions of reality and explains how true seeing has nothing to do with the eyes at all. The second part consists of a grand exchange of spiritual experiences in which twenty-five bodhisattvas and arhats give personal accounts of the particular methods by which they achieved enlightenment, although in the end they agree that the meditation on sound used by the bodhisattva Avalokiteśvara is the best of all.

There are a number of possible reasons for the attraction of the *Śūraṃgama Sūtra.* One is its fluid and eloquent language (which lends credence to the idea that it was originally written in Chinese rather than translated from Sanskrit). A second reason is that it is a highly eclectic text that weaves together material drawn from Hua-yen metaphysics, Ch'an meditation techniques, Tantric dharanis, and Pure Land devotions, just to mention a few. As Tsuchida notes, in many ways it served as a handy synthesis of the different texts and schools that had been pouring into China in the course of the previous centuries. This quality may explain its particular attraction during the Sung and later among a growing number of lay Buddhists who, presumably, did not have the time or interest for a serious study of all of these various texts. Lo Yüeh (1137–1213), a contemporary of Chu Hsi, noted that the literati of his time were not as diligent as those of previous generations and that even when it came to studying Buddhism, they merely dipped into some of the better-known Buddhist texts like the *Śūraṃgama Sūtra,* the *Yüan-chüeh ching,* the *Vimalakīrti Sūtra,* and the *Ching-te ch'uan-teng lu.*[37] This is a charge that Chu Hsi levels against Su Shih as well.

A third and equally important attraction of this text was surely its deeply transcendental metaphysics. The *Śūraṃgama Sūtra* fully embraces the idea of the *tathāgata-garbha,* the luminous, profound awareness that is beyond the control of causes and conditions and is "spotless, pure, perfectly complete, and of firm and solid substance, unchanging *(ch'ang-chu),* and indestructible like the royal diamond."[38] One can see the attraction of this idea: indeed it forms the basis for most of the major religions of the world. It offers the possibility of complete self-transcendence and of a changeless, unconditioned absolute.

According to Tsuchida, the *Śūraṃgama Sūtra* also provided an apparently more satisfactory answer to the perennial question why, if the entire world and all the beings within it are inherently infinite, undefiled, unchanging, and pure, do they still manifest themselves as finite, defiled, and changing? The answer provided by orthodox T'ien-t'ai doctrine was that fundamentally there is no difference between them, that the absolute is contained in the relative and the relative in the absolute. However, this position can easily become an elitist one in that "it is possible . . . only in the spirit which is willing to reach out for the absolute openness, to face a total negation of what he takes for a being."[39] The *Śūraṃgama Sūtra,* by positing the relative—the finite, defiled, and changing—as nothing more than illusory clouds, obscuring a primordially pure luminosity or absolute, provided its readers with at least the "appearance of a stable framework: the path is unambiguously laid out from the finite to the infinite. It also inspire[d] piety and yearning for the transcendent."[40]

In this overwhelming emphasis on the unchanging absolute beyond form, form itself becomes little more than a defilement, a cloud that obscures the inherent luminosity of the *tathāgata-garbha.* Indeed, phenomena are regarded as purely illusory creations of the mind: in the words of the *Śūraṃgama Sūtra,* "they are but creation and destruction appearing and vanishing within the permanent, wonderfully bright, immutable, all-embracing, and profound . . . nature of the Tathāgata store wherein neither coming nor going, neither delusion nor enlightenment, and neither birth nor death can be found."[41] What is lost is the tension between form and emptiness, *shih* and *li,* samsara and nirvana, the world and the mind that characterizes classic Mādhyamika thought. Or, as Tsuchida puts it, the spiritual movement is "not into the world but into itself, to enstasis (samadhi) not to ek-stasis, not into a thorough openness by completely emptying oneself, not towards a communion with other beings, not into history."[42] It is not difficult to see why Chu Hsi would have found this stance profoundly objectionable. But what about Su Shih, who not only studied (and copied out passages from) the *Śūraṃgama Sūtra,* but referred to it constantly in his writing? I would suggest that although he might not have been as conscious of its epistemological implications, there is a certain ambivalence—if only indirectly expressed—in Su Shih's response to this text. It was clearly of intellectual and aesthetic interest, offering imagery to feast on and ideas to play with. George Hatch notes, for example, that intellectually, "nothing delighted Su Shih more than the destruction of common sense perception in Buddhist epistemology, whereby the eye might gaze inwardly on itself, the mind dwell thoughtlessly upon its own awareness."[43] He fails to point out, however, that it is not "Buddhist" epistemology in general that Su is responding to, but that of the *Śūraṃgama Sūtra,* which is particularly concerned with the nature of perception, and especially the true seeing which "transcends all external conditioning forces."[44]

On a more personal level, the fact that Su's references to the *Śūraṃgama Sūtra* appear to increase as his life becomes more beset with difficulties and uncertainties suggests that the idea of an unchanging, undefiled, transcendent absolute beyond the vagaries of a life of change might have offered a spiritual consolation. Yet Su Shih continually laments his inability—or rather his psychological reluctance—to "leave the world," and even as he praises certain monks who appear to have gone beyond the stage of "coming and going," he notes, almost with relief, that they still understand the importance of "human feeling."

Other characteristics of T'ien-t'ai Buddhism were also reflected in Su Shih's life and works. It would seem that the T'ien-t'ai teachers of the Northern Sung were particularly open to the idea of the compatibility of Confucianism and Buddhism. Chih-li, for example, in a letter to one of his disciples, notes that although Confucianism and Buddhism represent different paths, they shared the same concern for self-cultivation and spiritual practice.[45] Later Su Shih writes with great admiration of his good friend the T'ien-t'ai master Pien-ts'ai Yüan-ching (1011–1091):

> Alas! Confucianism and Taoism are different gates; Confucianism and Buddhism separate mansions. Furthermore the Ch'an sects fight among themselves. I observe how the Great Ocean has its north, south, and eastern [boundaries]; and the rivers and streams although they may differ one from the other, have the same destination. Although [Pien-ts'ai] is a great dharma master, he has forsworn fixed dogmas. There are no rules to be upheld or broken; filth and cleanliness are both without substance. He speaks [quietly] without engaging in noisy debate. [For him] practice and theory are one.[46]

Pure Land Buddhism

Su Shih's religious life—and indeed that of many of his contemporaries—could not help but be touched by concepts, images, and practices generally associated with Pure Land Buddhism. It was not simply a matter of his mother's being a devout believer; most of the eminent Buddhist monks with whom he associated—whether Ch'an or T'ien-t'ai—were also strong advocates of these practices. Su's friend Pien-ts'ai, for example, was a particularly zealous Pure Land practitioner. He burned three fingers on his left hand and two on his right (something he discouraged his followers from emulating) to show his determination to be reborn in the Pure Land. As Leo T. K. Chan puts it, "The Chinese Pure Land school was so amorphous and versatile that it accommodated itself easily and spread along paths of least resistance, coexisting with the dominant school of the time, Ch'an, as well as the T'ien-t'ai, Hua-yen, and Vinaya schools."[47]

Although there were a number of formative figures before him, the traditional first patriarch of the Pure Land School in China is Hui-yüan (334–416), who together with a number of lay literati, including the famous poet Hsieh Ling-yün (385–443), is said to have founded the White Lotus Society (named after the two lotus ponds Hsieh built on either side of the temple on Mt. Lu where the devotees gathered). This group vowed to be born in the Western Paradise and met regularly, probably to meditate. Hui-yüan was by no means a proselytizer, and even this association seems to have been an informal one. Nevertheless, the idea of getting together with others to engage in devotional practices was an attractive one, and eventually Pure Land societies would begin to spring up all over China, becoming especially popular during the Sung. There were a number of important figures after Hui-yüan, including T'an-luan (476–642), Tao-cho (562–645), Shan-tao (613–681), and Hui-jih (680–748, also known as Tz'u-min). The latter is particularly interesting. He went to India and lived there for thirteen years teaching Indian Buddhist scholars. In his *Ching-t'u tz'u-pei chi* [Collected essays on Pure Land compassion], in three fascicles, he advocates the concurrent practice of discipline, learning, and meditation as a balanced approach to religious training. One of the reasons for this emphasis on balance was his strong objection to cer-

tain followers of the Southern Ch'an school, whom he felt were
immoral, nihilistic, and generally a danger to the average seeker of
truth.[48] This emphasis resurfaced in later teachers interested in integrating Pure Land and Ch'an teachings, such as Yung-ming Yen-
shou (904–975). This synthetic tendency would continue to grow
and flourish during the Sung dynasty.

The major figure of early Sung Pure Land was Sheng-ch'ang
(959–1020), who began by studying the doctrines of T'ien-t'ai
before devoting himself entirely to Pure Land. When he died in
1020, the eminent T'ien-t'ai monk Chih-yüan compared him to
Hui-yüan of the third century. Sheng-ch'ang first headed the Shao-
ch'ing temple (ssu) on West Lake in Hang-chou, where he established a "pure behavior society" (ching-hsing she), the head of
which was the prime minister at the time, Wang Tan. Such societies,
composed of laity and monks, literati and commoners, were
extremely common during this time.[49] Another famous society, said
to have consisted of over 100,000 members, was organized in Loyang by Wen Yen-po (1006–1097), an eminent man of letters who
was a member of the conservative faction and an old friend of the
Su family. In fact, the Pure Land compendium Lo-pang wen-lei
[Assorted essays on the Land of Bliss], compiled by Tsung-hsiao
(1151–1214), describes a veritable explosion of such religious
societies, especially in the southeastern provinces of Kiangsu and
Chekiang. One of the largest of these was the Ching-yeh she, established between 1068 and 1077 by Vinaya Master Yüan-chao (1048–
1001), which had nearly 20,000 members, both lay and monastic.
The Lo-pang wen-lei quotes Yüan-chao: "[When it comes to] establishing societies and organizing groups, there is no distinction
between rich and poor, old and young: all of them take sincere refuge in Pure Land. Whether it be practicing visualization, or reciting
[Amitabha's name], or fasting and engaging in spiritual disciplines
. . . never since ancient times has Pure Land so flourished."[50]

Another important expression of piety in Pure Land Buddhism
was the presentation of Buddhist images to temples for the purpose
of accruing merit either for oneself or, as was more often the case,
for a departed loved one.[51] Many of Su's Buddhist-related poems
are written on just such an occasion—one of these was written in
Hang-chou at the instigation of Yüan-chao himself. Su is also said
to have taken a painted image of Amitabha Buddha along with him

on his final exile to the south as a kind of "passport to paradise" in case he should die en route. Later Pure Land proselytizers nonetheless refer to Su again and again as an example of a lay devotee of extraordinary spiritual potential, who, unfortunately, did not sustain his practice and so was unable to be born in the Land of Bliss.

THE VINAYA SCHOOL

Despite his close association with Pure Land Buddhism, Yüan-chao was a famous scholar of the *Ssu-fen lü,* which by the early T'ang had become the most authoritative text of the Vinaya school of Chinese Buddhism. The founder of the school—a title awarded him posthumously by Yüan-chao—was Tao-hsüan (596–667, also known as Nan-shan). Although the *Fo-tsu t'ung-chi* traces this school back to Dharmagupta, the reputed compiler of the *Ssu-fen lü,* it probably did not take shape as a school until the Sung, largely owing to men such as Ts'an-ning (911–1001) and later Yüan-chao. The latter, whom Su Shih knew in Hang-chou, had begun his monastic career as a T'ien-t'ai monk before becoming one of the primary exponents of Vinaya (and Pure Land) in the Northern Sung. He wrote numerous commentaries and often used T'ien-t'ai teachings to explain the Vinaya texts. He believed that the Vinaya, Ch'an, and doctrinal schools (Hua-yen and T'ien-t'ai) all issued from the same source and were therefore fully complementary. Or, as he put it, "The Vinaya [school] is what the Buddha [uses to] regulate [the dharma]; the doctrinal [schools] are what Buddha [uses to] explain [the dharma]; and the Ch'an [school] is what Buddha [uses to] express [the dharma]."[52]

HUA-YEN BUDDHISM

The Hua-yen school is a Buddhist tradition of purely Chinese origin. Like T'ien-t'ai Buddhism, it represents an attempt to present the standard Mādhyamika understanding of the relationship between emptiness and form in a more positive and affirmative manner, emphasizing the interdependence and interrelationship between all things. It differed from T'ien-t'ai primarily in that it spoke not of an inherently pure mind underlying all things, but rather of the "nonobstruction between thing and thing" *(shih-shih wu-ai).*

Based, as its name indicates, on the *Avataṃsaka Sūtra* (Ch. *Hua-*

yen ching), the school traces its beginnings to Tu Shun (557–640), to whom is attributed the important Hua-yen text titled *Fa-chieh kuan-men* [Meditation on the Dharmadhatu], which sets out the heart of the Hua-yen teachings. However, the person responsible for systematically ordering the texts and doctrines of the Hua-yen school was Fa-tsang (643–712), a tireless translator, writer, and commentator known as the third patriarch of Hua-yen Buddhism. Fa-tsang assisted Śikṣānanda (652–710) in his Chinese translation of the *Avataṃsaka Sūtra* and is perhaps best known for his "Essay of the Golden Lion." Another important figure was Ch'eng-kuan (738–839), who is famous for his eighty-fascicle commentary on the *Avataṃsaka Sūtra,* but whose most notable accomplishment was, according to Robert Gimello, "to have laid a foundation on which Hua-yen could consort with other kinds of Buddhism," including Vinaya, T'ien-t'ai, and Ch'an.[53] This syncretic tendency becomes even more pronounced with the emergence of Kuei-feng Tsung-mi (780–841).

Tsung-mi began life as a Confucian scholar, and he was about to take the exams when he met a Ch'an master in 807 and turned to Buddhism. Later, inspired by a commentary on the *Avataṃsaka Sūtra,* he devoted himself to Hua-yen Buddhism and became famous for his eloquent preaching and his insightful commentaries. He was also a bridge builder. In his *Yüan-jen lun* [Inquiring into the origins of humans], a reply to Han Yü's critique of Buddhism, Tsung-mi found a way to include not only the various sects and schools of Buddhism, but also Confucianism and Taoism into his overarching classification of religious practice. Himself a student of Ch'an, he also advocated a coming together of the Ch'an, or meditational schools, and the doctrinal schools of T'ien-t'ai and Hua-yen. Significantly, Tsung-mi also drew from the *tathāgata-garbha* schools of thought in effecting this bridge. Thus, although Tu-shun used the term *li* to indicate the principle that all forms are empty, with Fa-tsang "*li* becomes associated with the one mind of the *Awakening of Faith,* an association that becomes even stronger with Ch'eng-kuan and Tsung-mi, in which case it is more appropriately translated as 'absolute.' "[54] In other words, *li* becomes almost like the one mind of T'ien-ta'i in that it represents, underlies, and is even the source of all reality.

After Tsung-mi's death, the ruthless supression of Buddhism led to a general decline of the school. However, it experienced a revival during the Sung with Tzu-hsüan (965–1036). Tzu-hsüan began his religious studies with the T'ien-t'ai school, then studied with a teacher of the Ch'an Lin-chi school, before settling on the Hua-yen school. However, he continued to use the ideas of Ch'an Buddhism to interpret such sutras as the *Śūraṃgama Sūtra*. His major disciple was Ching-yüan (1001–1088), who also studied the *Avataṃsaka Sūtra* and the *Śūraṃgama Sūtra,* and, like Tsung-mi, strongly emphasized the connections between Ch'an and Hua-yen. Ching-yüan headed the Hui-yin ssu in Hang-chou between the years 1068 and 1085, during which time Su Shih knew him.[55]

Su Shih's primary connection with Hua-yen Buddhism appears to have been less with its teachers than with its texts. For example, he seems to have read Tu Shun's *Fa-chieh kuan-men.* This particular text, as Peter Gregory explains, is divided into three sections: the discernment of true emptiness *(chen-k'ung kuan-fa),* the discernment of the mutual nonobstruction of principle and phenomena *(li-shih wu-ai-kuan),* and the discernment of total pervasion and inclusion *(chou-pien han-jung kuan).* The first of these represents an understanding of the inherent emptiness of reality, the second demonstrates that this emptiness *(li)* can only realize its actuality by means of phenomena *(shih),* and the third shows how both *shih* and *li* are transcended and one enters the Hua-yen world of total interpenetration in which "each and every phenomenon is not only seen to contain each and every other phenomenon, but all phenomena are also seen to contain the totality of the unobstructed interpenetration of all phenomena."[56] Su was particularly fascinated by these ideas and often drew from them in his writings.

The most important textual influence was, however, the *Avataṃsaka Sūtra* itself. This sutra inspired more Chinese translations and commentaries than almost any other Buddhist text. Together with the *Śūraṃgama Sūtra* it is among the Buddhist texts from which Su Shih benefited most; both intellectually and aesthetically his writings are replete with allusions, imagery, and vocabulary drawn from it. It is not difficult to see why. The *Avataṃsaka Sūtra* is less a work of great philosophical import than one of imagination and almost miraculous vision. This is particularly true of the famous final chapter of the sutra, referred to as the "Gaṇḍavyūha," or "Sudhana's Pilgrimage." Here is recounted the spiritual journey of the youth Sudhana, who visits fifty-three spiritual friends and guides before finally reaching his destination, the abode of the bodhisattva Samantabhadra. His journey culminates in an overwhelming vision of interpenetration inside Vairocana's tower. This spectacular vision—and it is a vision seen from the perspective of Buddhas and bodhisattvas rather than from that of ordinary sentient beings—is of the *dharmadhatu,* the "quick-silver universe of the visionary perspective wherein all is empty and therefore is seen as a flow lacking hard edges," a universe in which "the solid outlines of individuality melt away and the feeling of finiteness no more oppresses."[57] As Su Shih's own life was increasingly marked by frustrations and obstacles, he was greatly attracted to this vision. He was also greatly influenced by the writing style of this sutra. In fact, some traditional Chinese critics compare the well-known spontaneity of Su's best prose to the flowing style of the *Avataṃsaka Sūtra.*

> When reading Su Shih's writings—blandly laid out and straightforwardly narrated, like a great quantity of silvery water flowing along the ground, then [suddenly] bursting forth—I thought that in neither the past nor the present had there been such a writing style, flowing like an unleashed torrent without banks or boundaries. [However,] lately I have been reading the *Avataṃsaka Sūtra,* which is as vast as the misty sea, with nothing left out and nothing left unexhausted. Then, heaving a sigh, I said, Su Shih's writings surely were inspired by this.[58]

It is hard to know precisely what these commentators meant, but they are probably describing the flowing spontaneity of Su's best writing—he often compared his own writing to water, which effortlessly assumed the form of whatever terrain it found itself in. They might also have been thinking of Su Shih's use of some very striking metaphors and similes, which he enjoyed piling up, one on the other. This technique was often used in Buddhist writing, perhaps most effectively in the *Avataṃsaka Sūtra,* and Su was undoubtedly inspired by this sutra's dynamic prose style and its rich use of metaphoric and descriptive language. The eminent Ch'an Buddhist monk Ta-kuan Chen-k'o (1542–1603) writes: "The narrative proceeds in a free-flowing and swift way [until] with a twist one perceives the central idea. This [style] is most effectively utilized in the

Nan-hua [i.e., the *Chuang-tzu*] and the *Avataṃsaka Sūtra.* Tung-p'o's old-style poetry customarily makes use of this method."[59]

Su Shih was also intrigued by the mind-boggling notions of time and space in the *Avataṃsaka Sūtra,* where the Buddha "has the miraculous power of . . . revealing the whole history of all the worlds in the ten quarters from their first appearance until their final destruction."[60] Su Shih was much interested in metaphysical questions. He had encountered these in the writings of Chuang-tzu, but not on the cosmic scale to be found in many Buddhist texts. In poem after poem, he examines, often with great effect, the notion of "the world in a grain of sand," an idea similar to the T'ien-t'ai concept of "all three thousand realms immanent in an instant of thought."

Although by no means oblivious to sectarian differences, Su found friendship and intellectual and spiritual stimulus in monks from all these different schools, just as he found poetic inspiration and philosophical consolation in many different types of Buddhist texts. He becomes thus an interesting mirror of his times, reflecting their diversity and complexity in a way perhaps no other Northern Sung figure does quite as well.

3. Of Arhats and Altruistic Monks

ONE NIGHT shortly before Su Shih was born, Su's mother dreamed that a Buddhist monk blind in one eye came to her door requesting lodging. Eight or nine years later, her young son had a dream that he was actually a monk from Shan-yu. More than forty years later, a Buddhist friend informed Su Shih that this half-blind monk was none other than the Ch'an master Wu-tzu Chieh, a second-generation disciple of the great Yün-men Wen-yen (864–949).[1] This association was quickly adopted by the world of Ch'an Buddhism, probably as an excuse to claim this eminent man of letters as one of their own: it appears in almost every reference to Su in the traditional Buddhist hagiographic collections.[2] Wang Chi-hsiu (d. 1173), an ardent Pure Land devotee and author of *Lung-shu tseng-kuang Ching-t'u wen* [Lung-shu's essays on broadening the Pure Land], claims that the reason Su Shih was born with such special intellectual gifts was that as Wu-tzu Chieh he had seriously engaged in spiritual cultivation. However, because he had neglected his Pure Land devotions, he was at the same time fated to suffer great hardships.[3] Yet another source, a product of the popular imagination, explains that the reason this Wu-tzu Chieh, in all other respects a spiritually advanced monk, was reborn as the layman Su Shih was because he had illicit relations with a young woman right in his own temple![4] Despite their differences, all of these stories reflect the traditional perception that Su was closely linked with Buddhism and yet, for one reason or another, never attained (or desired) full membership in its ranks.

In fact, much of what we can glean of the young Su's earliest responses to Buddhism come, like his dream of the one-eyed monk, from memories of events recorded many years after they occurred. In 1098, for example, while living in exile on the southern island of

Hai-nan, Su acquired a painting of *lohan* (Ch. *arhats*) by a late T'ang painter of Buddhist subjects from Szechuan, Master Chang of Chin-shui. This unexpected acquisition brought back memories of a similar painting of *lohan* by the famous Buddhist monk-painter-poet Kuan-hsiu (Master Ch'an-yüeh, 832–912) that had hung in the family home when Su was a boy. Su recalls how offerings of tea were placed daily before the painting and how the tea would miraculously turn a milky white color or congeal into the shapes of pear, peach, or chrysanthemum flowers. He then explains more fully the nature of his family's connection with the *lohan:*

> My maternal grandfather, Master Ch'eng, when he was young took a trip to the capital. On his return, he found Shu [i.e., Szechuan] in a state of turmoil, with food supplies cut off. Unable to return home, he remained in hiding at an inn. Then sixteen monks arrived [at the inn], saying that they were from the same county. Each [monk] gave him two hundred coins, thus enabling him to return home. He never found out where these monks came from but said that they were the [sixteen] *lohan* and four times a year would make a large offering [to them]. By the time he was ninety, he had made over two hundred offerings.[5]

Strictly speaking, the *lohan* is, in Theravada Buddhism, an enlightened being who differs from the Buddha only in that he has had a teacher, whereas the Buddha achieved enlightenment without one. The *lohan* attains his enlightenment through meditation and the purification of consciousness, a process that often results naturally in the acquisition of supernatural powers. Because of this belief in the miraculous powers of the *lohan,* over the centuries they took on a more legendary cast and became objects of worship.[6] In China, their popularity appears to have begun in the T'ang dynasty with Hsüan-tsang's (600–664) translation of the *Record of the Abiding of the Dharma,* which contains a description of these arhats.[7] During the Late T'ang and Five Dynasties periods the cult apparently gained even greater momentum after Kuan-hsiu recorded the images of the *lohan* as he had seen them in a dream: it is these images that became the basis for most later paintings. Master Chang, however, seems to himself have had a personal glimpse of the *lohan:* "Master Chang," Su Shih writes, "was famous for painting *lohan,* and during the late T'ang, his artistry was praised

throughout the empire. . . . The people of Shu all say that these
lohan took human form in his family"—which, presumably, is why
he was able to render their figures so convincingly.[8]

The worship of *lohan* continued to be very popular during the
Sung. In fact, it appears to have been encouraged by none other
than the great Confucian statesman Fan Chung-yen, who on an
official trip to Shansi in the 1040s is said to have discovered an
ancient Buddhist text titled *Shih-liu ta a-lo-han yin-kuo shih-chien
sung* [Verses on the knowledge of cause and effect of the Sixteen
Great Arhats] lodged in the eaves of the inn at which he was staying. Fan wrote a preface to this text, which was probably a Sung
dynasty creation, and commissioned a Buddhist monk to make a
copy of it for preservation. Subsequently, it appears to have
enjoyed wide circulation, and according to one author, it is "evidence for the prevalence of the worship of the sixteen *lohan* among
the people of that time."[9]

It is clear that both Su's maternal grandfather and his mother felt
more than an aesthetic appreciation of the painting of *lohan* hanging in their home. Su appears to have absorbed this spirit of venera-
tion: when late in life he acquired the above-mentioned painting by
Master Chang of Chin-shui, despite his "straitened circumstances,"
he "had it mounted and placed a lamp, incense, and flowers [in
front of it] in order to pay it homage."[10] Su retained this partly aesthetic, partly religious fascination with the figure of the *lohan*
throughout his life: he collected paintings and statues of them when
he could, and wrote a number of essays and sets of verses describing them, which I will look at more closely in later chapters.

There were other early influences as well. As discussed in the last
chapter, Su is most often associated with the Ch'an sect of Buddhism—not surprising since by the Northern Sung it had become by
far the most dominant and pervasive Buddhist school in all of
China. Su's first contact with the Yün-men school and indeed with
Ch'an in general would seem to have come through friends of his
father, Su Hsün. In 1047, after sitting unsuccessfully for the civil
service examinations in K'ai-feng, Su Hsün returned home by way
of Mt. Lu in Chekiang. He stayed in this famous Buddhist area for
nearly a month, visiting its many scenic spots and conversing with
its resident monks, in particular the Yün-men Ch'an master, Yüan-
t'ung Chu-no. Born in Szechuan, Chu-no studied poetry, calligra-

phy, and the Confucian classics as a child. He left home at eleven, and at seventeen he received full ordination under a Vinaya master. After teaching for some years, he heard about the Ch'an teachings from a Ch'an follower (probably a monk of the Yün-men sect) who had just come from the south and decided to leave Szechuan in search of further instruction. However, he ended up staying for almost ten years on Mt. Tung in Kiangsi province, where he studied the teachings of Hua-yen Buddhism with a master from Szechuan named Shao-ts'ung. In around 1037 or 1038 he went on to Mt. Lu, where he became a formal disciple of Ch'an Master Yen-ch'ing Tzu-jan, in the lineage of the famous Yün-men master Hsüeh-tou Chung-hsien. Although still a relatively young man, Chu-no soon became quite well known. For a time he was the head of the Kuei-tsung ssu on Mt. Lu and attracted many disciples and followers. Emperor Jen-tsung (r. 1023–1063), known for his personal patronage of Ch'an teachers, held Chu-no in high regard, as did his successor, the Ying-tsung emperor, who in 1049 invited Chu-no to the capital to head the new Ching-yin Ch'an ssu, the first major Ch'an temple to be built in the capital. Chu-no declined, however, on the pretext that his eyes were failing him and sent his senior disciple, Huai-lien (whom Su would meet later) instead. Chu-no later moved to the Yüan-t'ung monastery on Mt. Lu, where he remained for twenty years before finally retiring. Chu-no had considerable contact with the literati: the young Ou-yang Hsiu (1007–1072, the great conservative statesman and writer who would later become Su Shih's mentor) met with him in 1042, as did Su Hsün.[11] Chu-no was known for his highly eclectic thinking; he is described as one who "wandered in and out of the hundred schools even though he was fully committed to Buddhism" and is even said to have softened Ou-yang's rigid anti-Buddhist stance.[12]

Another of Su Hsün's Buddhist friends was the monk Wei-chien (1012–1095), also of the Yün-men school of Ch'an. In fact, Wei-chien belonged to the Su family clan: his lay name was Su Tsung-k'o. According to Su Shih's account, which is the fullest one we have of this monk, Wei-chien began his study of Buddhism at the age of nine.[13] By the age of nineteen he had been awarded the honorary Purple Robe, and by thirty-six he had been given the title Pao-yüeh (Precious Moon). Wei-chien was apparently not only a scholar, a poet, and a healer, but a man of great personal charisma

who had over ten thousand followers during his thirty-year teaching career. Among other things, he supervised the reconstruction of
173 temples and shrines, the carving of numerous religious statues,
and the building of twenty-seven bridges in the Ch'eng-tu area, all
done with profound humility and much "talk and laughter." Wei-
chien represents the "new breed" of Ch'an monk that appeared in
great numbers in the Sung and showed the influence of Confucian
values on Ch'an. They were known as much for their social
involvement, from healing the sick to building bridges and roads,
as for their purely spiritual attainments. Throughout his life Su
Shih made it a point to praise monks like Wei-chien, who exemplified Confucian-like virtues. Su Shih first met Wei-chien and a fellow Yün-men monk by the name of Wei-ch'ing on a trip to Ch'eng-
tu made in his late teens. Later Su Shih would recall this encounter:

> Once I took a trip to Ch'eng-tu, where I met the highly cultivated
> dharma master Wen-ya [Literary Elegance] Wei-ch'ing. He was a
> man of distinguished character, both lovable and generous. He
> could tell stories from the Late T'ang and Five Dynasties periods
> that were not to be found in books, which is why I enjoyed very
> much going on excursions with him. Wei-chien was a fellow
> monk. He was a keen and active man, more so than most, and in
> his devotion to Buddha and his [desire to] help sentient beings was
> as strict and diligent as [a conscientious man] toward his official
> duties. I loved these two monks![14]

In 1054 Su Shih married, and two years later he went with his
father and his younger brother Su Ch'e (1039–1112) to the Northern Sung capital of K'ai-feng to sit for the *chin-shih* exam. Su
placed second. While they were in the capital, Su's mother,
Madame Ch'eng, passed away. All three returned immediately to
Szechuan, where they remained for the duration of the traditional
mourning period. Madame Ch'eng had been, like many women of
her class, a devotee of Amitābha Buddha. In 1059, two years after
his wife's death, Su Hsün had six bodhisattva statues carved in her
honor and placed in the Hall of the Maitreya Buddha at the Chi-le
ssu in Mei-shan. Before leaving Szechuan with his sons, Su Hsün
composed a largely conventional prayer to his dead wife. In this
piece, he describes how his childhood innocence was shattered by
the realization of death as, one by one, friends and relatives began

to die, culminating in the death of his wife. He then expresses the wish that his wife's soul may be able to wander with the same sorrow-free ease in the Pure Land he himself hopes to be able to find in this world of the living.[15] Su Shih, whose earliest exposure to Buddhism had come from his mother, absorbed the language and imagery of her Pure Land piety, and, like his father, he would later produce conventional, although often quite moving, hymns and religious verses for various commemorative occasions. Although he would by temperament be drawn more to the wit of Ch'an and the philosophical speculations of T'ien-t'ai and Hua-yen, he would never completely lose touch with the more tangible religiosity of Pure Land.

Hatch notes that, despite the religious atmosphere in which Su's mother raised him, "she gave him no contentment of faith," and it would be many years before he found a form of religious belief that truly sustained him.[16] However, Su did have the opportunity to either hear about or personally meet a number of great Ch'an masters, and if he was too young to appreciate their teachings, he was certainly old enough to be impressed by the force of their personalities and characters as well as their achievements, whether building temples, curing the sick, or telling stories. This sensitivity to character (along with a gift for admiration) would continue to be part of Su's Buddhism. It also reflects the "conservative impulse" of certain aspects of Northern Sung Buddhism, with its renewed concern for unifying practice and theory, meditation and doctrine.

In 1060 Su Hsün and his two sons left Mei-shan again for the capital. The following year Su Shih and Su Ch'e both sat for a special examination—Su Shih sponsored by Ou-yang Hsiu and Su Ch'e by Ssu-ma Kuang, the famous Sung statesman, historian, and leader of the conservative faction. Su passed with third rank (during the Northern Sung, the first and second ranks were never rewarded, and the third was awarded only four times) and Su Ch'e with fourth. Su was immediately appointed assistant magistrate with the rank of Councillor of Justice at Feng-hsiang, in western Shensi province, where he arrived with his wife and three-year-old son in early 1062.

In Su's first official position, although there were duties to attend to, including reviewing criminal cases and praying for rain, he had a great deal of leisure time on his hands. This time he spent visiting local scenic sites and writing poetry. (During his three years at Feng-hsiang, Su would write 130 poems. There are apparently only four extant poems from the following eighteen months back at the capital.) It was also in Feng-hsiang that Su learned more about Buddhism. Su credits his introduction to the intricacies of Buddhist doctrine not to a Buddhist monk, but rather to a military man he met in 1063, Wang Ta-nien. Wang was famous for having fought heroically against the rebels in the North not long before.[17] Su, only twenty-eight years old at the time, clearly admired this hero, who, like so many of the great heroes of old, had never been fully honored for his bravery and courage:

> The last year of the Chia-yu reign [1063], when I took up office at Chi-hsia, I would often visit the honorable Wang Wei-p'eng [Ta-nien] of T'ai-yüan, who was military supervisor and lived in the area. At that time, Magistrate Ch'en Kung-pi was extremely strict with his underlings, and word of his power and severity spread to neighboring cities. Officials dared not look him straight in the eye. Wang alone would remain unruffled and at ease and was never humiliated by him, [and even] Kung-pi respected him. At first I had my doubts and asked around among those who knew him. People told me that he was the grandson of the military commissioner of the Wu-ning Military District, Wang Chuang-p'eng, and the son of the deputy military and surveillance commissioner of the Wu-sheng Military District, Wang Wei-chi. When he was a young man, he had gone with his father to fight the [Hsi-hsia] rebels in the hills of Kan-ling, attacking and fighting them outside the city walls. More than seventy rebels were killed, two of whom he slew with his own hands. Although his deeds were reported [to the higher authorities], he was never rewarded for them. When people urged him to tell them the story of how it happened, he would laugh and say, "I was fighting for my king and for my father, not for a reward!" When I heard this, I conceived a great admiration for him and began to engage him in long conversations. His learning was extremely profound and extensive; there was little he didn't grasp. He was especially fond of my writings. Every time I produced something, he would clap his hands with delight. At that time I knew nothing about the Buddhist dharma. He would explain it to me in very general terms and always in such a way that opened up the most mysterious so one could verify it for oneself, and so one was left convinced. It is probably thanks to him that I have a fondness for Buddhist literature.[18]

Su admired Wang's heroic exploits, his Confucian integrity, and his ability to stand up to Ch'en Hsi-liang [Ch'en Kung-pi], the stern prefect of Hang-chou who had arrived in Feng-hsiang in early 1063 and for whom Su had no great affection.[19] However, his conversations with Wang opened his eyes to new dimensions of Buddhist doctrine. Su admired above all the straightforward clarity with which Wang was able to expound ideas, the ability to grasp the essence, something on which Su also prided himself. It would appear that this encounter was by no means a superficial one. Su's later contemporary, the poet and critic Yeh Meng-te, noted that these conversations with Wang Ta-nien were not approved of by Su Shih's Confucian mentor, Ou-yang Hsiu. Yeh writes:

> At first Su Tzu-chan [Shih] did not know about the teachings of Ch'an. When he became administrative assistant of Feng-hsiang, there was a military official by the name of Wang [Ta-nien] who taught him [about Ch'an], and he began to [nourish] a great knowledge and love [for these teachings]. At the time Master Ou-yang [Hsiu] still didn't understand [Su's interest in Buddhism]. Tzu-chan, however, did not grieve over [Ou-yang's] disapproval. Later when he was appointed prefect of Hang-chou, he made a special trip to Ju-i, hoping to be able to persuade Master [Ou-yang]. Master [Ou-yang] just laughed and didn't reply. [For Su to later] abandon Master Ou-yang and follow instead a [mere] military official can be said to be very courageous! After this, he followed Pien-ts'ai and other [Buddhist teachers] in Hang-chou and entered into [Buddhist teachings] even more deeply. Tzu-chan's [Buddhist] reasoning was peerless—he was able to go in and out of all the sutras of the Mahāyāna tradition, and there was nothing he could not grasp. It was truly marvelous.[20]

It would appear that, apart from his meeting with men like Wang Ta-nien, Su Shih's principal exposure to Buddhism during these years was through Buddhist painting and sculpture, of which there were numerous notable examples in the Feng-hsiang area. One of Su's first visits in the area was to the T'ien-chu ssu, just northeast of Feng-hsiang. There Su admired a statue of Vimalakīrti, sculpted by the T'ang artist Yang Hui-chih, that depicted the famous Buddhist layman sage racked by illness and on the verge of death. Su wrote the following poem to express his response.

Once there was a Master Yü who lay ill and dying
So his friend Master Ssu went to inquire after him.
Tottering over to the well, Yü gazed at his reflection
And sighed, "What has the maker of things done to me!"
Now as I contemplate this ancient statue of Vimalakīrti,
Sick bones jutting out like a dried-up tortoise shell,
I see that realized men have transcended life and death,
And that this body comes and goes like drifting clouds.
Worldly men are satisfied only with achieving fame,
Though my health is good, my soul is already weary.
This old man is spiritually whole and needs nothing;
Laughing and chatting, he can tame the wildest beast.
When he was alive, when people asked about the Way,
He bowed his head in silence, in his heart he knew.
To this day this old statue has not said a word,
And, like Vimalakīrti, neither dies nor rots away.
None of the local farmers' wives think to fix it,
Sometimes a field mouse nibbles at its whiskers.
Seeing it makes people lose their heads and run away,
For who can stand up to him, this Master of No Words?[21]

In his discussion of a famous early poem Su wrote to his brother while in Feng-hsiang, Fuller notes how Su's argument that life is full of farewells "conveys the sense of a young man trying to discipline himself, trying to find the consolations of philosophy, but failing, as young men are apt to do."[22] The same half-successful attempt at philosophical self-discipline is evident in this poem. It begins with an almost verbatim quote from the Chuang-tzu story of Master Yü, who, looking at his reflection in the well water, cries out with the joy and unconcern of the realized man: "Wonderful! How the maker of things is turning me into this crumpled thing! He hunches me and sticks out my back, the five pipes to the spine run up above my head, my chin hides down in my navel, my shoulders are higher than my crown, the knobbly bone in my neck points up at the sky."[23] Su juxtaposes this image of the physically distorted Master Yü with Vimalakīrti, who although his body was wracked with illness, carried on illuminating and profound philosophical discussions with his eminent visitors. Su then contrasts these men who are physically ill, even dying, but spiritually free with himself, a young man in his early twenties who, despite being physically fit, is suffering from a general feeling of discontent and overall malaise. The young Su might well have been intrigued by the statue and the metaphysical truths it imparted, but, as the last two lines indicate, he was not yet really able to understand them. In fact, he finds their implications frightening. The phrase "lose one's head" comes from the Chuang-tzu story of the demonic shaman Chi Hsien, who, after Hu-tzu shows him "the absolute emptiness where there is no foreboding of anything" and "how it is before ever we come out of our ancestry," flees in utter horror.[24] As A. C. Graham points out, the reason the shaman leaves is that "for the uninitiated who cling to life, the merest glimpse of this state overwhelms with the horror of self-dissolution in ultimate solitude."[25] It is this horror of self-dissolution, I believe, that lies at the heart of Su's reluctance ever to commit himself wholeheartedly to the nondualism of Vimalakīrti, which in urging people to "see one's original face before it was born" is asking for the same drastic leap of consciousness from the familiar sufferings of samsara to the distant and unknown bliss of nirvana. It is a reluctance shared by a great many other contemporaries, however, as is evidenced by the growing popularity of texts such as the *Śūraṃgama Sūtra,* which, based on the theory of the *tathāgata-garbha,* offered a more positive, if inevitably more dualistic, view of salvation.

Vimalakīrti appears again in another of Su's poems, inspired by a portrait by the famous T'ang artist Shih K'o (active mid-tenth century). Shih K'o, a student of Chang Nan-pen (874–889), belonged, along with the monk Kuan-hsiu, to the group known as the Masters of Shu who had fled Ch'ang-an and come to Szechuan during the Buddhist persecutions commanded by Emperor Wu-tsung in 845. Shih's painting style was swift, erratic, even eccentric, and executed largely in monochrome, a style that contrasted with the detailed, colored Buddhist paintings of his contemporaries. In this poem Su Shih is clearly interested in the aesthetic dimension of Shih K'o's painting, although we do not realize until the end of the poem that Su is equating the artistic skills of Shih K'o with the spiritual skills of Vimalakīrti.

> I contemplate this master among mere quacks,
> Men who claim this medicine for that disease.
> Sometimes the humors blow cold, sometimes warm,
> As lungs and liver, kidneys and intestines fight.
> The doctors come with prescriptions piled high,

But there is no medicine that will cure death.
The Great Physician only smiles, claps his hands:
No need for doctors, the illness is cured.
I contemplate the thirty-two bodhisattvas,
Each with his own interpretation of nonduality.
Vimalakīrti is silent and says not a word,
Thirty-two opinions collapse in a moment's time.
I contemplate what [Vimalakīrti] means to say:
Never has he debated in any other way.
It is like a candle made of oil and wax,
Unless it is lit, it will never burn.
Suddenly, in this silence, this wordlessness,
The thirty-two arguments go up in smoke.
If the followers of Buddha will read this sutra,
They will surely see that this is the way.
I contemplate Vimalakīrti in his ten-foot room:
Where nine hundred thousand bodhisattvas stand,
And thirty-two thousand lions crouch,
At ease and never in each other's way.
I marvel how he divides one begging bowl of food
Giving each one in the multitude his fill.
Desireless, one can hold the realm of deep joy,
As easily as a sliver of palm leaf in one's hands.
They say the bodhisattva was beyond all conceptions,
Exercising divine power from the place of Great Liberation.
I contemplate Master Shih, this worthy recluse,
With hempen shoes, tattered hat, and elbows bare.
He has produced a Vimalakīrti from a brush tip:
His divine power must surpass the bodhisattva's!
If you say this painting does not [embody] Absolute Reality,
Then what happened in Vaiśāli is also untrue!
Since this Buddhist (Shih K'o) has produced an image of
    Vimalakīrti,
I should make sure this meditation is a correct one![26]

In this piece the verb *kuan*—to observe or contemplate—is used to mark the poet's movement from scene to scene and thought to thought. The poem expresses what will be one of the primary influences of Buddhist ideas and texts on Su Shih's poetic consciousness: the fascination with those relativities of time and space that Chuang-tzu delighted in and to which the Buddhists added stunning cosmic dimensions. Throughout his life, Su in his poetry often uses the notions of the small being extended to encompass the large or the large being contained in the small—the world in a grain of sand. In other writings, too, Su refers to the miraculous manner in which Vimalakīrti, through the power of concentration, is able not only to fit all of the myriads of bodhisattvas and other beings into his tiny room but to feed them all from his single bowl of food.

The last object of Su's contemplation is the painter behind this portrait of Vimalakīrti, Shih K'o himself. Su Shih is not yet ready to admit that the power of the painter (or the poet) is inferior to that of the bodhisattva. Rather, the miracle of producing a Vimalakīrti from the tip of a brush is for him fully comparable to Vimalakīrti's own miracles. It is implied that Shih K'o, the worthy recluse, had to undergo the same rigorous discipline and concentration as did Vimalakīrti in order to accomplish his creative feat. This idea of poetry, painting, calligraphy, and ultimately life itself, as a form of skillful means *(upāya),* a glorious if ultimately illusory celebration of the form born from emptiness, is one for which Su found ample confirmation in Buddhist writings and one that appears again and again in Su's later Buddhist-related writings.

Another sanctuary in which Su spent much time recuperating from the stress of official life was the Ka'i-yüan ssu, which lay just north of Feng-hsiang. Built in the first year of the K'ai-yüan period (713) of the T'ang, it housed a number of masterpieces by T'ang artists that Su must have spent a good deal of time contemplating. He was most impressed by the frescoes of the famous T'ang painter Wu Tao-tzu (active early ninth century), whose paintings he had first seen in Ch'eng-tu.[27] Wu Tao-tzu was one of the greatest painters of Buddhist subjects of his day (the Taoists adopted him as well and even gave him a place in their pantheon of deities). His more than three hundred frescoes depicting scenes from the life of the Buddha were to be found all over China until most were destroyed in the Buddhist persecution of 845. In 1085 Su could only think of three surviving works that could safely be ascribed to this master. One of these was a fresco depicting the Buddha's *parinirvāṇa* in the K'ai-yüan ssu, which, although it must have been in a state of considerable disrepair, was still able to provide a powerful aesthetic, if not purely religious, experience.[28] Su Shih gives an account of the visit he made to the temple in the early morning hours of the first full moon of the year 1063: "Seen in the shifting flickering light,

the figures of the picture seemed to be moving of their own accord.
I stood for a long while gazing in fascinated wonder!"[29] The next
day, he wrote the following poem:

> The True Man from the West, has anyone seen him?
> His robes decorated with the Seven Treasures;
> A pair of great lions following at his heels.
> Yet he too once cultivated the Way
> With no small effort and diligence.
> [Sitting until] willows sprouted from his elbows
> And birds nested on his shoulders.
> [His enlightenment] at first misty and obscure,
> Like jade hidden away in the mountain depths.
> Then slowly it began to shine brightly,
> Like a lotus emerging from the water.
> The Way realized, in a single day
> He reached the state of nirvana.
> From the four directions people gathered,
> And both heaven and earth grieved.
> The sound of feathered creatures in mourning
> Shook the woods and valleys,
> While beasts and demons clawed the ground,
> And wept into the streams.
> This man with white brows and deep-set eyes:
> Whose son was he?
> Gazing around him, in a snap of the finger,
> His nature becomes spontaneously complete.
> As he disappears like a cold moon
> Fading into the clear dawn,
> In the emptiness a faint glow
> Marks the ancient orbit of sun and stars.
> In the spring I go to this old temple,
> To shake off the dust of the world.
> This old painting has long ago
> Been stained by the smoke of incense.
> The artist did not sign his name,
> But they say it was painted by Tao-tzu.
> Whether cross strokes or vertical,
> They surpass those of Ch'en and Sun—
> Huge alligators swallowing river minnow.
> As to the paintings of Mañjuśrī and Samantabhadra,
> To which you refer in your poem,

We'd have to hang them side by side,
In order to compare the two.

In this poem Su is primarily interested in the descriptive and dramatic possibilities of the scene so skillfully depicted by Wu Tao-tzu, an artist known for his dynamic portrayal of such things as barbarians, demons, and wild beasts. In the opening Su Shih uses lines from the same passage in *Chuang-tzu* referred to in the first poem on Vimalakīrti. But here he combines them with the Buddhist story of Sakyamuni sitting for so long in meditation that birds built nests in his hair. He also alludes to an inscription written by the T'ang poet Wang Wei in memory of a Buddhist monk who sat so long at meditation that "lotus flowers sprang from his feet" and "willow trees sprouted from his elbows."[30] The description of the Buddha's gradual cultivation of the dharma (and of his sudden enlightenment) are striking. The Buddha-nature of the historical Sakyamuni, obscured at first by the haze of ignorance, after long and arduous cultivation shines forth at last in all its inherent glory.[31]

The lines that follow, to judge from the description in the *Wen chien hou lu,* seem to have been inspired more by the dynamism of the painting itself than by Su's particular creative genius, although one can sense the delight Su took in describing the dramatic qualities of the scene as well as his penchant for personification, found in a great deal of his verse. He accentuates the inherent tension between the sorrowful weeping of the still-unenlightened followers and the quiet imperturbability of the Buddha. This description concludes with two lovely images that parallel those used to describe the Buddha's initial enlightenment experience. The moon is an important and much-used Buddhist symbol: according to one legend, the great philosopher Nāgārjuna once turned himself into a full moon in order to demonstrate the Buddha essence, or *dharmakāya,* which is inherent in all things. Su was always fond of the moon as a poetic symbol, although not always in a strictly Ch'an sense. Here, however, the moon symbolizes the *dharmakāya* of the man Sakyamuni that "disappears" into the clear dawn (of enlightenment) the way a drop of water "disappears" into the sea. The afterglow in the sky indicates that although the Buddha has entered nirvana, he (or rather his dharma body) still exists, just as the moon that "disappears" into the morning sky does not actually cease to be. In the concluding section of the poem, Su Shih expresses his deep appreciation of Wu Tao-tzu's artistry, comparing it favorably with the paintings by Sun Chih-wei and Cheng Yin, two early Sung painters famous for their paintings on Buddhist subjects. Su reserves judgment, however, on the apparently anonymous Buddhist painting of two of Buddha's attendants, Mañjuśrī and Samantabhadra, which his brother has described to him but he has not yet seen.

These luminous images are as much indebted to the original description in the *Nirvāṇa Sūtra* and to Wu Tao-tzu's artistry as they are to that of Su Shih. And much of both the imagery and the language is fairly conventional. However already in this early poem there is a fascination with the idea of the absolute contained within the relative, the transcendent within the immanent. The metaphor of the jade hidden in the mountain, like the jewel hidden in the beggar's coat, is often used not only in the *Lotus Sūtra,* but in texts like the *Śūraṃgama Sūtra* that emphasize a return, like the moon disappearing into the dawn, to the pure and unchanging *tathāgata-garbha* behind and beyond all changing phenomena.

In another poem, Su Shih once again refers to the frescoes on the wall of the K'ai-yüan ssu, although in this poem he compares them with the paintings of bamboo by the celebrated T'ang poet-painter Wang Wei that were located in a pagoda behind the temple.

> Where can one see the frescoes of Wu Tao-tzu?
> At the P'u-men and K'ai-yüan temples.
> East of K'ai-yüan Temple is a pagoda,
> In which is kept the handiwork of Wang Wei.
> Judging from all the paintings I've seen
> None can compare with these two masters.
> Tao-tzu is virile and far-reaching
> Sweeping up like the waves of the sea.
> Beneath his brush the wind and rain quicken:
> Even his empty spaces are full of vitality.
> From between the two towering *sala* trees—
> The luminous glow of a many-hued sunrise.
> The Realized One speaks of enlightenment.
> Those who understand weep with compassion,
> Those who don't clasp their hands in awe.
> Barbarian lords and demon kings
> In the many tens of thousands

> Straining forward to catch a glimpse,
> Their heads like those of tortoises.
> [Wang Wei] was at heart a poet,
> "Girdled and cloaked in sweet grasses."
> Today I contemplate this fresco,
> It is pure and sincere like his poems.
> The Jetavana monks, skinny as cranes,
> Their hearts like ashes forever dead.
> In front of the gate two stands of bamboo:
> Snowy joints linking frosty stalks.
> Crisscrossed branches, a confusion of leaves,
> Yet in each leaf can be seen its origin.
> Although Master Wu is wonderfully fine,
> Still he is but an artisan-painter.
> While Mo-chieh has transcended mere appearance:
> The Immortal Crane breaking out of his cage.
> I think about how both were divinely inspired.
> Although when it comes to [Wang Wei]
> I can only bow in wordless homage.[32]

This is a very consciously constructed poem, and in many ways it recalls Su's gifts as a writer of prose. It readily divides into sections that are interwoven with considerable deftness. The introductory section sets the scene and introduces the two major characters, Wu Tao-tzu and Wang Wei (Mo-chieh). The rather colloquial opening is characteristic of Su Shih and reminds one of a storyteller's opening line, designed to catch the audience's attention. The two sections that follow are devoted to a discussion of the art of Wu Tao-tzu: the first treats it in theoretical terms; the second describes the work itself. However, Su's focus on the scene is more visual than philosophical.

The fourth section turns to a discussion of Wang Wei, describing him once more in general terms. The flower imagery, a line from one of Wang Wei's own poems, seems somewhat out of place here, recalling more the character of the hapless protagonist of the *Li Sao* attributed to Ch'ü Yüan (fourth century B.C.). However, perhaps Su is trying to contrast the gentleness and somewhat "feminine" and impressionistic quality of Wang Wei's painting with the more virile and masculine and realistic character of Wu Tao-tzu's artistic style.[33] Here too he emphasizes that the qualities he admires in Wang Wei's paintings are the same ones he admires in his poetry, *ch'ing,* translatable as fresh/clear/pure, and *tun,* sincere/authentic. These are terms that will recur repeatedly in his descriptions of poetry and painting he admires, especially that of monks and Buddhists.[34]

In the fifth section, Su turns his attention to the Wang Wei painting itself. Here Su's description of the monks of the Jetavana (a monastery donated to the Buddha by a wealthy man) is based on the description of the Realized Man in the "On Making All Things Equal" chapter of *Chuang-tzu:* "Their hearts like ashes forever dead." He then describes the bamboo at the gate of the monastery. Here his description of Wang Wei's artistry brings in metaphysical as well as aesthetic truth. Each one of the innumerable bamboo leaves can be traced back to a single source *(i i k'o hsün ch'i yüan).* In other words, the totality of the whole can be found in a part. Michael Fuller discusses this image mainly in terms of the *li,* or inherent pattern, that runs through all things.[35] However, I would suggest that this image may also reflect the central Hua-yen concept of *shih shih wu ai,* or nonobstruction between object and object, best captured perhaps in the famous analogy of Indra's net, in the knots of which are placed multifaceted jewels, each of which reflects the net itself as well as all the other jewels. Seen from this perspective, the reason the masses of bamboo leaves do not obstruct each other despite the circumscribed space they occupy is that they are all inherently "empty" *(k'ung).* It is an idea that appeared above in the poem about Shih K'o's Vimalakīrti poem, where Su writes: "I contemplate Vimalakīrti in his ten-foot room / Where nine hundred thousand bodhisattvas stand / And thirty-two thousand lions crouch / At ease and never in each other's way." It will also reappear many years later in Su's description of a thousand-armed Kuan-yin, each arm of which is able to carry out its different function because each is ultimately rooted in emptiness.

In 1065 Su Shih was called back to the Northern Sung capital of K'ai-feng. Although the new emperor, Ying-tsung (1064–1068), greatly admired Su's writings and wanted to appoint him to the Han-lin Academy, Premier Han Ch'i (1008–1075) blocked the move, saying that such a high office would not be to the advantage of the young man. Instead, Su was appointed to the Bureau of Historiography. It was at this time that Su met another eminent Buddhist monk of the Yün-men sect of Ch'an, Ta-chüeh Huai-lien.[36]

Originally from Fukien province, Huai-lien had studied for ten years with Ch'an Master Lung-t'an Huai-teng (who was, in turn, the disciple of Yün-men Wen-yen's dharma heir, Wu-tzu Chieh, the monk whose reincarnation Su would later claim to be). He then went to Mt. Lu, where he became the disciple and personal attendant of Master Chu-no of Yüan-t'ung Monastery. In 1050, when Chu-no was asked to come to the capital to head the Ching-yin Ch'an ssu, he sent Huai-lien instead. Like Chu-no and Wei-chien, Huai-lien was a friend of Su's father, and after Su Hsün's death, Su Shih gave Huai-lien the Kuan-hsiu painting of the sixteen *lohan,* saying that it was only right that he should present a man for whom his father felt such deep regard something that his father had held particularly dear.[37]

Huai-lien was a man of considerable erudition and highly developed literary skills. He was also very popular in literati circles: like Chu-no, he was one of those Buddhist monks of the Sung who attempted to make Buddhism more palatable to the literati by demonstrating its basic congruence with Confucian and Taoist principles and beliefs. Su writes:

> At this time the Buddhists of the North were all stuck in external phenomena and limited by [their concepts of] karmic cause and effect. For this reason the literati all looked down on their words, which they took to be those of the foreign barbarians. Huai-lien alone [was able] to point out the marvelous [aspects of Buddhist doctrine] and make them compatible with [the teachings of] Confucius and Lao-tzu. His speech and writing were truthful, his actions and character were straightforward, and so all the literati of the time delighted in spending time with him.[38]

Huai-lien was greatly admired by Emperor Jen-tsung, who so valued his presence that when Huai-lien petitioned to be allowed to return to the south, the emperor refused to let him go. It was only after the Ying-tsung's accession to the throne in 1064 that the monk was finally allowed to return home to the Chekiang area. There he settled down on Mt. A-yü wang (Mt. Aśoka), where a large hall was built to house a set of seventeen poems personally written for him by Jen-tsung. Later, Su Shih wrote a memorial inscription for this hall, which was named the Ch'en-k'uei Pavilion.

Elsewhere Su recounts with admiration the story of how Huai-

lien refused an elegantly carved alms bowl presented to him by the
emperor, saying that his faith required only tattered and discolored
robes and a bowl made of clay. In this again is seen the concern on
the part of Su Shih and others like him to defend and perhaps to
some extent justify friendship with these monks by ascribing to
them virtues that were as much Confucian as Buddhist. Despite
Su's considerable interest in Ch'an teaching, he often spoke with
the greatest admiration of those monks who engaged in outwardly
verifiable and virtuous religious activities such as building temples,
carving religious statues, and providing vegetarian feasts for the
faithful.

Su was not destined to remain long in the capital. In 1065 his
wife, Wang Fu, died at the age of twenty-seven (she had borne Su
one son, now six years old), and the following year his father, Su
Hsün, also passed away. As a consequence, both Su Shih and his
brother were forced to withdraw from official life and return to
Mei-shan for the duration of the traditional mourning period. Not
long after Su Hsün's death, Wei-chien came to Mei-shan to visit the
family, at which time Su presented him with a set of four Wu Tao-
tzu panels painted with bodhisattvas that he had acquired in Feng-
hsiang. These panels had originally belonged to a temple in Ch'ang-
an. According to Su's own account, the temple had been looted and
burned during the disturbances of 880 and 881, but the four panels
had been rescued by a monk who fled with them as far as Feng-
hsiang. Eventually, they were purchased by a wealthy man, who in
turn sold them to Su Shih. Su then gave the panels to his father,
who, he writes, prized them very highly.[39] When Su Hsün passed
away, Su entrusted the panels to Wei-chien, who built a commemorative pavilion in which to house them. In his account of this transfer, Su shows not only what Hatch calls a "taste for light, delicious
satire,"[40] but also Wei-chien's own gift for repartee! After giving a
short history of the panels, Su asks the monk how he expects to preserve the panels when even the great T'ang emperor Ming Huang
was unable to do so. When Wei-chien promises to protect them
with his life, Su asks him what he will do if he should be killed by
robbers. Then, replies the monk, I will send my spirit to guard over
them. But, Su reminds him, there are those who have no fear of
spirits. The monk is finally forced to resort to Confucian principles

of filial piety, claiming that since all men have fathers, none would dare steal what had been given by a son in honor of his father.

In 1068 Su paid a visit to Wei-chien in Ch'eng-tu only to find that Wei-qing, the storyteller-monk, had passed away. During this period, Su traveled a great deal, once as far as Ch'ang-an, where, in the home of Ch'en Han-ch'ing, he admired a fine painting of Sakyamuni Buddha by Wu Tao-tzu. Over ten years later he would acquire this painting for his own collection.[41] It was also in 1068, at the end of the three-year mourning period, that Su Shih married a cousin of his first wife, Wang Jun-chih. His new wife was a Buddhist devotee, and later Su would often celebrate her birthday with the traditional Buddhist practice of liberating a live fish and dedicating the merit thus gained to her. At the close of the mourning period, Su and his wife left Mei-shan and returned to the capital. He would not return home again, except by means of his dreams and his poetic imagination, for twenty-two years. However, his early exposure to the piety of his parents, the practicality of laymen like Wang Ta-nien, the socially engaged work of monks like Master Wei-chien, and the mysterious, thunderous silence of Vimalakīrti did much to shape the direction of his multifaceted engagement with the world of northern Sung Buddhism.

4. In Buddha Country

Su SPENT the next two years in the capital. His writing consisted mostly of memorials and official correspondence. It was during this period that Wang An-shih, the head of the New faction, attained enough political power to begin to enforce the series of reform measures known as the New Laws. The promulgation of these laws would before long polarize the political world and force the literati to take sides. In 1070 Su Ch'e decided that he strongly disagreed with the new policies and in order to avoid possible confrontations found himself a post away from the capital in Ch'en-chou (present-day Huai-yang in Honan province). Su Shih, who was also very unhappy with Wang's policies, nevertheless hung on until 1071, at which time he was finally awarded an official post in Hang-chou in Chekiang province.

In Hang-chou Su came into close contact with the people and the policies he had so forcefully and eloquently written about during his time at court. Su opposed the relatively radical reforms proposed by Wang An-shih. Although by no means an ideological reactionary, he generally preferred a slow and measured approach to change, feeling that all too often it was the common people who suffered most in the execution of quick reforms. Nevertheless, he arrived in Hang-chou determined to fulfill his official duties conscientiously, and these duties often included implementing Wang An-shih's policies. He therefore reserved his criticism for greedy commissioners and wasteful farmers. His high official standing combined with his literary fame led to an extremely active social life, which no doubt helped to ameliorate the frustrations of his job. Despite the beauties and cultural richness of Hang-chou, however, it was a difficult time for Su, and it is not surprising that his poetry begins to reflect darker feelings not only of individual despair and frustration, but of a deepening awareness of human suffering per se. It is fair to say that it was in Hang-chou that Su, whose mind up until then had been, according to Hatch "quite vacant of religious feelings,"[1] began to develop a less detached, more personal interest in Buddhism. In his writings from this period, expressions of frustration and even despair are accompanied by a yearning if not for transcendence, then at least for peace of mind.

Hang-chou was popularly known as *Fo-kuo,* or Buddha country, because of the over three hundred temples and monasteries that dotted its scenic hills and bordered its lovely lakes. Su began to spend a great deal of time in these temples, not only finding solace in their tranquil settings, but also becoming interested in the stories and legends that surrounded many of them. A poem written in 1072, titled "An Excursion to Mt. Ching," is a good illustration.

Mt. Ching, located about fifty *li* northwest of Hang-chou, was the northeast peak of the T'ien-mu range that runs through Chekiang province. It was associated with the T'ang dynasty Ch'an master Kuo-i Fa-ch'in (also known as Master Ching-shan Tao-ch'ien, 714–792). Legend had it that Master Fa-ch'in arrived at Mt. Ching in 769, nearly three hundred years before Su's visit. One day as he was sitting in meditation on a bed of stones, a simply dressed old man appeared in front of him and respectfully bowed, saying that he was in fact not a man but a dragon. When Fa-ch'in asked him what he wanted, the dragon-man told him that since Fa-ch'in had come to the mountain, he felt obliged to leave. Before leaving, however, he showed the monk a large pond saying, "If I leave, this pond will dry up and leave but a small puddle of water. However, if you do not cover it up, I will return to protect the Master whenever necessary." Thereupon the sky grew dark and cloudy, and the wind and rain blew for several days without stopping, and the waters of the pond dried up, leaving a small spring called Dragon Well Spring, the waters of which were later believed to be efficacious for the eyes. Subsequently, Fa-ch'in found a grass hut on the northern corner of the mountain where the old man had been living and settled down with the two white rabbits who kept him company.

In his poem, Su ties this story in with several miraculous tales. One of these is about the old Confucian scholar who appeared one day at Fa-ch'in's doorstep asking for help in defending the Buddhist dharma in Ch'ang-an. When Fa-ch'in asked him what skills he had, the scholar replied that he was an adept at the recitation of the mantras of Avalokiteśvara. When asked for a demonstration, the man proceeded to shatter the stone cliff behind them into three pieces. Realizing he was not an ordinary person, Fa-ch'in ordained him as a Buddhist monk and sent him back to the capital to battle the (presumably) Taoist magicians on their own terms. Another story is about a monk who spent nearly twelve years alone in the mountains reciting the *Lotus Sūtra*. One day the bodhisattva Avalokiteśvara (Kuan-yin) appeared to him in the form of a woman dressed in colored robes and carrying a basket containing a white pig and two huge bulbs of garlic. Saying that she had come into the mountains to gather herbs, she asked the monk if he would give her shelter for the night. Apparently, he passed the test of both compassion and virtue, and the next day the woman's colorful robes were transformed into lovely clouds, her white pig into a white elephant, and the bulbs of garlic into lotus flowers. Finally there is the story of the Chin dynasty thaumaturge Fo-t'u-teng (arrived in northern China ca. 310), who when there was a drought would burn fine incense and recite incantations. After three days of this, a tiny dragon five or six inches long would appear to acknowledge the prayers, and soon after there would be a great rainfall. In yet another story, a contemporary of Fo-t'u-teng named Monk She would chant and a tiny dragon would descend into his begging bowl and there would be a heavy downpour.[2] These kinds of stories fascinated Su Shih: he knew a great number of them and used them liberally in his poetry.

The opening lines of "An Excursion to Mt. Ching" describe the dramatic landscape, which is made even more mysterious by a particular phenomenon of light that causes a mirage in the shape of terraces and towers. The poet then draws on a wealth of Buddhist legends and local lore to deepen the sense of mystery and the felt presence of dragon kings and powerful holy men of the past. This finally brings him to his own situation and his increasing sense of constriction and disillusion.

> This group of peaks emerges from the T'ien-mu range,
> With the power of steeds galloping over level land:

Midway their thousand-*li*-a-day legs begin to falter,
As golden whip and jade stirrups spin round and round.
People say where there are mountains there is water:
Below, a very ancient horned-dragon lies in the depths.
The holy man with his heavenly eye recognized his kingly air,
Built a grass hut and meditated on this desolate mountain
    peak.
[Seeing] his zeal could break the mountain's stone face
    asunder,
The Heavenly Maiden with a face like a lotus came down to
    test him.
Under the chill window, the rabbits snuggled under his warm
    feet:
At night he sat with his bowl and chanted as rain dragons
    descended.
A snowy-browed old man in the morning came knocking at
    his door,
Requesting to become a disciple and practice extended medi-
    tation.
Since then more than three hundred years have come and
    gone,
With people flocking to Chekiang to offer up their gold coins,
Soaring towers and a flood of halls have blanketed the moun-
    tain slopes,
The morning bells and evening drums startle dragons from
    their sleep,
In the clear emptiness, I lift my head and gaze at the mirage,[3]
As the sun sets, several sparrow hawks head for the village.
All life dwells together supported by earth and covered by
    heaven.
How vexing that the grease and the torch are both burned up.[4]
Lately I've become more aware of constrictions of the world's
    ways,
So each time I find a wide-open space, I feel happy and at
    ease.
Alas, I am old now, and have no use for all the world's
    affairs:
But seeking out the old learning, my mind becomes vast and
    boundless.
I wish to ask the dragon for water with which to rinse my eyes,
So that I can make out tiny characters even in my waning
    years.[5]

This same hint of world-weariness is evident in a poem written in 1073 to match a poem written by Su's brother. The previous year Su Ch'e had gone to Loyang to sit for a special examination and while there had visited Kuang-ai ssu, where he saw a relief by Yang Hui-chih depicting the Buddha's sermon on Eagle Peak as described in the *Lotus Sūtra* and a painting of the bodhisattva Mañjuśrī done by the late T'ang artist Chu Yao (a native of Ch'ang-an who was skilled at painting Buddhist and Taoist subjects in a style similar to that of Wu Tao-tzu). The three verses of Su's poem refer, respectively, to Master San-hsüeh, the residing monk of Kuang-ai ssu, Yang Hui-chih's relief, and Chu Yao's painting.

> Lodging in the world, the body is like a dream,
> If one lives in peace, a day can be like a year.
> Trying to sleep, I toss and turn on the worn-out mat,
> And pace around and around in my tattered monk's shawl.
> The Master suggests I make my bed among the wind and
>   bamboo,
> And have a drink beside the waters of the rocky spring.
> A nod of the head, and all worldly affairs seem wrong.
> Laughing at myself, I understand the wisdom of the Master.

> Although the marvelous lines are difficult to trace,
> Still I can make out several layers of mountains,
> A jumble of peaks, like shell-spiraled locks of hair,
> Faraway streams, and mountain peaks swathed in clouds.
> Just like a painting, it has captured the essence.
> Gazing into emptiness, I long to ask the monk about it.
> If I don't learn the meaning of the reclusive life,
> I can but sigh with regret until the day I die!

> Chu Yao was a painter of the late T'ang,
> Who developed a technique of profound grandeur,
> Traces of which remain neglected in this temple:
> Who is there to appreciate his painstaking efforts?
> The hallways resound with the patter of rain,
> The crumbling walls tremble with the clang of bells.
> The endless affairs of this world rise and fall,
> In another year, I shall return to lament today.[6]

Although these verses are primarily appreciations, they are also introspective. Su uses this occasion and these works of art to articulate his growing disillusionment with the world and his longing for inner peace—a theme that will continue to resonate through his later writing. In the second verse we see that the vision of emptiness, both aesthetic and metaphysical, no longer frightens him as it did when he viewed Yang Hui-chih's sculpture of Vimalakīrti some years earlier. Rather, it intrigues him and he feels a desire to "ask" more about it. This he begins to do in Hang-chou, which was full of Buddhist masters and monasteries of all kinds. In an official memorial written in 1070, Su Shih had lamented that "nowadays the literati all regard the Buddha and Lao-tzu as sages; booksellers in the marketplace will sell nothing but books of Chuang (tzu) and Lao (tzu)." He then went on to say that he could not help but feel skeptical of their avowals of transcendence and detachment; in his experience it was human nature to find "tranquility" in licentiousness and "joy" in boastful talk. Moreover, he said, if everyone were truly to be like Chuang-tzu and "regard as equal life and death, to see no difference between slander and flattery, to disdain wealth and position and delight in poverty and low status, then the emperor's differentiation of rank and status, that which by the world is mined and the dull sharpened, will [have to be completely] abandoned."[7] Here Su is expressing the concern not only that the outward appearance of transcendent detachment merely conceals selfish indulgence, but that without the distinctions of social rank and hierarchy based on merit, there would be no order in the world. It is a moral and social concern that he would express many times. However, as he came to know more and more Buddhists and Taoists personally, his blanket condemnations of "Buddhism and Taoism" were gradually replaced by selective criticism and a more conciliatory approach. Perhaps because there were so many Buddhists, it was important to choose one's friends carefully. As Su writes: "There were probably more Buddhists than anywhere else under heaven, [but] the principled and wise men were mixed in with the fraudulent and [merely] clever ones."[8]

However, there were clearly a number of Buddhist monks in Hang-chou of unimpeachable integrity and genuine spiritual attainment, and for these Su Shih was unstinting in his admiration and praise. In fact, it was his friendships (and, although there were a few that were particularly important to him, he met over one hundred of these monks) that contributed most to Su's deepening interest in Buddhist ideas during this period.

The monk Su spent the most time with on first arriving in Hang-chou was Master Nan-p'ing Fan-chen (1047–1089), one of the three major disciples of the great T'ien-t'ai master Chih-li. Since 1072 he had been abbot of Hsing-chiao Temple on Mt. Nan-p'ing, where he established the Nan-p'ing line of T'ien-t'ai Buddhism. Abbot Fan-chen was widely celebrated not only for his religious attainments and eloquent preaching, but also for his secular learning: Su spent many hours with him drinking tea and discussing history and the classics and, presumably, Buddhism. Su particularly admired Fan-chen's prodigious memory: the monk always remembered those portions of the classics Su had himself forgotten.[9] Other T'ien-t'ai monks Su knew were K'o-chiu (1013–1093) and Ch'ing-shun, who lived at the Hsiang-fu ssu south of Hang-chou. K'o-chiu, famous for his skill at writing poetry, was also a deeply contemplative monk. Su Shih recounts how one New Year's eve he stole away from the noise and merriment of the festivities outside the temple and found the monk seated in his darkened room in complete silence and tranquility, unperturbed by the noise outside. Like other Confucian literati, Su could not help but admire not only the secular learning of these monks, but also their evident calm and ability to live on almost nothing, virtues that were after all not alien to Confucian ideals. The following pair of poems was written in 1072. Su, who was out of town on official business, stopped for the night at a Buddhist temple, where he penned the poems for Ch'ing-shun, probably because Su felt he would appreciate their mood of stillness and solitude. In both of these poems, the first six lines describe the poet's own situation, and in the concluding two lines his thoughts turn to Ch'ing-shun.

I

Grasses hide the riverbanks, rain obscures the villages.
The temple hides among the slender bamboo: is there a
  gate?
Gathering kindling, boiling herbs: I pity the monks who
  are ill.
Sweeping the ground, burning incense to purify this guest's
  spirit.
The farm work not yet done and already a bit of snow has
  crept in.
The altar light has just been lit announcing the yellow
  dusk,

As the years go by I slowly understand the flavor of solitary
    life,
And long to sit with you, good sir, on facing mats and talk
    about it.

II

I have often begrudged bells and drums disturbing the
    lakeside hills,
But here in this solitary and secluded place, it seems quite
    natural.
Alms rounds in the village can truly provide enough to fill
    one's belly,
But facing the guest without saying a word is not neces-
    sarily Ch'an.
Looking for the path in, I had to beat my way through
    brush and mud:
I wash my feet, close the doors, and fall asleep to the sound
    of rain.
I imagine that in a previous life you were the impoverished
    Chia Tao,
Shrugging his shoulders against the night chill and writing a
    poem.[10]

In the second of these two poems, Su makes use of two paradoxes,
the first that poverty can in fact mean a full belly and the second
that the wordless conversation between Vimalakīrti and Mañjuśrī
was, in fact, not true Ch'an at all. Su's idea is not to dispute the
idea of a silence beyond duality, but rather to create a *kung-an*
(koan) of his own. In the last line, Su compares the solitary and frugal poet-monk Ch'ing-shun to the T'ang monk-poet Chia Tao
(779–843).

Also among the first monks Su visited in Hang-chou were Hui-
ssu and Hui-ch'in, who lived on Mt. Ku. Hui-ch'in had long been a
close friend of Ou-yang Hsiu, a man who, as Su points out, had no
special fondness for either Buddhism or Taoism, but who greatly
admired this monk's wisdom, erudition, and poetic gifts. Nor was
it merely an intellectual relationship: Su often mentions the deep,
often tearful emotion with which the two men spoke of each other.
Ou-yang seems to have placed upon Su the responsibility for assuring that Hui-ch'in and his poetry were properly appreciated by Su's
fellow literati, which Su fulfilled by writing a preface to the monk's
collection of poems.[11] At the time Su met Hui-ch'in in 1074, the
monk had just retired from administrative duties at his temple:

because of the tremendous growth in the number and size of Buddhist institutions, many Buddhist masters found themselves caught up in the tedium of bureaucratic administration. This seeming parallel between the monk's life and that of the official, normally considered polar opposites, was not lost on Su Shih.

> The high-flying crane of Mt. Ch'ing-t'ien
> Felt depressed inside his cage of bamboo.
> As long as he was fettered by worldly things,
> He was in the same boat as the rest of us.
> But from today he can leave it all behind:
> A laugh, and the myriad affairs are like nothing.
> His new poems are as if rinsed in clear water,
> Untouched by the dust and delusion of the world.
> A clear breeze enters between his two lips,
> And emerges in words like wind in the pines.
> Frosty hair sprouts from his bony temples,
> As hungrily he listens for the noon bell.
> "Poetry is not what impoverishes a man,
> The impoverished man produces fine poetry."
> I really believe these words to be true,
> I heard them spoken by the "Drunken Old Man."[12]

An adjective Su often uses in describing the poetry of his Buddhist friends is *ch'ing,* meaning clear, fresh, and pure. As Yu Hsin-li points out in his study of Su Shih's poetics, Su often used the term *ch'ing* along with the term *ch'un,* which in general means "pure," but specifically refers to the process whereby wine is refined, "purified," and left to mellow before drinking. It also refers to the product of this process, a good wine (or a good poem) that helps to create and sustain a particular mood or world. This process of purification required not only talent and some source of inspiration (a marvelous landscape, for example) but much disciplined effort: "Pure [ch'ing] poetry requires refining in order to extract the silver from the lead."[13] In speaking of the poetry of his monk friends, Su Shih is referring not only to their poetic discipline, but also to their spiritual, often ascetic discipline and their relative unworldliness. He is also referring to the poverty and hardship associated with the monastic life, as we see from the last few couplets of the poem. Su quotes the comment from Ou-yang Hsiu (who called himself "the Drunken Old Man") made in reference to the poet Mei Yao-ch'en (1002–1060) about poverty being the reason for good poetry rather than the other way around. Su clearly subscribed to this view, for he repeats it in many of his poems and writings. It is perhaps worth noting the ease with which Su Shih applies these basic Confucian values to his Buddhist friends, something Ou-yang Hsiu might not have approved of. Elsewhere Ou-yang writes:

> I have heard of exiled officials who were so distressed by their difficult circumstances that they rushed to embrace Buddhist doctrines. They learn to equate humiliation with honor and failure with success. Then their hearts are at peace. How deluded this is! . . . Confucius praised Yen-tzu this way: "He had only a small container of rice and a gourdful of water, others could not have borne such distress, but Yen-tzu's was the way of the sages of old. They never allowed themselves to be sorrowful. What difference does honor or humiliation, success or failure make to them?"[14]

Su did not quite see it this way. I would suggest that he saw no real difference between the imperturbability of Yen-tzu and that of many of his Buddhist friends. Thus he writes of his friends the monks K'o-chiu and Ch'ing-shun: "These were all friends of mine with whom I used to exchange poems in my days as magistrate of Hang-chou. Pure, frugal, and extremely poor, they barely had enough to eat and often not enough to wear. However, I never once saw them looking depressed."[15]

We see from the poem addressed to Hui-ch'in that this imperturbability, however, was the result not so much of self-discipline, of not allowing themselves to be sorrowful, as of insight into the fundamental unreality of "worldly things."

If Su Shih admired the poetry of these monks and saw no inherent conflict between poetry and spiritual cultivation, he also admired those men who seem to have been able to transcend the "addiction" to poetry and go "beyond words." The Buddhist abbot from Szechuan Su Shih met in Hang-chou to whom the following poem is addressed may not in fact have transcended words —he was happy to spend the day in conversation with his compatriot—but the poem does express this ideal of wordlessness.

> The many-*li*-distant hills of home are like a dream;
> And my son has slowly come to speak with the accent of Wu
> Every time I meet this man of Shu, we talk the entire day;
> And I can almost see the O-mei hues sweeping the sky.

This Master has long forgotten words, has truly found
   the Way.
But if I gave up writing verse, I'd have nothing left at all!
If next year I go and gather herbs in the T'ien-t'ai moun-
   tains,
I'll want even more to write poems, enough to fill the east of
   Chekiang.[16]

The idea of *wang yen,* or "forgetting words," derives originally
from the *Chuang-tzu* passage "Where can I find a man who has
forgotten words so I can have a word with him?" In the above
poem, Su speaks of the monk who, having attained the Way, no
longer feels the need to write poetry; he has, in effect, obtained the
fish and left the fish trap behind (which, presumably, is why he can
spend the entire day having a word with Su Shih). Su, in contrast,
finds that he is still very much caught in the "snare" of language. It
is a lament that is repeated again and again in his writings, and
although in part conventional, it also points to a deeply felt gap
between Su's transcendent ideals and his actual practice.

Su plays with the question of words versus wordlessness again in
an appreciation written for Six-Meditation Hall of Liao-hsing
(known more familarly as Old Man Ch'ui-tz'u), a monk from
Hang-chou who was a "specialist" in the meditations on the six
symbols of impermanence: dreams, magical illusions, bubbles,
dew, shadows, and lightning. The concluding lines of this piece
revolve around the symbol of the flash of lightning:

> In the space of a lightning flash,
> The world is built and established.
> The Buddha's words are like that lightning:
> The words come out, the meaning gathers.
> The Buddha is one with all sentient beings:
> In the enlightened state no confusion or harm.
> Old Man Ch'ui-tz'u
> Often engages in this meditation.
> Beginning with one, arriving at six,
> The six that give birth to the numberless.
> Because it gives birth, it has no end,
> Because it is one, it is not confused.
> Since Tung-p'o has no mouth,
> Who has composed this piece?[17]

Interestingly, Toshihiko Izutsu, in his discussion of the problem of articulation in the Zen context, reminds us that in Mahāyāna Buddhism in general, and Zen Buddhism in particular, a fundamental distinction is always made between two levels of reality: the relative and the absolute. The relative or secondary reality refers to "the common-sense view of Reality as it appears to the eyes of ordinary people," whereas the absolute or primary reality is "disclosed to man only through the actual experience of enlightenment." Izutsu goes on to say that language in the Zen context (best exemplified by the seemingly nonsensical language of the *kung-an*) is rooted in primary reality, which dissolves all distinction between speaker and hearer: "What is actually seen is a spectacle of words flowing out from no one knows where, glittering for a moment in the air like a flash of lightning, and immediately disappearing into the eternal darkness."[18]

Su Shih never followed up on this idea in any systematic fashion. His attempt to resolve the apparent paradox between speech and wordlessness, between writing poetry and seeking the dharma was ultimately a choice between living in the world and leaving it. However, his interest in reconciling himself to apparent opposites appears very clearly in the many poems addressed to Pien-ts'ai, the Buddhist monk with whom perhaps Su felt the closest connection in Hang-chou, and who exemplified the ecumenical spirit Su so admired.

Born in the Hang-chou area, Pien-ts'ai had left home to become a monk at the age of ten and had his first experience of enlightenment when listening to teachings by T'ien-t'ai master Tsun-shih's head disciple, Master Ming-chih.[19] Soon afterward Pien-ts'ai began preaching. He was clearly not only a silver-tongued speaker, but also a man of great charisma who attracted a large and loyal following. When Su first met him, he was the abbot of Upper T'ien-chu ssu on Mt. T'ien-chu, located just west of West Lake. As Su writes,

> In Ch'ien-t'ang there was a great dharma master who was called Pien-ts'ai. At first he lived at Upper T'ien-chu [from where] he transformed all of Wu-Yüeh [southeast China] with his T'ien-t'ai teachings. The people of Wu-Yüeh all flocked to him for refuge as if he were a Buddha come to earth, and they served him as they would their own parents. Gifts of money and cloth came to him

without his having to ask for them. . . . I have heard that when
the master first began to teach the dharma, [his words] sang out
[in response to one's] inquiry like a thousand stone chimes, and
[his responses were always] perfectly timed, like the tides of
the sea.[20]

Here Su speaks of the monk's popularity and of his gift of being
able to respond spontaneously to the needs of his followers by
means of his teachings, much as Su aspired to the same degree of
uncalculated spontaneity in his writings. Elsewhere, Su likens the
monk to Chuang-tzu's "True Man," who instead of attempting to
distinguish the many different noises made by the wind, the "hoot-
ing, hissing, sniffing, sucking, mumbling, moaning, whistling, and
wailing," is able to hear the heaven behind them all.[21]

Although [Pien-ts'ai] is a great dharma master, he has forsworn
fixed dogmas. There are no rules to be upheld or broken; filth and
cleanliness are both without substance. He speaks [quietly] without engaging in noisy debate. [For him] practice and theory are
one. He is like an unmovable mountain, like an endlessly sound-
ing bell, like a moon reflected in the water, like the wind blowing
through ten thousand holes. He is eighty-one years old, but
although his life is approaching its end, when meeting objects he
yields to them, giving he is never exhausted.[22]

Su also appreciated Pien-ts'ai's healing powers, which, if the
accounts included in his biographies are true, were considerable. In
the summer of 1073, Su, anxious because his son Su Kuo, who had
been born in 1070, had not yet begun to walk, took the boy to Pien-
ts'ai. The monk stood in front of a statue of Kuan-yin, placed his
hands on the boy's head, and recited some prayers. Not long afterward, the boy was able to walk and run about with no problem at
all. At the time the boy was also given a Buddhist name, and when
he was older, he showed a particular affinity for things Buddhist.
Su describes the incident in the following poem:

> South and north, sharing a single mountain gate,
> Above and below, two temples both named T'ien-chu.
> Dwelling therein is an old dharma master,
> Built tall and skinny like stork or swan.
> I do not know what practice he engages in,
> But his green eyes reflect the mountain valleys.

Just looking into them makes one feel fresh and pure,
As if all one's baneful vexations had been cleansed.
I took my seat among all the people gathered there,
Men and women come to pay homage to this white-footed
    monk.[23]
I had a son who was born with an elongated head,
Cheek and jawbones high like the tusk of a rhino.
When he was four [*sui*] he still couldn't walk,
And had to be carried about on people's backs.
But when the Master came and rubbed his head,
He could stand and scamper about like a deer.
Thus I know that these restraints and regulations
Can be wondrously used as a means of release.
What need is there to preach the *Lotus Sūtra,*
When one can feign madness and eat meat![24]

This combination of healing powers and eloquent preaching explains why Pien-ts'ai was so popular in Hang-chou that an envious
monk initiated a campaign of slander that resulted in Pien-ts'ai's
being forced in 1079 to leave the Upper T'ien-chu ssu, where he had
lived for nearly seventeen years. However, as soon as he left, his
followers also scattered, and the usurping monk was left isolated
and empty-handed.[25] The affair came to the attention of the court,
and a year later, Pien-ts'ai was reinstalled at T'ien-chu and his loyal
followers returned. Su wrote the following poem about the event:

When this Man of Tao left the mountain,
The mountain turned as gray as ashes;
The white clouds hid away their smiles,
And the blue pines were filled with grief.
Suddenly came news of the Man of Tao's return,
And bird song burst open the mountain valleys.
A divine light radiates from his precious temples,[26]
And a dharma rain washes away the swirling dust.[27]
I'd like to see the south and north mountains,
And the flowers blooming in the front and back
    terraces.
In sending a message to ask after the Man of Tao
I will use a Ch'an technique, make a little joke:
"What did you hear that impelled you to leave?
What did you see that impelled you to return?"[28]
The Man of Tao laughs, but he does not reply,

For what it means is to dwell in peace.
In the past he never lived here at all,[29]
Nor has he on this occasion ever returned.
These words in the end are not what matter;
Let's dine on these white arbutus berries![30]

In this poem there appear a number of ideas in Buddhist teaching that Su found very congenial and that will recur again and again in his poetry. One of these is the relativity of concepts of coming and going, departure and return, when viewed with the enlightened spiritual eye of the nonabiding person who makes a home in the dharma rather than in the world. As Michael Fuller points out, the word *chu* means both "to dwell" (or, in more modern terminology, "to reside") and "to cling to" or "to be attached to."[31] Thus, when one dwells *(chu)* in that which has no boundaries, in the absolute, it can then be said that one is no longer attached *(pu-chu)* to anything, nor does one dwell anywhere in the relative, particular sense.[32] Su found this idea of a state of mind that transcended "coming and going" very attractive, and its appeal would only grow as his own life became increasingly unstable. We see these same ideas in a poem written in 1073 in commemoration of a visit to a scenic spring called Tiger Run Spring located at a temple on Nan-shan, about ten *li* from Hang-chou. According to legend, Ch'an Master Hsing-k'ung (Huan-chung, 780–862) came to this spot in 819 with the intention of building a temple, but he found that there was no water in the area. An immortal appeared to him, however, and promised a quick solution to his problem. The next day, two tigers appeared and began to paw the earth until they had made a hole from which water began to gush out. (Legend also has it that this spring was originally located elsewhere and was moved to Nan-shan by the divine power of the gods.) Su weaves in related stories as well, in this case that of the Monk T'an-chao (419–492), who was visited one day by the dragon king in the guise of an old man. When the monk mentioned that there was no water in the area, the old man clapped his hands and a spring burst forth. A shrine was erected on the spot and many centuries later, in 938, a temple as well. In the following poem, Su compares the Buddhist monk to the spring, which, coming as it does from nowhere (no-mind) without any apparent karmic cause or conditions, is beyond conventional concepts of time and space.

Tall and lofty stands the stone tower atop the eastern
peak;[33]
When this old man first arrived, he was greeted by a
hundred gods.
And tigers transported this spring here for this wandering
monk;
Like when the dragon created a spray of water by clapping
his hands.
To this day travelers stop here to wash their face, hands,
and feet.
Lying down to listen to the water like tinkling jade on
empty stairs.
So I understand how this old man was like this Tiger Run
Spring:
He didn't think, as most men do, in terms of coming and
going.[34]

Su addresses the same theme in a poem written shortly after Su's
departure from Hang-chou. This poem is addressed to a monk
from Szechuan named Abbot Lun, who lived on Mt. Chiao, not far
from Hang-chou.

The dharma master lives here at Mt. Chiao,
And yet, in fact, has never lived here at all.
I've come here to ask about the dharma,
But the dharma master sees through me and says nothing.
It isn't that the dharma master lacks the words,
But that I do not understand the nature of his reply.
Look, sir, at how your head and your feet
Are capped and shod without a second thought.
It is like the man who had a long beard,
But did not anguish at its length
Until one day someone asked him
How he arranged it when he went to bed.
Then he put it inside then outside the coverlet,
The whole night spent looking for the best position.
So he tossed and turned until the dawn of day,
And in the end wanted only to chop it off!
Although this fable is light and humorous,
Still it contains a much deeper meaning.
When I asked the dharma master about this,
He gave a smile and nodded in assent.[35]

Here, in characteristic fashion, Su Shih attempts to explain the paradox of dwelling without dwelling that the abbot himself prefers to be silent about. He does so not with abstruse theology, but rather with a simple parable about the old man who became so obsessed with where he should put his beard when he went to bed at night that he was unable to sleep at all. The moral of the story is that once one begins to think about one's "proper place," inevitably one will begin to anguish about it. As Fuller rightly notes, this poem is "essentially social verse, an amusing composition."[36] Despite the jocular tone, however, it raises concerns that will reappear later in more sober and contemplative contexts. Just as Su Shih cannot forbear using words to explain the unexplainable, so he cannot help but anguish about his "proper place" in the world—a problem that will only get worse as his own life situation becomes increasingly insecure. Thus, in many ways his admiration of the seeming ability of his Buddhist friends to transcend the limitations imposed by geographical circumstance is often paralleled by his own feelings of constriction and frustration. These feelings are very clear in some of Su's comments about a fellow monk of Pien-ts'ai by the name of Hui-pien (also known as Dharma Master Hai-yüeh, 1014–1073).

> At a time when there was trouble in the southeast and a great deal of official business, I had little leisure time. Moreover, in those days I was full of youthful vigor and chafed under the constraints of office. Each time I visited him, I would sit, feeling purified. Often hearing just a single word would make my many anxieties disappear, and I would feel peaceful in body and soul.[37]

Hui-pien was, according to Su's description of him, a man of great equanimity who never demonstrated extremes of anger or pleasure. He was very popular among both monks and laymen, and he devoted much time and energy to educating the lay public in Buddhist theory and practice. And, like many of his contemporaries, he was a strong advocate of Pure Land Buddhist practices. In fact, he appears to have been one of those monks who, for the benefit of lay followers such as Su Shih, attempted to integrate the *ch'u shih* and *ju-shih* approaches to life:

> If everyone flocks to the world,
> who then will be a hermit?

> If everyone abandons the world,
>   who then will manage the world?
> There is none like this Great Master
>   who dwells between the two,
> Neither defiled, nor pure; neither Vinaya, nor Ch'an,
> There is none like Hai-yüeh.[38]

However, Su Shih was not able to spend much time with the monk. In 1073 Hui-pien suddenly fell ill, and he passed away soon after. Su, pained that he was not able to see the monk before he died, wrote a series of poems that go beyond a merely conventional expression of mourning.

> When I pay my respect to your remains, tears drench my
>   collar,
> Even knowing that you were never born and so could never
>   die.
> On the night Master Sheng preached, the hall glowed like
>   the moon,[39]
> But now the entire hall is as before—frigid as frost.

> Life and death last no longer than an arm bent then
>   stretched again.
> Feelings are left to ordinary men like us, which makes
>   things hard.
> Le-t'ien did not seek to be a guest in the Isles of P'eng-lai;
> But took refuge in the Western Paradise, where he became
>   a host.[40]

> I'd like to ask the reason why "drifting clouds" form only
>   to dissolve.
> They have no cause and yet they manifest like a body in a
>   dream,
> After Wang Wen-tu's friend revisited him and put his heart
>   at ease,
> What further need had he to ask about this principle?[41]

These poems show a deep receptivity to the Buddhist explanation of death, although the predominant tone of the poem is less detachment than great feeling, which "makes things very difficult indeed." The opening couplet of the second poem is an allusion to the words of Wang Heng (256–311), who, upon the death of his child, lamented the fact that "[since] the sages have forgotten feeling, and the lowest [of beings] have not attained to it, the place where feelings converge is right here among us." Thus ordinary human beings, trapped as it were between the ignorance of the animal world and the wisdom of the sage, are seemingly fated to experience the pain of loss and separation. This emphasis on the inevitability, and indeed the importance, of human feelings runs through all of Su's writings, and it is not surprising that it should appear in those that deal with Buddhism even though the religion repeatedly warns against being deluded by emotion.

In the last verse Su speaks of the body as a drifting cloud that disintegrates into the atmosphere, leaving no trace, an image drawn perhaps from the *Vimalakīrti Sūtra,* where the body is compared to "a cloud, being characterized by turbulence and dissolution."[42] Then he refers to the story of Wang Wen-tu (Wang T'an-chih, 330–375) and his friend the monk Fa-ch'ien. The two men promised each other that the one who died first would return and tell the other what the afterlife was like. As it happened, the monk died first and later appeared to Wang in a dream and assured him that there were indeed such things as good and evil and karmic consequences, so that he should continue to follow the Way and to aspire toward enlightenment. In making use of this allusion, Su reveals an understandable desire for more tangible "proof" of what happens after death.

This reluctance to give up human attachments and human feeling is seen once more in a poem Su wrote two years later upon hearing of the death of a Buddhist monk who, like Su Shih, was from Szechuan. During his time in Hang-chou, Su made three visits—and wrote three poems—to this monk. The first two visits found the monk aged and ill; the third visit found him gone.

> When I saw him last, he was hardly recognizable,
> Having become as skinny as a crane;
> Now suddenly he has vanished like a cloud—
> No place to seek after him.
> Three times I have come to his door,
> First he had aged, second he had grown ill,
> and third he had died.
> The snap of a finger contains it all—
> Past, Future, and what is called Now.
> Accustomed now to the sight of both living and dead,

> I found myself unable to shed a tear.
> But the villages of home are hard to forget,
> And I feel my heart still moved.
> I long to go to the River Ch'ien-t'ang,
> Pay a visit to the monk Yüan-tse,
> And from the bank of the River Ko-hung,
> Await the deepening of autumn.[43]

The closing couplets refer to the well-known story of the monk Yüan-tse and his friend the high official Li Yüan, both of whom lived in Loyang. One day the two were on an excursion to Mt. O-mei in Szechuan when the monk suddenly announced that his hour had come but promised that twelve years hence, on the night of the Mid-Autumn Festival, he would meet his old friend outside the T'ien-chu temple in Hang-chou. Sure enough, twelve years later, Li Yüan encountered a young ox herder on the banks of the Ko-hung River outside of Hang-chou, who turned out to be none other than his friend the monk. Again, although Su recognizes that his friend has, like the clouds, disappeared into the unknowable and that, as the *Vimalakīrti Sūtra* says, "the Buddhas are neither past, nor present, nor future; their enlightenment transcends the three times," he cannot help but fall back on more traditional ideas of transmigration for consolation.

There is one more poem, written in in the fall of 1074, that expresses with particular poignancy this deep-seated desire for continuity. Su wrote this poem in memory of a reclusive monk who lived in the hills just outside of Hang-chou. This monk, known as Ācārya Yün, had spent the last fifteen years in virtual seclusion reading and reciting Buddhist texts.

> After Master Yün arrived at Mt. Pao,
> He stayed for fifteen autumns straight,
> Reading his texts behind closed doors,
> Not lifting his head even for guests.
> Last year, I visited his quarters,
> Where sitting purely, I forgot my cares.
> At first I had nothing to say to him,
> And the Master also had nothing to reply.
> Today I come and knock again at his door:
> Nothing but wind sighing through empty rooms.
> They say he has passed into extinction without residue:

When the firewood is finished, the fire is gone.
Still, I cannot help wonder whether these rooms
Will not always contain the presence of this man.
Is not everything one encounters but a dream?
The matter passed, what is it I still seek?[44]

Not all holy men died without leaving any traces, however.
Shortly after Su's arrival in Hang-chou, another great Buddhist
monk also passed away. This was Ming-chiao Ch'i-sung, perhaps
the most influential and famous representative of the Yün-men sect
during the Northern Sung. Su writes the following about Ch'i-sung
and Hui-pien, who died the year after Ch'i-sung did:

> Ch'an Master Ch'i-sung was always angry-looking—no one ever
> saw him smile. Hai-yüeh Hui-pien was always cheerful—no one
> ever saw him angry. When I was in Ch'ien-t'ang [Hang-chou], I
> personally saw the corpses of these two men after they had trans-
> formed [died] in the midst of meditation. When Ch'i-sung was
> cremated, [his body] would not burn, and it was necessary to pile
> on fresh kindling and light the fire again. In the end there were
> still five [bones] that would not burn. Hai-yüeh was buried, but
> [after being exhumed] his face was as it was when he was alive,
> still carrying the trace of a smile. Thus, one can see that, although
> one was stern and the other cheerful, both did the Buddha's work.
> Men of the world treat their bodies like gold and jade, and yet in
> an instant they revert to dung and dirt. Enlightened men are just
> the opposite. This is what I understand of the dharma: If we are
> attached to [the body], it is destroyed, and if we let it go, it will
> last forever. Is this not so?[45]

Su Shih's concern for something that "lasts forever" may in part
reflect the consoling message of *Śūraṃgama Sūtra,* which upholds
the existence of a permanent, unchanging, Buddha-nature *(tathāgata-garbha)* that is not subject to birth and death. In a discussion
with King Prasenjit, the Buddha (who here sounds more like an
Upanishadic sage) explained how despite the changes undergone by
the body as it evolves from childhood to old age, there is something
"that is free from wrinkles and is unchanging." Happy and
relieved, King Prasenjit then "realized that, after death, one abandoned one life but took on another" *(she sheng ch'u sheng).*[46] In
other words, what Tsuchida calls the "radical negation and openness" of the *Vimalakīrti Sūtra* in the *Śūraṃgama Sūtra* becomes a

virtual dualism, easier to understand and accept perhaps but also a retreat from the full implications of *śūnyatā*.

Pien-ts'ai and Hui-pien were associated primarily with the T'ien-t'ai school of Buddhism, Ch'i-sung with the Yün-men school of Ch'an Buddhism. Ch'i-sung came from a remote area in the south of China and was largely self-educated.[47] After entering the monastery at thirteen, he studied under the esteemed Yün-men Ch'an master from Szechuan Tung-shan Shao-ts'ung (also the teacher of Su Hsün's friend Yüan-t'ung Chu-no) and became himself a highly esteemed master. As a young man, Ch'i-sung demonstrated remarkable intelligence and literary ability. He so impressed Li Kou (1009–1059), a man known for his staunch anti-Buddhist sentiments, that in 1032 Li introduced him to Ou-yang Hsiu, who subsequently allowed Ch'i-sung access to his personal library. There he immersed himself in the study of Confucian ideas and literary expression, which enabled him to "understand Confucian thought and its criticisms of Buddhism [and therefore formulate] his synthetic approach and understanding of religions, thus establishing sounder ground for his arguments in defense of Buddhism in debates with Confucian scholars."[48] It is not surprising, then, that he earned the respect and admiration of many Confucian scholars and statesmen, Su Shih among them.

All of these Buddhist friends of Su Shih, whether T'ien-t'ai or Ch'an, were engaged in spiritual practices normally associated with Pure Land Buddhism. During the T'ang dynasty, Hang-chou had been an important center of Buddhist activities and the base for many eminent Buddhist monks and masters. It flourished even more during the Five Dynasties period, when the north fell into chaos and the south emerged as the new cultural center of China, reaching its zenith as a Buddhist center during the reigns of Jen-tsung (1023–1064) and Shen-tsung (1068–1086). It would seem that for a long time Hang-chou Buddhism was characterized by an emphasis on Pure Land devotional practices and works of merit (in contrast to the Buddhism of Mt. Lu in Kiangsi, for instance, which, while by no means rejecting Pure Land devotions, placed equal emphasis on Ch'an Buddhist meditation).

Pure Land was extremely popular in Su's day, and religious societies of various kinds were everywhere, some small, some consisting of over a hundred thousand members. Many of these

societies were organized by prominent literati, such as the society in
Loyang headed by Wen Yen-po (1006–1097), an eminent man of letters who was a member of the conservative faction and an old
friend of the Su family. In Hang-chou, one of the largest societies
was the Ching-yeh she, established between 1068 and 1077 by the
Vinaya master Yüan-chao (1048–1116), which had nearly twenty
thousand members.[49] Although there is no evidence that Su was a
regular member of any of these societies, it was primarily at Yüan-
chao's instigation that Su commissioned a painting of the Amitābha Buddha, which he dedicated to his parents, in particular his
mother, and for which he wrote the following hymn.

> The Buddha in His Complete Realization
> Fills worlds as many as the sands in the Ganges.
> While we, our thoughts all inverted,
> Rise and fall between life and death.
> It is said that with but a single thought,
> One can attain rebirth in the Pure Land.
> Thus is created that which has no beginning,
> And which arises from but a single thought.
> If it can arise from but a single thought,
> Then it can be extinguished in a single thought.
> When both arising and extinguishing cease
> Then will we and the Buddha be as one.
> Like tossing water into the sea,
> Like pumping bellows into the wind;
> Even if we had the wisdom of a sage,
> We would be unable to tell them apart.
> I pray that my mother and my father,
> Together with all sentient life,
> May dwell in the Western Paradise,
> And that they may encounter only joy.
> May all enjoy longevity without end,
> Without either coming or going.[50]

Although it was written primarily as a conventional expression of
filial piety, I see in this hymn the influence of the *Śūraṃgama
Sūtra*, which speaks at great length of the inverted views of ignorant men and women who fail to realize that all phenomena are
"but creation and destruction coming and going within the eternal,
wonderfully bright, unchanging, all-embracing, and marvelous

essence of the Tathāgata store *(ju-lai tsang)*. In this true and unchanging essence, there is no coming or going, delusion or enlightenment, birth or death to be found."[51]

As Su's life became increasingly difficult and subject to change, the idea of an unchanging absolute not subject to "coming and going" began to appeal to him more and more. By the same token, however, he and many of the better known of his Buddhist friends were very busy not only trying to make Buddhist teachings more accessible to the lay world, but also becoming actively involved in social activities of various types. Some of these friends, Pien-ts'ai, for example, provided models of people who had found a way to be in the world and yet not of it. It is of these Buddhists that Su writes with the greatest of admiration. Many of the Hang-chou writings show a growing tension between a desire to transcend the limitations of the human (and political) situation Su finds himself in and a realization that such transcendence is neither practical nor even possible. This tension is illustrated well by the following famous poem, which Fuller calls "a bemused confession of contradictory impulses."[52]

> The wind sings in the tall pines, the evening rain falls lightly,
> The east hermitage half obscured, the west hermitage
>   closed.
> I've traveled all day in the mountains without meeting a
>   soul,
> Pungent and permeating, the wild plums fill our sleeves with
>   fragrance,
> The mountain monks laugh at my fondness for this
>   unsullied landscape.
> For they are weary of the deep mountains they are unable to
>   leave.
> Although I do love these mountains, I laugh at myself as
>   well.
> Traveling alone breaks my heart and it is difficult to go on.
> It would be better to be at West Lake sipping fine wine,
> With crimson apricots and jade peaches, coiffed topknots
>   so fragrant.
> I send a poem in apology to the old men gathering wild
>   greens,
> I've never wished to avoid other people; how could I leave
>   the world?[53]

Su Shih here gives a description of a solitary, contemplative walk from Pu-chao ssu to two smaller hermitages located on the temple grounds. It is in the final lines that the contradiction emerges, as Su suddenly turns from the quiet melancholy of the landscape and reassures his readers that, in the end, he much prefers the gaiety of a drinking party on the banks of West Lake. Since he never wished to get away from people, why should he want to leave the world as the mountain monks have? However, as Fuller perceptively notes: "The very fact that this assertion occurs at the end of a poem about a solitary walk through secluded hills . . . gives it a slightly wishful ring. Su Shih here creates a persona who seems to be trying to tell himself and his audience that he really does not need to seek out 'pure scenes' ('unsullied landscapes')."[54] One can sense an echo here of Su's response a decade earlier to the image of the silent Vimalakīrti: he is profoundly attracted but also somewhat frightened by the implications—in particular the existential loneliness—of a life committed completely to the search for enlightenment. This tension between what one might call the "urge for transcendence" and the gravitational pull of the world—whether moral, social, aesthetic, or emotional—lies at the very heart not only of Su's religious life, but of much of his writing as well.

5. In a Wilderness of Mulberry and Hemp

By 1074 Su's term of office in Hang-chou had come to an end. He was, however, in no great hurry to return to the intrigues of court life. Instead, he petitioned to be transferred to Shantung province in the hopes of being closer to his brother, Su Ch'e, who was living there at the time. Su's request was granted, and he was assigned to Mi-chou in southwest Shantung province, although at a greatly reduced salary. The contrast with his life in Hang-chou could not have been greater.

During the Han dynasty, Mi-chou had been a bustling economic and cultural center, but with the rise of the south as the cultural heart of the country, it gradually reverted to what Su termed "a wilderness of mulberry and hemp." Almost immediately on Su's arrival, the area was visited by a plague of locusts, and one of his first official duties was to petition the court to suspend the collection of autumn taxes. Deprived of the external distractions and pleasures of Hang-chou and confronted with the grim realities of his new life, Su was often ill and depressed. In an effort to cope with this new and difficult situation, Su Shih began to make use of what, according to George Hatch, "becomes a characteristic device —the creation of another, sometimes self-consciously imaginary world in which to live, enriched by the company of friends and poets past, furnished by a literature of accommodation to any environment, sustaining optimism toward the future by committing oneself thoroughly to the immediate joys of the present."[1] The art of this accommodation involved, among other things, finding new heroes such as the famous recluse T'ao Yüan-ming (376–475), whose character and writings reflected more closely Su's own changing perceptions of the world. And, not surprisingly, the more existential and metaphysical aspects of Buddhism begin to interest

him in a way they had not previously. In general, it was a very introspective period.

Li I-p'ing, author of a recent biography of Su Shih, notes that
during this period Su seems to indulge in "superstitions and
dreams . . . produced as an emotional reaction [to a situation or
environment]. One function of dreams is to supplement that which
is lacking in everyday life [i.e., wish-fulfillment], while superstitious practices are used to fill an emptiness of spirit."[2] This is a
somewhat simplistic analysis of Su Shih's psychic state, but it is
true that Su's writings include numerous accounts of dreams—
many of which convey a painful sense of isolation and loneliness
and a deep longing to break through his feelings of constriction. We
also see in this period the beginnings of a pattern often to be
repeated—an instinctive move to escape life through dreams and
sleep followed quickly by a more pragmatic attempt not only to
accommodate himself to his situation, but even to derive pleasure
from it. The physical symbol of this growing urge for transcendence is a building Su fixed up in Mi-chou called the Terrace of
Transcendence (Chao-jan t'ai). The prose piece he wrote about this
building is largely a rebuttal of a piece written by Su Ch'e that
describes Mi-chou in very unflattering terms. Su Shih replies that it
is all a matter of perspective, that one can derive as much pleasure
from the ordinary as from the extraordinary, from the common as
from the fine, from eating vegetables fresh from the garden, fishing
in the local ponds, or brewing rice wine. In Mi-chou Su was given
a chance to practice the equanimity he so admired in monks
like Pien-ts'ai who were able to live anywhere at all without
being unduly upset. If life is indeed but a temporary sojourn,
then the wisest thing to do is to derive as much pleasure and joy as
possible from one's present circumstances. As Su writes in his
account:

> There is something worth observing in all things. Whatever merits
> observation can be enjoyable—it need not be unusual, awe-
> inspiring, or beautiful: one can get drunk both by eating less and
> by drinking thin wine; one can fill one's belly with either fruits
> and vegetables or plants and trees. Extending this analogy, where
> can I go and not find joy? Now, the reason we seek good fortune
> and avoid disaster is that we consider good fortune joyful and
> disaster sorrowful. Although what men desire has no limit, there

are things that can satisfy my desires. [Distinctions between] the beautiful and the ugly battle inside [one's mind], and one is [constantly] confronted with whether to accept or reject [something]. And so the things that bring joy are always few, whereas those that bring sorrow are always many. This I call seeking disaster and avoiding good fortune, [but] now how can it be human nature to seek disaster and avoid good fortune? There is something about things that obscures [their true nature]. [Most people's minds] travel within [the confines of] things and do not wander beyond them. Things are neither [inherently] large nor small, but when seen from within, they are all towering and huge. Now whenever I am confronted by their hugeness, I become confused and anxious. It is like watching a fight through a crack in the fence—how can one know who is winning and who is losing? And so [distinctions between] the beautiful and the ugly spring up everywhere, giving rise to sorrow and joy. Is this not a great shame?[3]

In this piece, Su reminds his readers (and, even more important, himself) that distinctions between the "beautiful" and the "ugly," the "large" and the "small" are relative and not absolute. This notion appears repeatedly in the writings of Chuang-tzu, but it can also be found in many Buddhist texts. As Su notes, "There is something about things that obscures [their true nature]." He may be referring to Buddhist texts such as the *Śūraṃgama Sūtra,* where the Buddha tells Ananda that ordinary (and false) perceptions of large and small, square and round are a result of observing what appears to be external (phenomena) from the standpoint of what appears to be internal (the ego or false sense of self). In order to see things as they "really" are, one must see things from the standpoint of the mind, which is neither internal nor external.

All sentient beings from beginningless time have been deluded by externals and, losing their original minds, have been turned around by objects. Caught up in this, they perceive large and small sizes. If they could [instead] turn objects around, they would be like the Tathāgata, and their bodies and minds would be in the state of complete illumination and unchanging [perfection].[4]

This was not the first or the last time that Su found himself being "turned around by objects." When he begins to feel confused and anxious, oppressed and confined, he often turns for comfort

and clarity to the psychologically liberating perspectives of both
Chuang-tzu and Buddhism.

In 1075 Su wrote the following poem, titled "Seeing Off Spring":

> A verdant spring in a dream—can one ever catch it?
> I long to take lines of poetry and bind back the lingering
> lights.
> Wine gone, the ill traveler thinks only of sleep.
> Honey ready, the golden bee is also loathe to fly.
> Thinning temple hair, meditation bench—forget all worldly
> schemes.
> I depend on you to send me the *Meditation on the Dhar-
> madhatu*
> With which to wash away the evils of all worldly affairs.[5]

The *Fa-chieh kuan-men* [Meditation on the Dharmadhatu] was a
Buddhist text that had recently been recommended to Su Ch'e by a
friend. It is a relatively short but rather difficult text (designed as a
meditation manual rather than a philosophical treatise) attributed
to Tu Shun (558–640), the first patriarch of Hua-yen Buddhism.
The text was extremely significant for the development of Chinese
Buddhism because it interpreted the Mahāyāna notion of śūnyatā
in terms of principle *(li)* and phenomenon *(shih),* two terms drawn
from the Chinese philosophical tradition. As Peter Gregory points
out, the use of these terms marks an "important shift towards an
affirmation of the phenomenal world."[6] This text discusses the different ways that phenomena and principle interrelate and shows
how, ultimately, the world is characterized by total interpenetration
in which "each and every phenomenon is not only seen to contain
each and every other phenomenon, but all phenomena are also seen
to contain the totality of the unobstructed interpenetration of all
phenomena."[7]

In "Seeing Off Spring" Su Shih appears to be more interested in
cleansing the defilements of the world than in realizing their inseparability from nirvana. However, other writings from this period
more directly reflect his interest in the Hua-yen philosophy of totality and the interpenetration of phenomenon and principle. An
example is an account (also written in 1075) describing the circumstances surrounding the construction of the Pavilion of the Great
Compassionate [One] in Ch'eng-tu. Su wrote this piece at the

request of a Buddhist monk by the name of Ming-hsing, who was the grandson of Master Chang, painter of *lohan,* and was himself a painter of Buddhist images. I translate a good portion of this account below, because it provides an excellent example of Su's more philosophical musings at this time. It also shows, yet again, the profound influence of the *Śūraṃgama Sūtra.* (Chüeh-fan Hui-hung quotes Su's piece entirely in his *Shou Leng-yen ching ho lun* [Combined discourses on the *Śūraṃgama Sūtra*], as does the Ch'ing critic Ch'ien Ch'ien-i in his collection of commentaries on this sutra.[8]) The hymn begins with a preface:

> The [bodhisattva of] Great Compassion is [one of the] transfor-
> mation-bodies of Kuan-shih-yin. Kuan-shih-yin achieved realiza-
> tion by means of [the sense-faculty of] hearing.[9] From the start
> [although] he listens, [yet] it is possible for there to be nothing
> that he hears. From the start [although] there is nothing he listens
> to, it is possible for there to be nothing that he does not hear. The
> reason it is possible for there to be nothing that he hears is that he
> is not incarnate. The reason it is possible for there to be nothing
> that he does not hear is that he has countless incarnate forms. [If
> this is true of the bodhisattva's ears] how much more [is it true] in
> the case of [the bodhisattva's] hands and eyes. Thus, if he were
> not nonincarnate, he would not have the wherewithal to support
> countless incarnate forms; while if he did not have countless incar-
> nate forms, he would not have the wherewithal to demonstrate the
> perfection of the nonincarnate [state]. For this reason, [no matter
> whether] he divides himself into countless incarnate forms or
> gathers together to form [a single manifestation composed of]
> 85,000 [hands in various] *mudrā*s and the 85,000 pure and pre-
> cious eyes, it is all but one single Way.[10]

Su describes how Kuan-shih-yin (whom I refer to here as "he" although I could also use "she") achieved enlightenment by means of the sense-faculty of hearing. This description is based, at least in part, on the section of the *Śūraṃgama Sūtra* in which Avalokiteś-vara (Kuan-shih-yin) himself relates how he attained enlightenment by fixing his attention first on the object of hearing, then on the sense of hearing, and finally on the organ of hearing itself:

> In this way, slowly and gradually both hearing and the object of
> hearing came to an end. [However, although] they had ceased, I
> did not stop there [but went on to the point where both my]

awareness of this state and this state itself were [as if] empty. When this awareness of emptiness reached completeness, both the emptiness and that which was emptied were extinguished.[11]

In the *Śūraṃgama Sūtra,* this experience, which is equivalent to fully realizing the *tathāgata-garbha,* or all-perfect, all-luminous Buddha-mind, makes it possible for the bodhisattva to assume the many different forms and respond to the countless needs of sentient beings:

> When I first attained the marvelous, marvelous hearing-mind *(miao-miao wen-hsin),* the essence of this mind *(hsin-ching,* i.e., the *tathāgata-garbha)* left hearing behind and there was no longer any distinction between seeing, hearing, feeling, and knowing: [it all] became a single all-pervading, clean, and pure Precious Awareness *(pao-chüeh).* For this reason I am able to manifest myself in so many marvelous forms.[12]

Su Shih in his piece dramatizes this ability to respond appropriately as follows:

> Suppose I have an ordinary human being swing an ax in his left hand while wielding a knife in his right, count the flying geese with his eyes while noting the beat of the drums with his ears. With his head he should be able to nod to a passerby [at the same time that] he is using his feet to climb up the stairs. No matter how intelligent he is, he will not be able to do all of this at once. How much more so if he had a thousand hands, each holding something different, and a thousand eyes, each looking [at something different]. Now when I sit in tranquility, my thoughts concentrated and still, deep like a great luminous mirror, then men, ghosts, and beasts of all sorts appear before me, [while] forms, sounds, smells, and tastes combine together in my body. Although my mind does not rise [to meet phenomena], there is nothing it does not connect with.[13]

Here Su explores the idea that spiritual detachment does not mean that one must abandon the world, or even the senses. Rather, you can sit quietly, and the world will come to you. By detaching oneself from (particular) things and realizing the One Mind, one is able to make connection with all things and to respond to the world around one.

Finally comes the hymn itself:

> I ponder over us mortals with two eyes and two arms,
> Who, when objects arise, are unable to respond.

With wild delusions and utter confusion,
We react by becoming filled with desire.
Distraught and beset by anxious thoughts.
Even though anxious thought is inherently unreal,
We might as well have no eyes and no arms!
The bodhisattva has a thousand eyes and arms,
But might as well have only a single eye and arm.
When objects arise, then the mind also arises.
However, the bodhisattva is never anxious,
But responds to whatever needs responding to,
And there is nothing that is not appropriately met.
A taut bow set with a white arrow.
Sword and shield made of maple wood;
Sutra scrolls and incense flowers.
A finger bowl made of green willow;
A large jeweled censer made of coral;
A white whisk, a vermilion hazelwood staff,
The bodhisattva understands all he meets,
And that which he grasps, he does not doubt.
How has the bodhisattva attained to this no-doubt?
Because his "self" is a self of no-mind.
If the bodhisattva still possessed a mind,
Then a thousand arms would mean a thousand minds.
And a thousand minds inside one single body—
What a terrible struggle that would cause!
How would the bodhisattva have time to respond?
But because these thousand hands have no-mind,
Each arm is able to find its own place.
Bowing my head to the Great Compassionate One,
I vow to help all sentient beings cross over.
That they may all find the Way of no-mind,
And all be of a thousand arms, a thousand eyes.

The poem carries on from the preface; it repeats and refers to ideas developed there. However, there is an integrity to the hymn itself. It begins with the "I observe" or "I contemplate" *(kuan)* that marks it as a meditative poem. The object of the poet's contemplation is the thousand-armed bodhisattva, the sight of which has brought to mind thoughts concerning mortal men, the same mortal men Su described in the preface as being hardly able to manage a hatchet in one hand and a knife in the other. Here he repeats much the same thing in a different way: although people have only two arms and two eyes, they are still confused and bewildered by

worldly objects; they do not know the art of response. The bodhisattva, however, with his thousand arms and thousand eyes, is neither anxious nor confused and thus can respond to all things with
compassion.

The first part of the poem, then, states the dilemma, the paradox
posed by the vision of this great statue of the thousand-armed
bodhisattva at Ch'eng-tu. Before he deals directly with the possible
reasons for this paradox, however, Su shifts the tempo of the poem
by moving from the meditative mode to a descriptive one, dwelling
in a leisurely and lyrical fashion on the various accoutrements of
the bodhisattva, interjecting color—white arrows, green willows,
white whisk, vermilion staff—into the grays of a purely philosophical discourse. Only then does the poet return to the root question:
how has the bodhisattva attained this state of no-doubt? And he
answers: because his "self" is that of no-mind. Quickly and with a
touch of his characteristic wit, Su then explains why this must be—
imagine the bickering and fighting if there were a thousand minds
struggling for control of a single physical body! Seemingly satisfied
with this explanation, he ends his hymn in time-honored fashion,
with a renewal of the bodhisattva vow that all sentient beings may
attain to the state of no-mind symbolized by this thousand-armed
statue of Kuan-shih-yin.

Su was not only interested in the ideas in the *Śūraṃgama Sūtra;*
although mostly written in prose form, it contains a number of
teachings in verse. One of the longest of these is delivered by the
bodhisattva Mañjuśrī; Lu K'uan-yü titles it "Mañjuśrī's *Gāthā*
Teaching the Appropriate Method for Human Beings."[14] It might
well have been the flowing, almost hypnotic style of this particular
gāthā that Su was attempting to emulate. The eminent Ming
dynasty monk and critic Ta-kuan Chen-k'o (1542–1603) apparently
believed this was the case. He writes:

> The fish are alive, but the fish trap is dead. Meaning is alive, but
> words and letters are dead. Therefore it is said that those who
> place all their faith in words perish, while those who are distracted
> by phrases are lost. However, when I read the "Hymn to the Great
> Compassionate One," I knew that Tung-p'o had attained to the
> living [i.e., the spirit] even as he made use of the dead [i.e., the
> words]. Thus that which was dead has come completely to life.
> Tung-p'o often praised the writing of the [*Śūraṃgama Sūtra*], say-

ing that there was nothing that matched it for delicate subtlety and marvelous style. Looking at these two [the *Śūraṃgama Sūtra* and Su's Shih's hymn], it is [clear that] the poet has grasped the wondrousness not only of the dead part [the language] of the *Śūraṃgama Sūtra,* but also of the living part [its spirit]. How is it that he has been able to fulfill the [requirements of] words and letters and yet divorce himself from words and letters in order to reveal [the essence of] the One of [a Thousand] Arms and Eyes?[15]

Su Shih was only in Mi-chou for three years. In 1076 he suddenly received word that he was to take up a new post in Hsü-chou in the southeastern province of Kiangsu. He met his brother along the way, and they traveled together for part of the journey. They had planned to stop at the capital, but, unexpectedly, they were denied entrance because of some new regulations and stayed instead at the home of their friend Fan Chen (Ching-jen), remaining there for a few months before setting out for Hsü-chou. It would seem that Su often was in the position of defending his interest in Buddhism with his more solidly Confucian friends, Fan Ching-jen among them. Su says that Fan, who was "no lover of Buddhism," went so far as to "slander" the Buddha's teachings.[16] Fan was a skeptical person and insisted that he would not believe anything he could not see with his own eyes. Su, however, is said to have once reminded his friend of his willingness to believe his physician when he tells him that his internal *ch'i* is in need of balancing—even though he himself has never actually seen this vital energy! Why then does he insist on seeing the Buddha before believing in his teachings?[17] Su notes that, despite Fan's lifelong antipathy toward Buddhism, in the end he was such a pure and circumspect person that he came to embody Buddhism's most essential principles.

The period at Hsü-chou was filled with official duties that began as soon as Su arrived. He was immediately confronted with a devastating flood caused by a break in the dikes of the Yellow River, an emergency that he handled so effectively that he received an imperial commendation. While at Hsü-chou Su also produced many well-written and judicious memorials to the court.

It was also in Hsü-chou that Su finally met the Buddhist poet-monk Ts'an-liao (Tao-ch'ien, 1043–ca. 1116), who would become a good friend. Ts'an-liao (posthumously given the title of Great Master Miao-ts'ung) was born in Yü-chien, outside of Hang-chou. He was moved to become a monk at an early age, it is said, after reading the *Lotus Sūtra*. He was also an accomplished poet. He is regarded by Chinese Buddhists as one of the eight Buddhist poets of the Sung, but he was often criticized by his contemporaries for writing what seemed to be overly secular poetry for a monk. Su no doubt was attracted by Ts'an-liao's poetic talents as well as by his personality, which was in some ways much like Su's. He was apparently extremely outspoken and did not hesitate to offer unsolicited criticism. Su, however, would defend his friend, saying that when he scolded someone, he did so without feeling any personal anger, so that it was like being hit by "an empty boat." He describes the monk's somewhat paradoxical personality as follows:

> There is no one like Master Ts'an-liao. He is poor of body but rich in the Tao. He is eloquent when he writes, yet stutters when he speaks. On the surface he is meek and mild, but inside he is strong and virile. He does not compete with people, yet he likes to criticize his friends' errors. A withered form, an ashen mind, and yet he delights in playing with phenomena, unable to forget completely the language of feeling. These are five reasons why Master Ts'an-liao is not easily understood.[18]

Su's many poems and letters addressed to Ts'an-liao, although not free from the conventions expected of writings addressed to a Buddhist monk, seem to reflect a deeper affinity. The following poem was written in 1075.

> The breast of this man of Tao is as pure as the mirror-
> waters,
> From which myriad forms arise and disappear without
> a trace.
> Living alone at the old temple, he plants fall chrysan-
> themums,
> I long to dine on the fallen flowers with this man of
> Sao.[19]
> Where in this world of men is there a north and a
> south?
> How can a flock-bound wild goose vanish alone into
> the blue?
> His doors closed, he wears a hole in his meditation
> cushion,

While above his head the months and years pile up
   unnoticed.
This year he happened to leave his room in search of
   dharma,[20]
Wishing to polish and hone the Sword of Discrimina-
   tion.
His robes so torn and patched they look like hills and
   streams,
His ragged frost-white whiskers frighten off the
   children!
Dukes and lords seek in vain to make his acquain-
   tance,
And so realize that his homely face is not for the
   buying!
The autumn wind carries my dream across the River
   Huai,
And I imagine I see the oranges hanging in the empty
   hall.
Friends that find themselves at opposite ends of the
   sky;
Gazing toward each other like scattered morning stars.
How can this old magistrate of P'eng-ch'eng be worth
   the trouble?
Now that I pass the time of day with farmers and
   country folk.
Undaunted by the thousand hills between you and my
   rustic hut,
In your desire to see me, your feet fly like gibbons.
Line after line of silken words pour forth endlessly.
He still has the sinuously intricate feelings of a poet.[21]
The gibbon's call and the heron's cry have no special
   meaning;
They are unaware that below them a traveler walks by.
The rain on the empty stairs is also completely
   innocent,
What then plays on my heart like an orphan's cry?
I long to gather herbs in the mountains of the
   immortals,
But instead sit and sigh, "When will this basket be
   filled?"
Piles of papers, official responsibilities fill my days,
Only at night is there time to share a little tea and rice.

I beg you to use your Mani pearl to cleanse this turbid
   water,[22]
As together we watch the setting moon tilt like a
   golden bowl.[23]

This poem is interesting in terms of the added perspective it gives
on Su's poetic ideas, and it is also profoundly satisfying aesthetically. Although one must shy away from using the term "sincerity,"
one can sense a depth of feeling in this poem that does not depend
on the knowledge that Su Shih and Ts'an-liao were very close
friends. There is also an aesthetic coherence to this poem, which I
think may derive from the firm thread of emotion that binds
together lines that are not particularly lyrical.

   There is a careful organization to this rather long poem. The first
four lines are a general description of Ts'an-liao. Su considers him
first and foremost a man of considerable spiritual development; the
term *shui ching* (waterlike mirror) is often used in Confucian texts
to refer to a person's particular perceptiveness, discrimination, and
vision. This meaning is not lost here, although it is enriched by the
Buddhist metaphor of the mirror, which reflects all the phenomena
of the world faithfully without possessing them or being attached
to them. It is a vision unclouded by ignorance, ego, or attachment.

   The following two lines contain a Buddhist image that contrasts
the unenlightened view of time and space with the enlightened one
(seen before in the quote from the *Vimalakīrti Sūtra*). And in the
Platform Sūtra, Hui-neng recounts how, when he first arrived at
East Mountain to study with Hung-jen and told him that he was a
commoner from the south, the master reproved him saying: "If
you're from Ling-nan [the south] then you're a barbarian. How
can you become a Buddha?" Hui-neng's reply was: "Although
people from the south and people from the north differ, there is no
north and south in Buddha nature."[24] In the next line Su refers to
geese, which he uses elsewhere as a symbol of enlightenment in that
they leave no tracks behind them as they soar through the heavens.
Here, however, even they cannot escape the distinction between
north and south. These two lines introduce the theme of this poem,
which is the friendship between the two men and the delight the
poet feels at the prospect of a visit. He is saying that although he
knows that there is a different way of looking at the question of

time and space, when it comes to being parted from a friend, he is still human and still acutely aware of the distance that separates them, the difference between north and south.

The subsequent lines return to Ts'an-liao, this time in both a narrative and a descriptive vein, setting the background for the monk's visit. Su describes Ts'an-liao's long years of solitude and spiritual cultivation and his decision to go back to the world of men, part of the Mahāyāna Buddhist injunction to return to the marketplace. The lines descriptive of Ts'an-liao's appearance are very typical of Su Shih; his tattered robes are compared to old paintings, for which Su nursed a special fondness, and his uncut whiskers frighten the children. There is a spontaneity and informal feeling about these lines that is characteristic of Su, and it shows the depth of feeling between the two men: the poet's respect for Ts'an-liao does not hinder him from describing the monk's rather homely appearance. The next four lines express this affection more fully. The geographical obstacles to travel were by no means negligible in those days, not to mention the general lack of control even the highest government official had over where he was placed or what he would be doing. Ts'an-liao endured much hardship in order to visit Su Shih, especially during Su's periods of exile, and in these lines we can see how much the poet appreciated these expressions of friendship.

Once together, the two men spent many hours in conversation and writing poetry. The following lines refer to Ts'an-liao's poetry. Despite his rather forbidding appearance and his long and arduous spiritual discipline, he is capable of writing "embroidered words," i.e., lyrical and emotional rather than simply dryly "religious" verse. However, once more Su makes oblique reference to the detachment or emptiness that is at the root of Ts'an-liao's verse. Thus, like the cry of the gibbon, the weeping of the crane, the sound of rain on empty steps, it gives the appearance of being completely unpremeditated, completely spontaneous, and unaware of the effect it will have on the travelers walking below. This "pure" spontaneity is surely Su Shih's highest aesthetic ideal, whether or not he achieved it in his own work. The next four lines contrast the apparent freedom, inner and outer, of Ts'an-liao, with Su's own situation, being caught up in the onerous duties of the bureaucratic life and longing to leave it all behind and retreat to the hills—a longing that expresses itself more and more frequently in Su's poetry. The poem ends beautifully with a plea to his friend to share his Buddhist clarity, if only for a moment, and shed a little spiritual light (and emotional companionship) on his own turgid existence. The sun setting in the final lines makes for a simple but somehow very satisfying conclusion to the poem.

Ts'an-liao was a great inspiration to Su, but at the same time he seems to have made Su even more aware of his own limitations. A poem Su wrote to match one written by Ts'an-liao expresses this feeling very beautifully:

> Nature's artisans have not yet discussed the many
>   bridges of Su-chou;
> They head first for the winter plum and turn them
>   upside down.
> The snow thaws south of the Yangtze, spring mists begin
>   to rise.
> Melting away the ice-flowers, cooling down my feverish
>   brain.
> The wind is refreshing, the moon sets, and no one here
>   to watch!
> The fresh-faced Lo-fu maiden slips away at the break
>   of day.[25]
> No one left but, flying overhead, a pair of white egrets;
> Jade feathers on a coral branch vying for loveliness.
> Wu Mountain's man of Tao has a heart as clear as water.
> His vision a spotless void with nothing there to sweep
>   away.
> He can use marvelous language to express the many
>   emotions.
> His strategies are just a test for this Old Man Tung-p'o.
> But Tung-p'o's wordly addictions are not yet completely
>   cured;
> At times he writes long prose pieces and small grass
>   characters.
> He can still shake the long branches and dine on fallen
>   blossoms:
> His hunger does not yet warrant calling out to the
>   heavens.[26]

Here we see, with considerable poignancy, the nature of Su's poetic friendship with Ts'an-liao, the very deep admiration he felt for the monk and his poetry, and his sincere wish to emulate him. There is also the conception of language as a form of skillful means, a strategy for inducing enlightenment, that was to become widely subscribed to by both Buddhist and lay poets in the Sung. In the end, however, there is Su's acknowledgment of his own limitations or, rather, of his own deep-seated reluctance to take the necessary step away from the realm of emotions and attachments—and art. In the last lines we see a man who is determined to rely on his own powers, who does not yet feel driven to the point where he must make a decision. He is not hungry enough spiritually to call out to the heavens.

This idea of calling to the heavens for help appears in a hymn of praise Su wrote for a friend by the name of Chu Shou-ch'ang, who was separated from his mother at the age of seven, zealously dedicated himself to Buddhist devotions, among them writing out sutras with his own blood, and was ultimately rewarded by finding his mother again when he was over forty years old. In the preface to this poem, Su writes:

> I have observed that most of those in this world who have attained the Tao have done so because of their sufferings. When their sufferings become unbearable, they have no one to tell them to, so they call out to their fathers and mothers. [If] their fathers and mothers do not listen to them, then they raise their heads and call out to Heaven. [If] Heaven is unable to save them, then they must entrust their lives to Buddha, the World-honored One. The Buddha in his great compassion [uses] skillful means to enlighten them and cause them to understand that all sufferings stem from desire.[27]

Even though he is not prepared to undergo the same religious discipline as Ts'an-liao (who "wears a hole in his meditation cushion, while above his head the months and years pile up unnoticed"), Su realizes the potential power, both personal and aesthetic, in the kind of "emptiness" Ts'an-liao embodied. Because Ts'an-l'iao is "as pure as the mirror-waters," his poetry can fully reflect the world, even the world of emotion and feeling. The implications of the contemplative state for the writing of poetry continued to concern Su Shih deeply. Another very well known poem, also addressed to Ts'an-liao, deals more directly with the question of the relationship between Buddhism and poetry.

The Reverend Master has investigated suffering and
   emptiness,
In you, the hundred thoughts are already as cold as ash.
The hilt of a sword can produce only a wheeze,[28]
A scorched seed will not sprout again.
So why do you seek out people like me,
Comparing your words with ours for richness and
   brilliance?
Your new poems are like jade-white snows;
The words you speak are of a startling purity.
T'ui-chih commented on someone's running script,
"Endless affairs as yet unrestrained;
Anxiety and sorrow, an unbalanced *ch'i;*
All of it lodged in the sweep of the brush.
I sometimes wonder about these Buddhists
Who look upon the self as an empty hill-top well.
Lazy and lethargic, grounded in the still and bland.
But can they produce something dynamic and strong?"
I've considered this carefully and find I don't agree.
Genuine skill is more than mere illusion.
If you wish to make your poems marvelous,
You must not despise emptiness or stillness.
For it is in stillness that all movements are completed;
And it is in emptiness that all worlds are contained.
Observing the world, when walking among men;
Contemplating the self, when resting on cloudy peaks,
The salty and the sour both contain many fine flavors
And among them can also be found the constant flavor
"Poetry and the dharma do not cancel each other out"
This is a statement I must ask you more about.[29]

    The organization of this poem shows the hand of a master essay-
ist. The first few lines are a description of Ts'an-liao's spiritual
attainments; he has evidently been able, through Buddhist meditation and inquiry, to see through the illusory nature of emotional
and worldly experience. Thus, his heart (mind) is ash-cold. The
poet then asks the inevitable questions (1) Why does a person who
has achieved the state of wordlessness still seek out poets like himself and join in their literary rivalries? and (2) How does a person
who has presumably gone beyond the emotion that is generally the
prime impetus for writing poetry manage to produce poetry of a
very high order himself?

Before tackling these questions, Su refers to his literary predecessor Han Yü. In a piece commenting on the cursive calligraphy of a certain Kao Hsien, Han Yü makes the point that it is precisely because the calligrapher combined a heart full of "anxiety, sorrow, and unbalanced *ch'i* with the mastery of his art and the ability to concentrate singlemindedly that he was able to produce such a powerful work of art."[30] In other words, it is the combination of deeply felt emotion desperate for expression and masterful technical skill that results in vigorous and dynamic poetry (or good art). Han Yü's theory seems to have been that "writing, especially poetry, results when external stimulation causes some imbalance in the writer's emotional balance."[31]

> In general, it is when things in the world are disturbed that they make noise. The trees and grasses are ordinarily silent, but when the winds buffet them they make noise. Water is silent, but when breezes stir it up then it makes noise. . . . Similarly, stone and metal chimes do not sound of their own accord. It is only when someone strikes them that they make noise. It is the same with regard to men and the words they speak. Words are uttered only when someone has no choice but to speak. When someone utters any sound whatsoever, it is because his heart is not at peace.[32]

Han Yü's argument is fairly convincing: the artist commits his skill and wisdom so single-mindedly to his work that external things do not stick to his mind. But he retains his emotions and perceptions of the world, which are expressed in his art. He does not have the same kind of detachment exemplified by the Buddhist monk who has cut all ties with worldly experience and, so says Han Yü, is quiescent and bland and cannot possibly create anything of any vitality or value. Han Yü seems to view art as a reaction to external stimulus, which differs greatly from Su's own developing views.

Su does subscribe to one part of Han Yü's argument, that is, the idea of "lodging," which is very close to the Buddhist teaching of nonabiding or nonattachment, the single-minded concentration of Han Yü's artist being comparable to the meditative state of the Buddhist monk. Here, for instance, is Huang T'ing-chien admonishing a Buddhist monk and would-be painter:

> The reason why Master Wu [Tao-tzu] surpassed his teacher was that he learned from the mind, so that whatever he did was excel-

lent. When Administrator-in-Chief Chang [Hsü] did not cultivate other skills, the use of his talents was undivided, so that he was able to become completely absorbed. . . . *For if the mind is able not to be distracted by external things, then one's original nature is preserved intact, and all things appear in abundance as if in a mirror.*[33] (italics mine)

But Huang and Su Shih reject Han Yü's assumption that Buddhists completely disregard emotion. Perhaps Ts'an-liao provided proof that a Buddhist's detachment from the world and his own emotions did not necessarily mean that he no longer experienced them. He was no longer *distracted* by them, perhaps, but he continued to feel them with a clarity and fullness perhaps denied to the man of *"unbalanced ch'i,"* no matter how superb his artistic ability. In fact, the monk's very detachment, acquired and maintained through contemplative stillness and emptiness, would seem to enable him to use these emotions that much more effectively for the writing of poetry. As Ronald C. Egan puts it:

> Su Shih does not reject the notion of "lodging," applied either to poetry or calligraphy. He objects to Han Yü's insistence about what it is that gets lodged in these arts. Instead of lodging emotions, Su Shih prefers to speak of lodging *i* ("intent, the mind") or *hsing* ("exhilaration"). If Han Yü's lodging seems a cathartic release of pent-up feelings, Su Shih's lodging is an entrusting of the mind or the personality to the art. Su is less apt to think of this artistic lodging as a purging of feelings than as a transcendence of self-centered concerns.[34]

In his discussion of this poem, Richard John Lynn notes, rightly, that Su is not only arguing for individuality and spontaneity in poetry, but also warning against imitation. "Although he does not seem to have ever explicitly formulated a 'sudden' approach to poetic success or 'enlightenment,' " Lynn claims, "the many references to freedom and spontaneity in his writings indicate that he surely would have been in the 'sudden' camp if he had to choose sides."[35] Although there is no question that Su Shih was far less concerned with rules and "correct" models than his contemporary Huang T'ing-chien (whom Lynn calls a "thoroughgoing 'gradualist' "), Su Shih also believed that spontaneity and freedom often came only after long years of practice. As he writes in his appreciation of Li K'ang-nien's calligraphic rendering of the *Heart Sūtra* quoted in Chapter 2: "If suddenly I am asked to write something in large and small seal characters, it is like trying to walk straight along the edge of a wall. After repeated practice, I get a rough grasp of it, and I try to manage a naturalness in the way I manipulate my brush." Only after repeated practice (which, it is implied, Li K'ang-nien spent many years on), the "mind forgets the hand, the hand forgets the brush, the brush naturally lowers onto the page, without the ego exerting any effort."[36] In other words, while the actual experience of enlightenment (or artistic creation) is sudden and completely spontaneous, it is often preceded by some kind of gradual cultivation. Thus, even Ts'an-liao is described in the following way: "His doors closed, he wears a hole in his meditation cushion / While above his head the months and years pile up unnoticed."

In 1079 Su Shih received notice of his transfer to Hu-chou, which was not far from Hang-chou in Chekiang province. He took advantage of the journey to see the sights, and together with some close friends, including Ts'an-liao, he traveled by boat down the Huai and Yangtze rivers, stopping off at Mt. Chin and Mt. Hui to visit some of his many monk friends and commemorating each occasion with poems. At this time he probably also visited the Buddhist monk Fo-yin Liao-yüan (1038–1098), perhaps the best known of Su's monk friends.[37]

Fo-yin was born in Shao-chou (Kiangsi province) to a family of Confucian scholar officials. Although the hagiographic claim that by age two he could recite the *Analects* and by five he could recite three thousand poems by memory is certainly exaggerated, he was clearly an exceptionally gifted child. He is said to have studied all of the Confucian classics as a young man and was noted for his mastery of their contents. At the age of fifteen, however, after reading the *Śūraṃgama Sūtra,* he abandoned these studies and left home to become a monk. He studied under a number of Ch'an Buddhist teachers of the Yün-men school, including Su Hsün's friend Yüan-t'ung Chu-no. Chu-no had particular regard for Fo-yin's literary talents and compared him to Hsüeh-tou Chung-hsien (980–1052), the highly gifted poet-monk whose verses form the heart of the koan collection *Pi-yen lu* (translated into English as the *Blue Cliff Collection*) compiled by Yüan-wu K'o-ch'in (1036–

1135). Fo-yin served for a time as Chu-no's secretary, a post left vacant when Huai-lien left for the capital. However, it appears that administrative duties, even monastic ones, did not agree with him, and Fo-yin left not only this post but Chu-no as well, returning to become a formal student of Ch'an Master K'ai-hsien Ch'ih-tao, a second-generation disciple of Wen-yen Yün-men. Finally, after many years of traveling from temple to temple, Fo-yin settled on Mt. Chin, an island mountain located in the Yangtze River in Chekiang province.

Fo-yin was not a man of conventional spirituality—he probably spent more time with his lay literati poet friends than he did with his fellow monks and more time drinking wine and composing poetry than doing meditation or preaching. One of his early contacts would appear to have been Chou Tun-i (1017–1073), an important figure in the Confucian revival of the Northern Sung, who held office in the Mt. Lu area for five and a half years beginning in 1069. However, it was Fo-yin's relationship with Su Shih that became famous, the subject of innumerable anecdotes, stories, legends, and even dramatic pieces.[38]

The exchanges between Su Shih and Fo-yin (many of which are no doubt apocryphal) often display the deft use of paradox and irony that one expects from a Ch'an master. One day Su Shih composed a *gāthā* of which he was particularly proud, since it seemed to have captured the "imperturbability" of the Ch'an spirit perfectly. He immediately had a servant deliver a copy to Fo-yin, then living at Mt. Chin, in order to learn his opinion. Fo-yin received the poem, but offered no comment whatever. Reluctant to return home without an answer, the servant asked Fo-yin to make some comment. Fo-yin finally said something quite disparaging about the poem. When Su Shih heard this, he was furious; he immediately set out for Mt. Chin and confronted the monk personally. It did not take Su Shih long, however, to realize the yawning gap that lay between his poem on imperturbability and his perturbation. The two men laughed heartily. The friendship between Fo-yin and Su Shih is known particularly for such humorous, light-hearted, yet somehow satisfying exchanges.

In the late twelfth century a compilation of these exchanges (many of them obviously apocryphal) titled *The Recorded Sayings and Question-Answer [Dialogues] of Layman Tung-p'o and Ch'an*

Master Fo-yin (Tung-p'o chü-shih Fo-yin Ch'an yü-lu wen-ta) was apparently very popular not only among the literati but in the entertainment districts as well.[39] In the *Chin-kang k'o-i pao-chüan,* a semipopularized version of the *Diamond Sūtra* attributed to a southern Sung monk by the name of Tsung Ching, Su is listed alongside such figures as Śakyamuni and the Sixth Patriarch as an example of those who have pursued the spiritual path. The reason he is so listed is that "he was often close to Fo-yin"![40] In the popular story of Su's transgressions in his previous incarnation noted in Chapter 1, Master Wu-tzu Chieh is admonished by a fellow monk. When Wu-tzu Chieh dies and is reborn in the body of a white rooster, this monk recognizes him and puts him in a cage near the temple door so the bird can listen to religious sermons. As a result, the rooster is reborn again as Su Shih. The fellow monk eventually dies and is born into a Confucian family, and although initially planning to pursue an official career, he ends up becoming a Buddhist monk: the dharma name he is given is Fo-yin. According to the story, Su was initially vehemently opposed to Buddhism but, thanks to an exchange of poems with Fo-yin, is eventually converted and takes up Buddhist spiritual cultivation!

Su greatly admired Fo-yin's poetic talent:

> Although I long to ride a winged chariot,
> And visit Master Red Pine in the east,[41]
> The isle of P'eng-lai cannot be reached,
> Over the thirty-thousand-*li*-long River Jo.[42]
> Better then to go and visit Mt. Chin:
> With just a light wind and sails half full.
> Amid the hills rises the Sumeru Terrace,
> Its cloud-covered peak standing all alone.
> If you look up at where the roads all end,
> Who would believe it was millstone-smooth!
> Inside this terrace there lives an old monk,
> With blue eyes that mirror window and chair.[43]
> Sharp and pronounced are his jadelike bones,
> Bright and gleaming his frost-white teeth.
> His probing paradoxes are not easily grasped;
> His thousand *gāthā*s gush out like spilled water.[44]
> What need is there to go in search of Te-yün,[45]
> When there is a monk like this right here?

I've been unable to learn the art of immortality,
So please teach me the way of deathlessness.[46]

Su had not been in office in Hu-chou for three months when he
was summoned to the capital to face very serious charges. His political enemies claimed that his writings contained slanderous and
subversive allusions to the emperor and the court as well as to current policies. Su was arrested in Hu-chou, taken to the capital, and
put in jail for over one hundred days. That Su was bewildered and
disoriented during his time in jail and fully expected to be executed
is evidenced by poems he wrote to Su Ch'e at this time. Not surprisingly, after he was finally released and exiled to Huang-chou in
Hupei province, his thoughts began to take a more somber and
increasingly introspective hue. This experience marked a major
turning point in his life, as he writes in a moving letter to a friend:

> Ever since I was accused of this crime, I have closed myself off to
> everything, and like a skiff floating among the grasses and set
> adrift between the mountains and the sea, I have been mingling
> with woodcutters and fishermen. I am often mocked and cursed
> for a drunk, but for now I am delighted that I am slowly becoming
> a stranger to men. From friends of a lifetime, I have not seen or
> heard a single word. When I write to them, they do not respond.
> Now you, sir, once again start up correspondence—it is not some-
> thing I had expected. The tree has its gnarls, the boulders have
> their vapors, and the magic rhinoceros has a stripe down its horn;
> [all of these] are used to attract [the attention] of men and [yet] all
> of them are [the results of] disease. Now that I am in exile, there is
> little to occupy me, so I have been engaging in silent and contem-
> plative introspection. Looking back over the past thirty years, all
> the many defects of my life, which you, sir, see, belong to the I of
> the past and not to the I of the present. How can you simply listen
> to the sounds and not consider the feeling [behind them] or gather
> the blossoms and toss away the fruit? It is impossible to explain
> my meaning fully in a letter without seeing you personally. Ever
> since I got into trouble, I have not dared to write.[47]

And, in fact, Su Shih did give up writing for a while, devoting himself to Buddhist meditation and the study of the Buddhist sutras. In
a letter to his literary disciple Ch'in Kuan (1049–1101), Su writes:
"Since I got into trouble, I've not written a thing and I am exercising considerable self-control. If I were to write again, it would be

like breaking down the walls of a dam—out would pour a torrent of words."[48]

When Su Shih did start to write again—and it was inevitable that he would—it was indeed like a dam giving loose: it is generally agreed that the poems written during the Huang-chou period are among his most compelling. Many of these poems are, not surprisingly, permeated with philosophical inquietude and concern. They also show the influence, both philosophical and imagistic, of some of the Buddhist texts he had been reading so intensively. As Ch'ien Ch'ien-i notes, "Before Huang-chou, Su's writing took its [inspiration] from Chuang-tzu; after Huang-chou, it derived [that inspiration] from Buddhism."[49] Su approached these texts selectively, drawing poetic inspiration from the vitality of their language and images, and spiritual sustenance and solace from their glorious visions of inner emancipation. He took more than a purely intellectual interest in them, as can be seen from the contents of a letter written to a friend at this time:

I've always enjoyed reading Buddhist books, but as I am ignorant and dense, I've never been able fully to grasp their marvelousness. Just once in a while, I manage to extract a very superficial and general idea, which I then use to purify and cleanse my mind. It is like a farmer pulling weeds: as soon as he pulls one out, another springs up in its place. . . . Although it may seem to be a useless task, in the end it is better than not pulling weeds at all.[50]

These modest claims must be taken with a grain of salt. It has often been noted that many of Su Shih's philosophical commentaries are brilliantly written, if rather unsystematic. However, as Christian Murck points out, this lack of rigorous intellectual analysis should be regarded not as an indication of Su's superficiality and reluctance to grapple with the issues but as an expression of his rejection of highly systematic and "dry" philosophical discourse.[51] The letter quoted above continues as follows:

Compared to the so-called transcendent and enlightened among the gentlemen of the world, I know nothing. In the past Ch'en Shu-ku [1017–1080] enjoyed talking about Ch'an and considered his [understanding] to be enlightened while disdaining mine for being superficial and limited. I would say to Shu-ku, "What you speak of is, to use the analogy of eating and drinking, like dining on dragon's flesh, while what I have learned is like [eating] pork. Of course, there is a difference between dragon's flesh and pork, but even if you talk the entire day about dragon's flesh, it cannot compare to being able to dine on pork [that is] truly delicious and filling.

Su's concerns are not so much scholarly as practical: although his understanding may be superficial in comparison to the truly enlightened, it is an understanding that can satisfy a spiritual hunger, a hunger whetted by the experience of exile.

6. An Ant on a Millstone

IN A POEM written in 1080 at the start of his exile in Huang-chou, Su compares himself to a tiny ant struggling for survival in a heartless universe.

> We are born between heaven and earth,
> Solitary ants riding a huge millstone.
> For all our paltry attempts to move to the right,
> We are helplessly turned by the wind wheel to the
>   left.[1]
> Although I have practiced benevolence and righ-
>   teousness,
> I have still not been able to escape hunger and cold.
> The sword-blade pot—a perilous way to cook rice![2]
> The spiked mat—no restful sitting there.[3]
> But do I not have these lovely mountains and
>   streams?
> Besides, in a blink of an eye, the storm will have
>   passed.
> Although one need not wait until old age to retire,
> How many men have had the courage not to?
> I am lucky to have been put out to pasture,
> Like a weary horse that has had its load removed.
> My family has the run of this river post house.
> At the tunnel's end, Heaven poked a hole through
>   for me:
> These good things balance out the hunger and
>   poverty.
> I have no need for either condolences or congratu-
>   lations!
> Tranquil and calm, I feel neither joy nor sorrow,
> And so won't turn these words about hardship into
>   song.[4]

The analogy of the ant riding on a millstone was a cosmological analogy used during Su's time to explain the movements of the sun and the moon. According to this theory, the heavens revolve toward the left, or west, while the sun and the moon revolve toward the right, or east. However, because the speed and power of the heavens (the millstone) are greater than those of the sun and the moon (the ant), the sun and the moon are pulled back down into the west. The wind wheel refers, in Buddhist cosmology, to the boundless circle of wind that lies beneath the circles of space, water and metal on which, in turn, the world rests.[5] The more commonly known wheel of Buddhism is the wheel of samsara, the winds of karma that rotate the world around an unending samsaric cycle of life and death. It is clear from the opening couplets of this poem that the poet feels trapped, as much by the vagaries of political change as by anything else. He tries to convince the reader—and probably himself as well—of the advantages of his political ostracism, the most important being that it has forced him to do what he always wanted but lacked the courage to do: to retire to a simpler life. Finally, in the closing line of the poem, he both identifies with and distinguishes himself from Ch'ü Yüan, the hapless third-century poet-official who at the end of the *Li Sao,* his long verse polemic against both official corruption and the crush of time, descends into utter despair. In many ways, the Huang-chou exile is a study in how to make creative and imaginative use of the temptation to despair.[6] Significantly, Buddhism had a considerable role to play in this process.

Su Shih's first actions on arriving in Huang-chou reveal a near obsession with purification, as if he wished to cleanse himself of the filth and grime of the world. There are intimations of this feeling as early as Hang-chou, but in Huang-chou it becomes much more serious. Su spent much time at the An-kuo ssu in Huang-chou praying, burning incense, and meditating.

> When I had more or less solved the problem of living quarters, and had some scant provision of food and clothing, I closed the door and made a clean start. I summoned my faculties and humbly reflected, seeking a way of renewing myself. I looked back on all my utterances and activities: they had all missed the *tao,* not just my recent offenses, and I did not know where to begin my reform. I sought them out methodically, and some I regretted

unendurably. So I sighed deeply and said, "My *tao* is not equal to controlling my spirit: my nature is not equal to mastering my habits. I am not digging at the roots, but only pruning among the branches. Even if I reform now, I will surely act the same again later. Why not restore my sincerity by becoming a Buddhist monk, and seek a complete purification?" I found a monastery south of town, called [An-kuo] temple, with fine woods and tall bamboos, ponds, and pavilions. Every day or two I went there and burned incense and sat in silence, investigating myself deeply. And I forgot the difference between myself and other things: my person and my mind ceased to exist. I sought to discover how my guilt was first born, but could not find it out. My whole consciousness was pure and clean, and the pollution fell away of itself. Inside and out I was free of any dependence or attachment. Surreptitiously, I delighted in this, and went there morning and night for five years.[7]

Although Su had no intention of becoming a monk, he was clearly shaken up by his recent brush with mortality, and he withdrew to recollect and investigate himself. The above letter indicates a sudden interest in the question of pollution and purification, after his recent contacts with the dirty world of politics. However, it seems that he knew this delight in purity was an escape and that a transcendence of the very concepts of purity and defilement was called for. This idea is explored in the following poem, titled "Bathing at An-kuo ssu."

> With old age, I've gotten lazy about things,
> But when I get dirty, I still think of bathing.
> Wispy hair that doesn't even reach my ears,
> Yet I still bother to bathe once every month.
> There is plenty of fuel in this mountain village,
> And the misty fog obscures this warm valley.
> How much longer can this worldly dust defile me?
> I wish I could just briskly shake off these fetters!
> After I dress, I go sit in the small pavilion,
> And let down my hair alongside the slender bamboo.
> The heart's ten thousand troubles are all empty,
> And a single bed is all a body needs for comfort.
> All one has to do is forget about both defilement and
>   purity,
> And wash oneself of the ideas of success and failure.

I return home in silence, there is not much to say.
I must meditate on this principle until it becomes
   second nature.[8]

Another manifestation of this concern for purification is a sudden concern with the question of meat eating. Su is known as a gourmand, and even today there is a dish, composed largely of highly seasoned pork fat, known as *Tung-p'o jou*. Su writes that sometimes during his first year in Huang-chou he made a trip to an area called Ch'i-t'ing, located about twenty-five *li* from Huang-chou. Once, on the way, he happened to meet his old friend Ch'en Chi-ch'ang. Chi-ch'ang, also known as Master Lung-ch'iu, was the youngest son of Ch'en Kung-pi, the official who had given Su such grief during his time in Hang-chou. As a young man Chi-ch'ang had been fond of drinking and swordplay and had neglected his studies. Later, however, he became a hermit at Ch'i-t'ing near Huang-chou, where Su met up with him. Not long afterward, Su made a second visit to Ch'i-t'ing. However, Su writes,

> I had for some time desisted from slaughtering [animals], and I was afraid that Chi-ch'ang would slaughter [an animal so as to prepare a special meal] for me. For this reason, I used the rhymes from the poem of the previous year [at the time of his first visit] to compose a poem in which I spoke of my renunciation of killing. [Not only did] Chi-ch'ang refrain from slaughtering [animals] after that; many people in Ch'i-t'ing were converted, and there were [even] those who gave up eating meat.[9]

Su goes on to note that in the four years he was in Huang-chou, he and Chi-ch'ang visited each other many times, each time composing a poem that made use of the ryhmes of the first one. Then, when he left Huang-chou, Su arranged some of these poems together into a poetic sequence and presented them to his friend as a parting gift. The following is the second in this sequence of verses inveighing against the eating of meat:

> I grieve for the frog caught inside the trap,
> With mouth closed, he guards the few remaining
>   drops.
> And I grieve as well for the fish in the net,
> With mouth open, he gulps down a bit of moisture.
> Ripping out their bellies causes both to suffer,
> When it gets to this point, I dare not think of it.[10]

Elsewhere Su Shih writes: "Last year I was released from prison, and since then I have not killed a single living thing. Whenever I am given food rations of shrimp or clam, I release them all into the river."[11] Su must have sympathized with the "frog caught inside the trap" in a new way because of his own experiences.

Also on a trip to Ch'i-t'ing, Su had a strangely disturbing dream during a night spent at a temple along the way. In this dream a monk whose face was torn open and covered with blood appeared accusingly before him. The following day, Su arrived at Ch'i-t'ing and there found that the local temple contained an ancient statue of a *lohan* with its face destroyed and ravaged. The painting of the *lohan* that hung in the Su family home was clearly an object of worship, and throughout his life Su regarded paintings and statues of *lohan* with particular respect—whether or not he actually believed in their divine powers. It is not surprising, then, that Su took the statue home, had it completely restored, and then installed it with great ceremony in Huang-chou's An-kuo ssu.[12]

Once the shock began to wear off, however, Su's life in Huang-chou settled into one of simple but intense pleasures: "He fished and waded the streams, picked herbs, mixed with the local people and their liquor."[13] It was a very difficult time for Su financially, and one way he tried to make ends meet was by arduously clearing and planting a five-acre plot of land that the district administrator had lent him for that purpose. He wrote his justly famous set of eight poems, the "Eastern Slope" poems, as a record of this experience, and, as he himself puts it, "to console myself in my labors." It was also at this time that he took the name of Layman of the Eastern Slope, or "Tung-p'o chü-shih," an open affirmation if not of Buddhism per se, then of the importance of the contemplative life.

Su did not live in isolation. As always, he had a regular stream of visitors, including his good friend the monk Ts'an-liao. The two men took many excursions together, the best known being the one to Red Cliff that inspired Su to write the famous set of prose-poems *Ch'ih-pi fu* that in many ways embody the spirit of philosophical accommodation that was ripening during this period.

To say that Su's Huang-chou poetry evinces a new maturity, integration, and depth does not mean that it shows greater consistency or continuity than his earlier poems. The period in Huang-chou can be seen rather as a gradual movement away from a primarily "reactive" attitude to life toward a more creatively "responsive" one, although he did not cease to derive intense intellectual and aesthetic pleasure from things as well. Several pieces from this period reflect the stylistic influence of the *Avataṃsaka Sūtra* and many of the ideas of the *Śūraṃgama Sūtra*. One of these is a piece penned in 1080 after a visit from a monk by the name of Wu-ch'ing, who had been sent from Szechuan by Su's old friend Wei-chien to request a piece of writing to be carved in stone for his newly refurbished sutra hall at the Sheng-hsiang monastery in Ch'eng-tu. Su had yet to see the building, but he wrote the piece anyway, based on Wu-ch'ing's descriptions but also, perhaps, on the descriptions in the *Avataṃsaka Sūtra* itself, especially the famous final chapter of the sutra, referred to as the *Gaṇḍavyūha*. Here is recounted the spiritual journey of the young layman Sudhana, who visits fifty-three spiritual friends and guides before finally reaching his destination, the abode of the bodhisattva Samantabhadra. His journey culminates in an overwhelming vision inside Vairocana's tower.[14] Su's description of the sutra library in Ch'eng-tu is very similar to this vision:

> It contained countless jewels, gold and cinnabar, porcelains and genuine pearls, all kinds of sandalwood incense [as well as] the solemn and awe-inspiring teachings of the Buddha and bodhisattvas. [Wei-chien has] built a great treasury of precious things, overflowing with more wonders than the sea. There was a great heavenly dragon, which supported [the roof on its] back, as well as numerous smaller dragons arranged in a circle around it. [There were] various transformation-bodies of bodhisattvas and protectors of the Buddha dharma staunchly defending its doors. [There were] devas, maras, demons, and spirits, each grasping their weapons as a defense against the inauspicious. These many treasures, together with the many Buddhas were resplendent and fragrant. From each one there arose a jewel-like radiance and a pervasive fragrance that, pleasing and delicate, wafted and wandered, giving rise to many different forms and endless transformations. . . . All those who see it will benefit from it, according to their nature and character.[15]

According to Hui-hung, this particular work flowed forth in a flood of inspiration after Su woke from a dream in which Wei-chien appeared to request a composition from him. According to Hui-hung, Su composed the "Account of the sutra-library of the

Sheng-hsiang yüan," which is more than a thousand lines long, in a
single sitting and without making any corrections.[16] In the prose
preface to this work, Su acknowledges this burst of creativity, and
tries to reconcile it with the Buddhist notion of the karma of words.

> There was a [certain] layman, whose forebears were men of Shu
> and who had a strong karmic affinity with this monk. He left [his
> home] and [began a life of] wandering. [Once] when he was in the
> region between the Yangtze and Huai rivers, he heard about the
> work of the Buddha that this monk was engaged in and wanted to
> do as others had and give up that which he was attached to. He
> looked all around his person as well as in his home in search of
> something he could give away, [until he] realized that there was
> not a single "thing." Like a sprout from a scorched seed, like a
> stone maiden, there was not the slightest thing to be relinquished.
> He then said to himself: "All I have is the speech karma I have
> [created through my attachments] from the Nonbeginning to the
> present: the perverted speech and worldly phrases, the debates
> and discussions on the past and the present, right and wrong, vic-
> tory and defeat. Because of this karma, the words and phrases
> that emerge are still like bells and chimes, the embroidered essays
> delight the ear and eyes. Like a man who is fond of gambling, the
> days grow more impoverished with each victory. . . . Today I
> relinquish this karma and compose this *gāthā* of the Treasury of
> Precious Jewels. I vow that in this very life, after composing this
> *gāthā,* all [causes for] future lives will be annihilated and all kar-
> mas, worldly causes, and evil thoughts, together with all the
> obstacles [dividing] phenomena *(shih)* and noumena *(li)* will be cut
> off forever. In all the worlds there will be no grasping and no let-
> ting go, no hatred and no love, nothing possible and nothing im-
> possible.

Like Po Chü-i before him, Su is trying here to rationalize his
"karma of words" by dedicating himself to the higher cause of
spreading the dharma and, ultimately, helping to accumulate the
merit that will allow him to go beyond words—if not in this life,
then perhaps in another. The hymn that follows this prose preface
is easily recognizable as a statement of the search for the inherently luminous Buddha-nature that, like the jewel hidden in the
beggar's tattered robes, is always present but rarely discovered.
Here Su Shih changes his metaphor to a jewel hidden in the mountains.

> I wander through the jeweled mountains,
> Seeing the mountains but not the jewels.
> Cliffs and valleys, grass and trees
> Tigers and panthers, dragons and snakes,
> Even if they knew where the jewels were,
> They couldn't get them if they wanted.
> There was also a seeker of jewels,
> Who claimed to have already found them.
> But he saw the jewels and not the mountain,
> He too was unable to get the jewels.

Apart from the familiar Buddhist analogy (and the subject of two of the Seven Parables of the *Lotus Sūtra*) of the seeker of jewels who ultimately finds them on his own person, again we see the strong influence of the ideas and the language of Hua-yen Buddhism, especially as expressed in the *Śūraṃgama Sūtra,* with its extended meditations on the six sense organs, including taste—which has no inherent nature of its own, "no independent substance apart from flavors (such as) sweetness and bitterness, and tastelessness"[17]—and sight—which "has no independent substance that exists apart from the two states of light and dark."[18] In the chapter on self-enlightenment, in which each of the bodhisattvas relates how he came to enlightenment, Aniruddha notes that having learned to perceive with the mind rather than the eye, he feels that the best means of perfection "is made possible by turning the organ of sight back to its source."[19] Here Su Shih is using the image of the jewels *(li)* and mountains *(shih)* to illustrate the fundamental unity between the relative and the absolute, which was basic to the *Śūraṃgama Sūtra* and many other Buddhist texts. He then continues with a different analogy, that of the dreamer. This analogy of the dreamer is a common one in Buddhist Mahāyāna literature.[20] The contrast is between the awakened state (identification with the absolute) and the dreaming state (identification with the relative).

> It can be compared to the man in a dream
> Who is still unaware that he is dreaming.
> For once he realizes that it is a dream,
> His dream will then change and melt away.
> I see "myself" and do not see the dream,
> And so consider "myself" to be awake
> Not knowing what true awakening is.
> Neither awakening nor dreaming exists.

Then, finally, Su moves to a third analogy, that of taste.

> I contemplate this Great Treasury of Jewels,
> It is like using honey to describe sweetness.
> Because sentient beings have not yet been taught
> They still use sweetness to describe honey.
> Although sweetness and honey are interchangeable.
> A thousand kalpas continue without end,
> From honey to the sweet sugarcane,
> To the sweet pear and the orange.
> One speaks of the sweet but gets the sour,
> And also the acrid, salty, and the bitter.
> Until suddenly one returns to the original flavor,
> And the root of the tongue as a sweetness.
> And then in silence I know myself.
> And no longer bother with finding analogies.

Here again Su is expressing an ideal, to return to the "original flavor" that lies beneath all flavors, the original silence that underlies all analogies. However, as he readily admits, he is still "far from the Way" and lacks the dharma eye that can see through the multiplicity to the unity. However, there is still a way. In the last few lines of this poem, Su touches upon a crucial element in the Ch'an Buddhist use of language that is not to be shunned or despised, but rather allowed to emerge from what Toshihiko Izutsu calls "a certain dimension of consciousness which is totally different from the dimension of speaking and not speaking," the dimension Master Pai Chang (720–814) was referring to when he urged his disciples to "speak in a state in which your throat, lips and mouth have been snatched away."[21] It is like Chuang-tzu, who searches for a "man who has forgotten words so I can have a word with him." In other words, speech is no longer simple *parole,* but rather a form of articulation that, within the specific context of a verbal exchange between master and student, transcends both speaker and listener and becomes "a momentary self-presentation of absolute Reality itself."[22]

> Today I recite this *gāthā*
> Knowing that I am still far from the Way.
> It is like the sense of sight seeing itself
> This kind of eye is not something I have.
> There must be a man without any ears,
> Who can listen to these tongueless words.

In the split-second of a finger snap,
My thousand-*kalpa* karma will be washed away.

Here again is a restatement of the fundamental message of the
Śūraṃgama Sūtra, to return to the primal ground of awareness that
is prior to the senses. In fact, as Tsuchida points out, although this
text "insists upon the unity already and always realized and immanent, it is a one-way transcendence."[23] The *Śūraṃgama Sūtra* often
uses the metaphor of the person whose vision of "blossoms in the
sky" is caused in fact by a problem with the eyes, a cataract, for
example. This means that the blossoms in the sky, worldly phenomena, are not real, since they disappear forever once the cataract is
removed. Su, however, seems to have been at least partly aware of
some of the potential problems of this emphasis on the absolute, as
we can see from the following piece.

A mind divested of all sense perceptions: this is the goal. It seems
to me that whenever the mind is so divested, there is already the
perception of truth. But this perception of truth, or *samādhi,* is
not something that exists or does not exist and is not to be
described by words. Therefore the masters taught their disciples
that they should stop there [without attempting to describe it]. It
is like removing a [cataract] from the eyes; the eye sees as soon as
the [cataract] is removed. A doctor has a way of removing the
[cataract], but he has no specific way of conferring vision upon
the eye. . . . People who do not understand sometimes describe a
state of animal unconsciousness as the state of Buddhahood. If
so, then when cats and dogs sleep after being well fed, their bellies
moving rhythmically with their respiration, these animals, too, do
not have a thought on their minds. It would obviously be incorrect
to argue that therefore the cats and dogs in such a state have
entered Buddhahood. . . . Am I correct in thus interpreting what
you have taught me? Just as I write this, outside my window there
is an angry wife pummeling her husband, the angry sounds of
cursing like sparks flying from the ashes, like pigs squealing and
dogs yapping. Yet, I know that there is a trace of enlightenment
[even] in the squealing of the pigs and the yapping of the dogs. [In
the same way] the mirrorlike nature of the rivers is contained in
the flying pebbles and rolling boulders [of a flash flood?]. Often I
seek [enlightenment] in ordinary tranquility, and just as often I
find myself lamenting that I cannot find it. Today, amidst this
uproar, I suddenly find I have grasped [the meaning] of this.[24]

Although Su states clearly his understanding of the "goal" of the
spiritual life as being transcendence, the return to the primal, inherent awareness that comes prior to and is the basis of all the senses
and their objects, he places greater emphasis on the dynamic quality of this relationship between the transcendent and the immanent:
the *tathāgata-garbha* can be found in "the squealing of pigs and the
yapping of dogs." He is reiterating the basic doctrine of T'ien-t'ai
Buddhism, which "conceives of the infinite absolute as absolutely
connatural, copresent, and interpenetrating with the finite, incho-
ate, and which, therefore, thinks of the truth only in a dynamic
movement itself of the spirit. . . ."[25] This dynamism is by no means
denied by the *Śūraṃgama Sūtra,* but, as Tsuchida shows clearly, in
its elevation of the pure, uncontaminated, undefiled absolute,
much of this dynamism is lost. In a way, many of the contradictions
and conflicts in Su's own religious life reflect this problem. Thus,
during the Huang-chou period, when he is both at the height of his
creative powers and the most profoundly engaged with Buddhist
texts and ideas, his writings reflect a struggle between two different
things. There is a yearning for an absolute transcendence and
purity that will make of all worldly objects and affairs but illusory
blossoms in the sky. In his retreat to An-kuo ssu and his valiant
efforts at self-reflection, although he was unable to find out "how
my guilt was first born," he did achieve a state in which he felt that
his "whole consciousness was pure and clean, and the pollution fell
away of itself." However, the "surreptitious pleasure" he took in
this retreat seems to indicate that he was aware that turning inward
could easily result in a turning against the world or, if nothing else,
a passive state of quiescence no different from that exhibited by
sleeping cats and dogs. And so, still drawing from Buddhist ideas
(rather than retreating to Confucian ones), Su also attempts to
locate poetically if not always to experience personally the transcendence within the immanent, the pure within the filthy, and the
silence within the uproar.

The interest in pure gnosis is always there, however. It appears
again in a commentary to the *Platform Sūtra* in which Su uses ideas
drawn directly from the *Śūraṃgama Sūtra* to explicate the meaning
of the three "bodies" of Buddha: the *nirmāṇakāya,* the *saṃbhogakāya,* and the *dharmakāya.* The *Platform Sūtra* is associated with
Hui-neng (638–713), the sixth Chinese Ch'an patriarch and tradi-

tional founder of the Southern school of Sudden Enlightenment. As Yampolsky notes, this sutra does not offer anything strikingly original: "For the most part they are phrases, terms, and ideas taken from the context of various sutras, and discussed, to a certain extent, in terms of Ch'an."[26] One of these basic ideas is that *prajñā*, or enlightened wisdom, is coexistent with rather than the result of meditation. "Thus, while *prajñā* is described as the "function" of meditation, it is at the same time explained as something akin to the original nature, wisdom of which is tantamount to enlightenment."[27] Another concept is that of sudden enlightenment, the "*samādhi* of oneness" and "direct mind" traceable to the *Ta-cheng ch'i-hsin lun* [Awakening of faith] and the *Vimalakīrti Sūtra,* respectively. There is also the doctrine of no-thought, which "is associated with non-form as the substance, and non-abiding, as the basis." As Yampolsky explains:

> These terms all seem to be pointing to the same thing: the Absolute, which can never be defined in words. Thoughts are conceived of as advancing in progression from past to present to future, in an unending chain of successive thoughts. Attachment to one instant of thought leads to attachment to a succession of thoughts and thus to bondage. But by cutting off attachment to one instant of thought, one may, by a process unexplained, cut off attachment to a succession of thoughts and thus attain to no-thought, which is the state of enlightenment.[28]

These ideas occur over and over again in Su's writing, in particular the idea of the power of a single thought to break the endless succession of thoughts. As he writes in the hymn quoted above, "In the split-second of a finger snap, my thousand-kalpa karma will be washed away." Su's discussion of this sutra, however, focuses primarily on instructions in the *Platform Sūtra* on how to realize the threefold body of the Buddha within oneself. According to the sutra, "Everyone in the world possesses it, but being deluded, he cannot see it and seeks the threefold body of the Tathāgata on the outside."[29] Moreover: "The *nirmāṇakāya,* the *saṃbhogakāya,* the *dharmakāya* / These three bodies are from the outset one body / If within your own nature you seek to see for yourself / This then is the cause of becoming Buddha and gaining enlightenment."[30]

In the sutra, the *dharmakāya,* the essence of the Buddha, is described as the innate purity of all beings, which is likened to the sun, moon, and blue sky, which are always bright even if they seem to be obscured by the "floating clouds of false thoughts."[31] In his commentary, however, Su Shih uses the analogy of the eye and the sense of perception from the *Śūraṃgama Sūtra:*

> What does it mean to say "one perceives the *dharmakāya*"? The quality of perception [associated with] the eyes is neither existent *(yu)* nor nonexistent *(wu).* A person who has no eyes will still perceive darkness: [even if] the eye is withered and the pupils dead, the quality of perception is not [thereby] destroyed: this then is [what is meant by] enlightenment [i.e., seeing one's original mind *(chien-hsing)*]. It has nothing to do either with the existence or nonexistence of the eye; it neither comes nor goes, neither rises nor is destroyed. Therefore it is said "one perceives the *dharmakāya.*"[32]

This passage is clearly influenced by the *Śūraṃgama Sūtra,* a great part of which deals with the question of the true nature of perception: the Buddha attempts to show how it is that the innate nature of seeing does not depend on whether there is darkness or light, or whether one has a physical eye or not.[33] The *Platform Sūtra* then discusses the *saṃbhogakāya,* or body of complete enjoyment, which is, strictly speaking, a physical body that does not take the gross, material form we are most familiar with. Being a physical body, it can be seen, but only by very advanced beings, such as the bodhisattvas, who have acquired this ability through long and arduous spiritual cultivation. However, since, theoretically at least, all sentient beings are potential bodhisattvas, they also are capable of perceiving the *saṃbhogakāya.* In the *Platform Sūtra,* however, the *saṃbhogakāya* Buddha within oneself is conceived of more as a state of mind: "As one lamp serves to dispel a thousand years of darkness, so one flash of wisdom destroys ten thousand years of ignorance. Do not think of the past; always think of the future; if your future thoughts are always good, you may be called the *saṃbhogakāya* Buddha."[34] Su, in his commentary, also refers to *saṃbhogakāya* as descriptive of a fairly advanced spiritual state. However, he continues to use the analogy of perception:

> What does it mean to say that "one is able to perceive the *saṃbho-gakāya*"? Although [one's] original mind exists, [since] the sense

organ is not completely [developed], therefore one cannot perceive it. However, if one is able to calm and nourish one's senses, not let oneself be obstructed by phenomena, and cause [the sense organ] to be luminous and completely clear, then [one's] enlightenment will be complete. Therefore it is said "one has the potential of perceiving the *saṃbhogakāya*."[35]

Finally, there is the *nirmāṇakāya,* or transformation body of the Buddha, a gross physical body that manifests "in whatever way is necessary for others" and "may teach any teaching, Buddhist or non-Buddhist, out of compassionate skillful means."[36] Sakyamuni Buddha is the best known of these transformation bodies but by no means the only one. In the *Platform Sūtra,* the *nirmāṇakāya* Buddha of one's own nature is none other than the *saṃbhogakāya* "observed from the standpoint of the *Dharmakāya*."[37] In other words, it is the awareness that one's thoughts create one's reality; "if you think of evil things then you will change and enter hell . . . but if a single thought of good evolves, intuitive wisdom is born. This is called the *nirmāṇakāya* Buddha of your own nature."[38] Su Shih also notes this idea that a single thought can, in a snap of the fingers, result in intuitive wisdom. Moreover, once one understands the power of the mind to bring about changes and transformations, one is no longer tossed and turned and controlled by these changes, but rather, like Avalokiteśvara, can make use of them as skillful means. "What does it mean to say that '[all] that one sees is the *nirmāṇakāya'*? When [one's] root nature is complete, then in a snap of the fingers, the myriad changes and transformations that one sees everywhere will all serve as skillful means [for the teaching of the dharma]. Therefore it is said that '[all] one sees is the *nirmāṇakāya.*' "[39] This last passage again shows Su's fondness for the idea of skillful means, which, in other contexts, he often uses to justify his love of poetry and painting. In general, this effort at scriptural commentary is superficial and even misleading. In fact, Chu Hsi's criticisms of Su Shih's Buddhist scholarship (despite his distaste for Buddhist ideas, Chu did study its texts with care) appear to have been quite well founded in this regard! However, there is no question Su delighted in this half-playful epistemology.

    This delight in epistemology is apparent in another piece Su wrote in response to a literary dare by his friend Ch'en Chi-ch'ang, who once remarked teasingly to his friend that for all his literary talent, the only thing he could not write was a Buddhist sutra. When Su asked why Ch'en thought he was incapable of this, Ch'en said, "Buddhist sutras flow out of the [experience] of *samādhi,* but the Master's would necessarily emerge from intellection." "You, sir, do not realize that I am not one who produces from intellection," Su replied. Ch'en then pointed to his hat, made from molded fish bone, and challenged Su to write a hymn about it in the spirit of the *Avataṃsaka Sūtra.*[40] Su immediately took up his brush to write a Buddhist-like hymn titled "The Fish-Bone Cap."

> If you take this lustrous and shiny fish-bone cap,
> And scrutinize it closely, what was it to begin with?
> Form and vital spirit just happened to come together,
> And, as a result, a fish suddenly came into being.
> Unluckily, this fish got caught in a fisher's net,
> And so got sliced open and had its bones removed.
> The moment the fish bones were removed,
> Then they were no longer the fish.
> Heat was then applied to mold the shape
> Of this tall-as-the-Wu-Yüeh-mountains hat.
> The moment the fish bones became a hat,
> Then they were no longer the bones.
> Creation and destruction go on forever:
> And ultimately there will be no hat either.
> Now supposing that before it had been destroyed,
> It was presented to a hairless man,
> If the hairpin has no hair to grasp,
> Then would it still be a hairpin?
> I contemplate this illusory form,
> As I've already meditated on dew and lightning.
> And so why not on things beyond form.
> Dew and lightning are already without existence.
> Because this Buddhist is compassionate and kind,
> I hope that he will accept this hat of mine.
> If he sees that this hat is not a hat,
> Then he will know that the "I" is not the "I."
> And he will live among the five *kleśas,*[41]
> Clear and pure and forever joyful.[42]

Although still a product of intellection, albeit a very spontaneous one, this hymn demonstrates a clear understanding of the basic

Buddhist principle of *anattā,* or lack of inherent self-existence, as well as the concept of dependent co-origination.

In 1084 Su Shih was called back from exile by order of Emperor Shen-tsung and appointed to office at Ju-chou in Hunan province. On his way from Huang-chou to Ju-chou, Su stopped by in Yün-chou to see his brother, then traveled on to Mt. Lu, where he stayed several weeks. At this time, he wrote the following poem, inspired by Wu Tao-tzu's famous depiction of the horrors of the Buddhist hells, called the "Transformations of the Hells."

> I have heard that when Wu Tao-tzu
> First painted his "Scenes of Hell,"
> People were so frightened of retribution,
> That for two months they slaughtered no animals!
> This was a mere painting, not the real thing,
> Brush and ink uniting to create an illusion.
> Those people had enough to eat and drink,
> What caused them to sweat with fear?
> But if one understands the Buddha realm,
> One knows it is but a creation of the mind.
> If people could just understand these words,
> The hells would shatter of themselves.[43]

This *gāthā* is quite interesting in that it is simultaneously an appreciation of Wu Tao-tzu's artistic skill and, like the previous poem, a subtle undermining—from the Buddhist perspective—of the entire creative enterprise. Thus, Wu Tao-tzu's art is seen as an illusion created by the union of brush and ink. It is such a convincing illusion, however, that it strikes fear and trembling into the hearts of the well-fed and complacent. In fact, it is said that this painting of Wu Tao-tzu's, done on the walls of an important temple in the capital city of Ch'ang-an, so frightened the inhabitants of that city that many of those involved in the butchering of animals actually did change professions. And Su himself says in an inscription for the Wu Tao-tzu painting: "Contemplating 'The Transformation of the Hells,' one sees not the ways in which [bad karma] is created, but rather the nature of the punishments suffered [because of it]. Tragic! Tragic! . . . I fear [the cycle of samsara] is like the grass by the side of the road, which although it is scorched by wildfires, comes up again when the spring wind blows."[44] Despite his interest in the more metaphysical approach of Ch'an Buddhism, Su never completely abandoned his concern for the conventional aspects of Buddhist morality, the question of karmic retribution in particular. Nor does the *Śūraṃgama Sūtra*. Here he seems to be referring to the spring winds of desire, which have a way of enticing the green shoots of love, life, and longing from even the most barren and experience-scorched of grounds! By the same token, for the Buddhist, the mind is also a great artist, and all of creation might well be considered its illusory masterpiece. Hui-hung mentions the case of a Buddhist monk who is said to have commented after his enlightenment experience: "That which I had been carrying around like a burden was just like the objects painted by [Wu] Tao-tzu. Although they seem to be full of life, actually they are nonexistent."[45] This is what Su seems to be saying in his poem as well, since he obviously found this rather phenomenological approach to life very congenial. The same view is expressed in the famous twentieth chapter of the *Avataṃsaka Sūtra:*

> In mind there is no painting,
> In painting there is no mind;
> Yet not apart from mind
> Can any painting be found.[46]

After arriving at Mt. Lu, Su visited the Yüan-t'ung temple, where his father had visited Chu-no more than forty years earlier. There he also met Master Tung-lin Ch'ang-ts'ung of the Huang-lung school of Ch'an Buddhism and had what might be called his "enlightenment experience." Master Ch'ang-ts'ung was from Szechuan province.[47] After his teacher's death, Ch'ang-ts'ung lived for a while at Mt. Lung-t'an, where he soon became quite famous: it was often said of him that he was "Ma-tsu come again," owing in part to his decided emphasis on direct insight rather than intellectual knowledge (the great Ma-tsu Tao-i (709–788) was a third-generation disciple of Hui-neng and a seminal figure in the development of early Ch'an Buddhism). In 1080, at the age of fifty-six, Ch'ang-ts'ung finally settled down at the Tung-lin temple on Mt. Lu, where he established a Ch'an center. A teacher of great skill and considerable presence, he attracted many followers, lay and monastic, Buddhist and non-Buddhist. Yang Shih (1053–1135), one of the most important students of the philosophers Ch'eng Hao and Ch'eng I, is said to have had many conversations with Ch'ang-ts'ung and

even to have adopted some of Ch'ang-ts'ung's views in his own formulation of Confucianism.[48] And Ch'ien Ch'ien-i writes of an official by the name of Liu Ching-ch'en who had never believed in
Buddhism, but who after talking with Master Ch'ang-ts'ung for
seven days took up the practice of Ch'an meditation and before
long had attained extraordinary results.[49] Ch'ang-ts'ung soon came
to the attention of the emperor, who asked him to come to the capital (the monk pleaded illness and refused the offer). In 1088 the
court awarded him the Purple Robe and the honorary title of Ch'an
Master Chao-chüeh. Ch'ang-ts'ung's immediate disciples included
many who were born in Szechuan. The most famous of these was
Yüan-wu K'o-ch'in (1063–1135) of the Yang-ch'i school of Lin-chi
Buddhism. Su Shih's name along with that of his literary disciple
Huang T'ing-chien are also among those listed under Ch'ang-
ts'ung's lineage. This affiliation does not necessarily mean that Su
was a formal disciple of Ch'ang-ts'ung, but it does show that he
was more seriously interested in Ch'ang-ts'ung's teachings than
most of his fellow literati-officials. Su was particularly impressed
by Ch'ang-ts'ung's ability to live in the world without attachment,
responding to life fully and completely, even while seated on his
meditation mat:

> Because loyal subjects are unafraid of death, they are able to
> accomplish great deeds in this world. Because courageous war-
> riors are unconcerned for their lives, they are able to achieve great
> fame in this world. These kinds of men have not yet attained the
> Tao, but they value righteousness and have little care for their own
> lives. Now if men can achieve things like this [by relying on princi-
> ple], how much more can [they achieve by] going beyond the
> Three Realms and fully understanding the ten thousand dharmas:
> no birth, no aging, no becoming ill, no death, responding to [the
> needs of] beings [yet being oneself] without emotion! Grave and
> dignified is this Master Ts'ung, a lion among monks. His breath is
> like the clouds; his sneeze is like the wind. Once I met with him
> and made a joke. Without rising from his meditation mat, he
> clapped his hands, chatted, and smiled, transforming the slopes of
> Mt. Lu into the palaces of the dragon kings Brahma and Sākya.[50]

Dōgen (1200–1253), who founded the Sōtō sect of Buddhism in
Japan, held Su Shih in very high regard and named an entire chapter of his *Shōbōgenzō* after an enlightenment quatrain penned by

Su after listening to Ch'ang-ts'ung's teachings. According to Dōgen, Master Ch'ang-ts'ung was once asked by a monk, "Do inanimate objects preach the Law?" The master replied, "Continuously." This exchange became a koan, which was given to Su Tung-p'o. Su spent an entire night wrestling with this koan and at dawn wrote a poem that he showed to Ch'ang-ts'ung, "who acknowledged his enlightenment."[51]

> The murmuring brook is the Buddha's long, broad
>   tongue.
> And is not the shapely mountain the body of purity?
> Through the night I listen to eighty thousand *gāthā*s,
> When dawn breaks, how will I explain it to the others?[52]

The "long, broad tongue" of the Buddha is referred to in many different sutras. In the following verse from the *Avataṃsaka Sūtra,* it becomes a metaphor for the Buddhist teaching, the *dharma,* which, in keeping with the basic Mahāyāna concept of *upāya,* or skillful means, is communicated in whatever form best suits people's needs.

> My tongue is broad and long, coppery red,
> Shiny like a jewel, pure;
> With it I communicate to beings according to their
>   mentalities:
> You should realize this wisdom.[53]

For Su Shih the murmuring stream is like the tongue of the Buddha in both its shape and its sound, a voice articulating the dharma to him in the form of "eighty thousand *gāthā*s" (the 84,000 different teachings of the Buddha designed to heal the 84,000 kinds of suffering to which sentient beings are subject). Having heard these teachings, Su Shih feels moved to pass them on to others, although, unlike the Buddha, he is not exactly sure how to go about it. Dōgen comments on this poem as follows:

> When [Su Tung-p'o] heard the sound of the valley stream, he was enlightened. Was it caused by the sound or by his master's teaching? Perhaps [Ch'ang-ts'ung's] teaching and the sound of the valley stream are mixed together; the water is proclaiming the Law by its sound—objectivity and subjectivity are unified. Is this unity [Su Tung-p'o's] enlightenment? Do the mountains and rivers manifest the Buddhist Way? When your mind is clear, you can

experience the sound and color that proclaim the teaching of mountains and rivers.[54]

Dōgen is pointing out that, in Su's receptive and responsive mind, the sounds of the water have become inseparably intertwined with the Ch'an master's sermon, so that it is difficult to tell who is the enlightened and who is the enlightener: phenomena and noumena have become one.

Dōgen clearly considered Su to have been a serious student of Ch'an Buddhism: he says that if Su had not "endeavor[ed] in right practice, he would not have had this experience."[55] Not everyone agreed, however. For example, the Ming official T'ang Wen-hsien, in his postscript to the *Tung-p'o Ch'an-hsi chi,* notes that this verse shows that Su Shih still stood outside the gates of illumination and had not yet plunged into that dark vastness beyond words and letters, the root of life and death. And there is also a story about a Chinese monk who brought Su's poem before a famous Ch'an master and remarked with a sigh, "It isn't easy to arrive at this stage [of spiritual insight]!"[56] The teacher merely commented: "[Su Shih] didn't even find the road [to enlightenment]; how can you say he arrived [there]?" The monk puzzled over this koan-like statement all night long and, when the temple bell sounded at dawn, took up his pen and wrote the following poem:

> Layman Tung-p'o is much too discursive;
> His self obscures the gate between sound and form.
> If the river is the sound [of the Buddha's tongue]
> And the mountain the form [of the Buddha's body]
> Then if neither mountain nor river existed,
> What a tragedy that would be!

This anecdote would seem to indicate that, in the end, Su Shih was really only a literary pantheist. He was quite willing to equate the form of the mountain with the *dharmakāya* of the Buddha and the river's singing with his long tongue (especially in the intensely Buddhist setting of Mt. Lu), but he stopped short of saying that all of these—mountain and river, body and tongue—are inherently empty. Ken Wilber calls pantheism "a way to think about 'Godhead' without having to actually transform yourself."[57] The problem, Wilber says, is that pantheism "mistakes the totality of the universe [for] that which is radically prior to or beyond the universe."[58] Or, as the monk asks, what would happen to the Buddha's body of purity if there were no Mt. Lu?

While at Mt. Lu, Su also visited Hsi-lin ssu with Master Ch'ang-ts'ung, and it is on the wall of that temple that he wrote his most famous quatrain, quoted in the Prologue to this study:

> Regarded from one side, an entire range;
>   from another, a single peak.
> Far, near, high, low, all its parts
>   different from the others.
> If the true face of Mount Lu
>   cannot be known,
> It is because the one looking at it,
>   is standing in its midst.[59]

This poem reveals Su Shih's fascination with changing perspectives: the notion that our perceptions of the world are formed not by what is actually there, but rather by our physical and, more important, mental locations. It is a poem greatly admired by Chinese critics for its spontaneity and apparent simplicity. Wang Wen-kao writes: "Such poems emerge from a moment's inspiration: to accomplish this [the poet] must hold the Buddhist sutras in his breast and only then can he refine them [like gold] in a fire. Because of this its tone is one of unalloyed simplicity."[60]

There was a special connection between Mt. Lu and Szechuan, and a number of Taoists made their way to this mountain as well. One of these was a certain Taoist master Ch'ien, who, in Su's eyes at least, had apparently reached what Chuang-tzu calls "the stage of being [a fellow man] with the maker of things, and [so roams] in the single breath that breathes through heaven and earth."[61] Some years later, Su wrote the following poem in praise of Master Ch'ien of Mt. Lu:

> Creatures endowed with consciousness should
>   observe their breathing.
> What is it that while in repose can still move in and
>   out?
> If one cannot travel within one's own mind, if one's
>   house has no exits,
> Then the six senses will be in conflict, wife and
>   mother-in-law will quarrel.[62]

This Taoist master has escaped from people,
retreated into Mount Lu,
In the mountains no one lives, so he can come and go
at will.
As soon as the one who goes is empty, the one who
returns is lost.
This life indeed exists between coming and going,
Like an endless gossamer thread stirred by a light
breeze,[63]
Inner and outer alchemies are realized in the snap of
a finger,
The mortal world—a nod of the head and three
thousand autumns have passed.
I will mount a crane and fly home to wander the
world with you.[64]

After visiting Mt. Lu, Su went on to Chin-ling (present-day
Nanking), where he had a pleasant sojourn discussing poetry and
Buddhism with his political arch-enemy Wang An-shih, former
head of the Reform party, who was living in retirement in the foot-
hills of the Chung-shan mountains. Su and his family of twenty
continued on to Ju-chou. Because the site was much too small to
support the large clan, Su made plans to buy land in nearby
Ch'ang-chou instead. However, it was not Su's destiny to settle
down yet. In 1085 Emperor Shen-tsung died and the ten-year-old
Che-tsung (r. 1086–1101) ascended the throne, with the empress
Hsüan-chen wielding power from behind the curtain. Like a game
of musical chairs, the reformers were sent packing and conservatives like Su Shih were recalled to the center of power.

Much more could be (and has been) said of the four years of
Huang-chou exile, which were, as George Hatch puts it, "a
uniquely intense biographical event."[65] In terms of Su's religious
life, however, it can be characterized generally as a period in which
Su grappled with questions about the meaning of life and death
with a seriousness and intensity lacking in much of his earlier work
—not surprising given his imprisonment and his close encounter
with death. This encounter in many ways brought to a head the tension between the transcendent and the immanent, the "pure" and
the "impure" present earlier in Hang-chou. This tension in turn
found release in an extraordinarily creative burst of writing, which

often found inspiration and confirmation in Buddhist texts. Although Buddhist personalities like Master Ch'ang-ts'ung made a great impression on Su Shih during this time, he was even more inspired by Buddhist ideas and, perhaps even more important, the language in which they were couched: the marvelous and even exuberant metaphors, images, and similes of the *Avataṃsaka Sūtra* and the *Śūraṃgama Sūtra*.

7. A Thousand Kalpas in the Palm of His Hand

AFTER LEAVING Ch'ang-chou, Su Shih briefly held the post of governor of Teng-chou (Wen-teng), a district located in P'eng-lai county on the northern coast of the Shantung peninsula. Although as it turned out he stayed only five days in Teng-chou before he was recalled to the capital, he took full advantage of his time there to visit the rugged mountains along the coast. One of the places he visited was P'eng-lai pavilion, which had been built high in the mountains overlooking the sea on the ruins of a temple dedicated to the Sea God. Below this spot was a high rock wall, pieces of which had been broken off by the pounding waves and, over time, smoothed into lovely small, round pebbles. Su collected some of these pebbles to take home with him. He also wrote a poem, dedicated to his friend the Old Man of Ch'ui-tz'u from Hang-chou, in which he explores the relativities of both space and time in a largely Buddhist context.

> In P'eng-lai a mountain peak overlooks the sea;
> The colors of which, like jade, never fade.
> It stands alone against the onslaught of the waves
> Which from time to time crush its "cloud-white
>   bones."
> Their hard corners softened by the god of the sea;[1]
> And the will-o'-the-wisp glowing brightly.[2]
> Row after row of these tiny stone pebbles
> So tiny and fine like pearls on a string.
> If the whole of our universe is but a single bubble,[3]
> Where is the distinction between true and false?
> I carry these pebbles back home with me,
> And in my sleeve there is the Eastern Sea!
> (Just as the eyes of the Old Man of Ch'ui-tz'u

Take in the entire world in a single glance.)
When they have been arranged in their containers,
I will have mountains and sea before me every day!
Although by next year the roots of the calamus
Will be inextricably intertwined with these stones,
There will always be the peaches of immortality,
Which you can expect to be ready in a single day![4]

The first part of this poem plays with the relativity of space, of large and small: the sea pebbles carried in one's sleeve become the Eastern Sea; arranged in a dish, they become the mountains. The last two lines play with the relativity of time. There is a famous legend about how the Queen Mother of the West once had seven peaches of immortality (that, like the pebbles Su has collected, were said to be produced miraculously from the sea). One day when Emperor Wu of the Han dynasty came to visit, the Queen Mother gave him five of the peaches; the remaining two she ate herself. When she saw that the emperor was saving the pits in order to plant some himself, she laughingly informed him that it would take three thousand years to produce a single one of the magical peaches. In his poem, however, Su collapses these three thousand years into a single day, the time between dawn and dusk. Su often used this technique of poetic miniaturization or "microcosmicization" by which the vastness of the heavens, the moon, rivers, and seas is brought down into the sphere of the personal—one's room, one's cup of wine, the sleeve of one's robe, and ultimately into the palm of one's hand.

Talking deep into the night, leafing through a
    thousand *gāthās*,
Making out a character, then a word: this self is
    truly the Buddha,
Hsi-ho and the Yellow Emperor are everywhere.[5]
The boat still, the river laps at my seat.
The tower empty, the moon falls into my cup.
So distant, yet it knows just where to find me:
Drunk on ink, beside this dilapidated wall.[6]

In this poem the still boat and the empty tower can be seen as metaphors for the stillness and emptiness of the meditative mind, which allows the greater world to enter into the personal world—

the moon into the wine cup, the river into the boat. Or, to put it more accurately, since the self is the Buddha, the moon is also the wine cup, and the river the boat: distinctions of large and small, cosmic and personal become irrelevant. But the poetic imagination too, when it is "drunk on ink," can lure this vastness into the personal sphere. Metaphysical support for these ideas can be found in various Buddhist texts. This process of miniaturization is illustrated vividly in the sixth chapter of the *Vimalakīrti Sūtra,* that favorite of Su Shih's:

> Then the Licchava Vimalakīrti thought, "Without rising from my couch, I shall pick up in my right hand the universe Abhirati and all it contains . . . its rivers, lakes, fountains, streams, oceans, and other bodies of waters; its Mount Sumeru and other hills and mountain ranges; its moon, its sun, and its stars. . . . Like a potter with his wheel, I will reduce that universe Abhirati . . . to a minute size and, carrying it gently like a garland of flowers, will bring it to this Saha universe and will show it to the multitudes.[7]

The assertion that "all things are Mind," as Izutsu reminds us, "does not mean that the whole universe comes into, or is contained in, the 'mind'. It simply means that the whole universe *is* in itself and by itself the Mind."[8] Thus it is not a question of reducing but of seeing things as they actually are, opening the Buddha eye and viewing the world from an entirely new dimension of awareness. A clear illustration can be found in the passage from the *Śūraṃgama Sūtra* where Ananda expresses his understanding of the fact that the original Buddha-mind completely permeates all time and space: "He turned around to look at the body given him by his mother and father, and seeing it in the emptiness of the ten directions, [it resembled] a particle of dust that was sometimes there and sometimes not, like a bubble floating on a vast limpid sea.[9]

Here again is evidence of the creative imagination that in Huang-chou had helped Su to overcome the physical and psychological constrictions of his everyday life. Although no longer in exile, he would continue to need this kind of perspective, as his life in the capital during this period was not particularly happy. Once again he found himself on the losing side among the contending political factions within the conservative government, and he was soon transferred to a politically less sensitive post in the Han-lin Academy. But this transfer did not solve his problems, for Su was also appointed one of two tutors to the young emperor, and the other tutor was the great Sung philosopher Ch'eng I, whose personality and philosophical views were diametrically opposed to those of Su Shih. Two factions soon grew up around them, the Lo faction supporting Ch'eng I's strict adherence to Confucian rites and rituals and the Shu faction supporting Su Shih's unorthodox and somewhat emotional interpretations of the classics. Fearful of being drawn into the maelstrom once again, Su reacted characteristically, requesting a transfer to a provincial post. However, his request was not accepted until 1089, nearly five years later.

During this time Su continued to read Buddhist texts, if not with the same sense of urgency as he had during those long days in Huang-chou's An-kuo ssu. In 1085, for instance, he wrote a post-script to an edition of the *Laṅkāvatāra Sūtra* that had been discovered by his old friend Chang Fang-p'ing (1007–1091) in the quarters of a Buddhist monk friend of his.[10] Su relates that no sooner had Chang read the opening lines of this sutra, penned as this copy was in fine and graceful calligraphy, than he gave "a great sigh of combined sorrow and joy, and subsequently entered the state of enlightenment." Nearly forty years later Chang presented the text to Su Shih, since by that time, as Su puts it, "[Chang] was seventy-nine years old, all of his illusions gone and his wisdom perfected,"[11] while Su had also aged owing to his many sorrows and "stood to learn from it." Chang also gave Su money to have the sutra printed and circulated in the Yangtze and Huai river regions. Later, at his friend Fo-yin's suggestion, Su had his postscript carved in stone and installed on Mt. Chin.

In his postscript Su Shih admits that this particular sutra is not at all easy to understand. In fact, Su was attracted to its relatively difficult and abstruse language, which he found intriguing. (Despite his growing fondness for free-flowing spontaneous *(tzu-jan)* and bland *(p'ing-tan)* language, Su Shih never quite lost his youthful love of the archaic and abstruse.) He writes:

> The *Laṅkāvatāra* is deep and unfathomable in meaning and in style so terse and antique, that the reader finds it quite difficult to punctuate the sentences properly, much less to adequately understand their ultimate spirit and meaning which goes beyond the let-

ter. This is the reason why the sutra grew so scarce it became almost impossible to get hold of a copy.[12]

The translation that Chang Fang-p'ing had given Su appears to have been the Guṇabhadra translation in four fascicles (*T* 670) of 443, the most widely circulated of the four translations made of this sutra. Although the other three (two of which were made in the T'ang) were of better quality, the Guṇabhadra was the shortest, which may account for its popularity. The great T'ang Buddhist scholar Fa-ts'ang (643–712) criticized this version for being unnecessarily obscure, but, as D. T. Suzuki points out, the main difficulty was its style, which resulted not, as Su supposed, from a "classical terseness," but from Chinese words being arranged in Sanskrit syntax. Another reason for the difficulty may be that the language of the *Laṅkāvatāra Sūtra* is not particularly poetic or symbolic, but rather is, to quote Suzuki, "straightforward in expression [noting] down in a somewhat sketchy style almost all the ideas belonging to the different schools of Mahāyāna Buddhism. It is partly for this reason that the sutra requires a great deal of learning as well as insight to understand all the details thoroughly."[13] Despite its difficulty, the sutra continued to be studied during the Sung, partly owing to Su Shih's own efforts to revive an interest in it. Su's poetry contains a great many allusions, direct and indirect, to this particular sutra, indicating that its language and philosophical content both made a lasting impression on Su Shih's literary mind.

Su also managed to keep up with some of his old Buddhist friends. In 1086 a Korean monk of royal descent by the name of I-t'ien came to China to visit various Buddhist temples and masters, Vinaya, Pure Land, T'ien-t'ai, and Ch'an, and to lecture on the *Avataṃsaka Sūtra*. Su Shih was one of the officials appointed to accompany the monk on his visit to the Hang-chou area, and he records what happened. The monk was treated ceremoniously at all the places he visited—all, that is, except Mt. Chin, where Su's old friend Fo-yin Liao-yüan refused to give the Korean any special consideration, observing that when I-t'ien left the world for monastic life, he also relinquished his right to special consideration because of his royal blood. Fo-yin might have wished merely to demonstrate the more iconoclastic Ch'an way, but he might have been touched with nationalistic fervor. In any case, although this treatment raised a bit of a furor, the emperor acknowledged the validity of Fo-yin's argument and let the matter pass.

In 1089 Su's request for a transfer was finally accepted, and Su was appointed prefect of Hang-chou. Needless to say, he was delighted to return to the scenic place where he had passed many happy hours almost sixteen years before. This time, however, his life was very different: his official duties included a major overhaul and repair of West Lake, which kept him extremely occupied. He was also confronted by a major famine and consumed many hours and much paper and ink trying to obtain relief for the people of Hang-chou. These duties seem to have taken all his energies; he produced no works of major literary merit. However, he did engage in various useful religious and social activities. He supported numerous local religious societies (which were characteristic of Hang-chou Buddhism) and their sponsorship of *chai,* or vegetarian feasts. Among these ceremonies was the *shui-lu chai,* or ceremony for the souls (of the "hungry ghosts" wandering lost) on land and sea. Su notes that because of all the famine and disasters suffered by the people in Hang-chou, "there are more *shui-lu* ceremonies [performed] here than in other places, since so many [more] people have died [here]."[14]

While in Hang-chou, Su revisited some of the monks he had befriended years earlier. Hui-ch'in, whom Su had sought out at Ou-yang Hsiu's recommendation when he first came to Hang-chou sixteen years earlier, was now dead, but Su composed a memorial piece for him, which was later inscribed on Mt. Ku, where the monk had lived. Su spent as much time as possible with Master Pien-ts'ai, whom he had known for over twenty years and who was living in retirement at the Shou-sheng ssu in Lung-ching. Pien-ts'ai was now more than eighty years old but still extremely alert. Su wrote several poems to commemorate their meetings. As a poet, Su was not a theologian or a philosopher but a man of deep feeling and a profound love of nature, words, and friendship. It was through words and friendship and the poetic imagination that he sought to transcend barriers of time and space. The following poem addressed to Pien-ts'ai shows once again his admiration for a man who had apparently done what Su would have liked to: transcend coming and going.

Sun and moon revolve like a pair of wheel hubs.
Past and present speed by like a fox on a hill.
There is nobody like this heron-thin old man;
Austere and stern, he no longer knows autumns.
He himself doesn't care whether he goes or stays
But man and heaven vie to keep him from leaving.
He leaves like a dragon coming out of the mountains:
The lightning and rain turn vast and mournful.
He comes like a pearl reentering the river:
Fish and turtles vie to greet him.
This life must be viewed as a temporary sojourn;
I have often suspected that fame was mere froth.
I am not as daring as Official T'ao [Ch'ien]:
And the Master grieves for this guest from afar.
Seeing me off back across the stream,
The stream that should flow in the opposite direction.
For now, I only ask that this Man of the Mountain
Remember how we two old men walked together
　　　today.
A thousand kalpas rest in the palm of his hand,
How could it be that he feels the pain of parting?[15]

There are a number of familiar themes in this poem. Again, Su expresses his admiration for someone who, because of his spiritual insight and detachment, is no longer emotionally perturbed by the passage of time and the proximity of death. In other words, he has reversed the samsaric flow and returned to his original nature. Su plays on the image of the stream of samsara and laments his own inability to "return"—not only like Pien-ts'ai but like T'ao Ch'ien, who gave up his official post and returned to his gardens and fields.

In a poem written a little earlier, Su refers to Pien-ts'ai's ability to transcend yet another set of apparent dualities: that between the writing of poetry and the life of the spirit. The closing lines of this poem read as follows:

I envy the Master's playful roaming through this
　　floating world.
He laughs at me: "Glory and decay both gone in the
　　snap of a finger."
And yet tasting tea and enjoying paintings are not
　　sinful pursuits,
Asking about the dharma and requesting poems are
　　not mutually opposed![16]

The predominant tone of these lines is characteristic, a mixture of admiration and envy for this "heavenly wanderer" who can live amid the froth of the world without being affected by it, this "utmost man" who, in the inimitable words of Chuang-tzu (as translated by A. C. Graham), rides "out on the bird which fades into the sky beyond where the six directions end, to travel the realm of Nothingwhatever and settle in the wilds of the Boundless."[17] Knowing that glory and decay both reside in the snap of a finger, Master Pien-ts'ai is undisturbed by the apparent tension between writing poetry and seeking the Tao, or between living in the world and forsaking it.

Much the same conclusion is reached in the following poem, which was written several years later, shortly before Pien-ts'ai's death, to match the rhymes of a poem by Ts'an-liao. Ts'an-liao's poem was written in 1079 on the occasion of a visit he and Ch'in Kuan made to Master Pien-ts'ai, who was then living in his retreat at Lung-ching in the mountains outside of Hang-chou. According to Su Shih, on this occasion Pien-ts'ai, who rarely wrote poetry, suddenly and spontaneously produced a poem like "the patterns and forms that spontaneously form on the water's [surface] when it is stirred up by the wind." The resulting poem so delighted Su that he remarked that "the poems of Ts'an-liao and others of my contemporaries are but clever embroidery in comparison!"[18] Although there is some confusion about the poem's authorship—it is included in Su's collected works although it was ostensibly written by Pien-ts'ai—it is worth quoting:

> My body as craggy as a stone, as a tree,
> My hair has already turned white,
> What men are these, friends from the past,
> Who have come to comfort me face to face?
> By nature, he [Ts'an-liao] shared the same mind-seal
> As Master Chou [Chiao-jan];
> Many are the times I think of Master Ch'in [Kuan]
> Whose mind is as complete as a pearl.
> And how [Ts'an-liao] that year walked in the
>   moonlight
> And came to this secluded valley;
> Dragging his staff, he pierced through the clouds,
> And braved the evening mist.
> Terraces and pavilions, mountains and forests:

There was never any difference between them.
It is for this reason that language
Is not to be distinguished from Ch'an.[19]

In this poem (which I have translated as if it were written in the voice of Pien-ts'ai), the Master Chou to whom Ch'in Kuan is favorably compared is the famous monk-poet Chiao-jan (730–799), whose writings represent the first extended treatment of the relationship between Buddhism and the literary arts. His literary critical work the *Shih-p'ing* [Evaluation of poetry] speaks of the "dharma of poetry" as something that transcends not only religious doctrines but even language itself, all of which provide but traces of the ultimate truth.[20]

In 1091, at the age of eighty-one, Pien-ts'ai summoned the monk Ts'an-liao (later to become a close friend of Su's) and informed him that in a week he would leave his body. He then refused to eat or speak. Seven days later, having composed his death poem, he bade farewell to his followers and passed peacefully away. After his stupa was built, Pien-ts'ai's disciple Huai-ch'u asked Su, who by then was back in the capital, to write the memorial inscription, but Su turned the task over to his brother, realizing, perhaps, that Su Ch'e's understanding and appreciation of Buddhism was deeper than his own.

In Hang-chou Su also visited with his old friend Master Huai-lien and gave him a three-legged bronze pot left to Su by his friend Chang Fang-p'ing. He was, however, distressed to hear that Huai-lien had been slandered and vilified by certain government officials, and he wrote a letter to the local magistrate protesting this treatment and reminding him how Emperor Jen-tsung had respected this monk. In 1090, not long after Su's arrival, Huai-lien passed away.

Su made some new friends as well. One of these was an unusual monk by the name of Chung-shu, who lived in Hang-chou's Ch'eng-t'ien ssu. An extremely gifted poet (unfortunately his collection of poetry, the *Pao-yüeh chi,* or *Precious Moon Collection,* is no longer extant), Chung-shu was especially known for his talent at writing *yüeh-fu,* or ballads, as well as very romantic and even erotic lyrics *(tz'u).* Before becoming a monk, Chung-shu had not only passed the *chin-shih* exam but had taken a wife. However, he found it almost impossible to stay at home, and one day his angry wife poisoned his meat. Chung-shu nearly died but cured himself by eating honey, which he continued to do for the rest of his life. Furthermore, doctors warned him that if he even touched meat again, the poison would reactivate and he would be dead. On hearing this, Chung-shu decided that he might as well become a monk. Even as a monk, however, he continued to write poetry of a distinctly secular sort, about which Su loved to tease him, calling his poetry "the honey of a thousand flowers." He must have been a rather complex person, however—in 1101, coincidentally the year of Su's own death, he committed suicide by hanging. Su wrote a number of poems to Chung-shu, including the following *yüeh-fu,* written in 1090:

> The old fellow of An-chou has a mind as resolute as
>   iron
> But still manages to retain the tongue of a child.[21]
> He will not touch the five grains, but eats only
>   honey:[22]
> Smiling, he points to the bees and calls them his
>   "donors"!
> The honey he eats contains a poetry men do not
>   understand:
> But the myriad flowers and grasses vie to transport it.
> The old fellow sips and savors and then spits out
>   poems,
> Poems designed to entice the ill "children" of the
>   world.
> When the children taste his poems, it is like tasting
>   honey,
> And that honey is a cure for the hundred ills.
> Just when they are madly rushing about grasping at
>   straws,
> Smiling, they read his poems and all their cares
>   vanish!
> Master Tung-p'o has always treated others with
>   fairness
> But still there are some who like him and some who
>   don't!
> Like a tea that some find bitter and others sweet,
> And unlike honey, which tastes sweet to everyone.

> So, Sir, I am sending you a round cake of Double
>   Dragon tea:
> Which, if held up to a mirror, will reflect the two
>   dragons.
> Though Wu during the sixth month is as hot as boil-
>   ing water,
> This old man's mind is as cool as the Double Dragon
>   Well![23]

Here Su is once again playing with the Buddhist notion of skillful means, a concept he, as a poet, found exceedingly attractive.

Another monk whose acquaintance Su apparently renewed about this time was Fa-yün Shan-pen (1035–1109), known familiarly as Hsiao-pen, "Little Pen," to differentiate him from a fellow monk also named Pen.[24] Shan-pen was a Yün-men Ch'an monk, a disciple of Hui-lin Tsung-pen (1020–1099). Hui-lin Tsung-pen was serving as the head of the Ching-ssu temple in Hang-chou when, in 1082, he was asked by Emperor Shen-tsung to head the Hui-lin Ch'an temple in the capital of K'ai-feng. He contributed greatly to the spread of Yün-men Ch'an. It is said that when the emperor invited him to court, Hui-lin Tsung-pen very nonchalantly seated himself in the lotus position, and when his tea arrived, he picked it up and drank it with the utmost informality and ease, despite the glares of the attendant officials. In time, he asked to return to Hang-chou, relinquishing his position in the capital to Fa-yün Shan-pen. Shan-pen came from a family of scholar-officials (descended from the famous Han dynasty official Tung Chung-shu) and had passed the *chin-shih* examination before deciding, in 1063, to become a monk. During his time in the capital he became known for his understanding of the *Avataṃsaka Sūtra*. He was then invited by Master Yüan-chao of Hang-chou to help him receive the many lay guests, mostly scholars and officials, who came to visit his temple. Just about the time Su arrived in Hang-chou, Shan-pen was given the name Ch'an Master Ta-t'ung and recalled to the capital to take charge of the Fa-yün ssu, a new Ch'an monastery built by the royal family. Understandably, the monk was at first quite reluctant to go, although he finally gave in to royal pressure. In a poem Su wrote to send Shan-pen off, he empathizes with a monk who still has many duties to keep him occupied even after he has "left" the world—a situation that was increasingly

common in the growing monastic bureaucracies of the Northern
Sung. The poet is no doubt projecting somewhat and perhaps
even rationalizing his own continuing attachment to the world
—if a monk cannot escape from all this, how can he be expected
to do so?

> As long as one dwells beneath this heavenly roof,
> No matter where one goes there will be dues to pay.
> Even if one lives peacefully with no business affairs,
> How can one pass one's life without trouble of some
>   kind!
> In mountain groves too there is worry and pain—
> Even official robes and carriages are part of the play.
> I have not yet been able to retire to the quiet life,
> But you, Master, should be living in peaceful
>   seclusion!
> The Imperial City is full of brilliant scholars,
> Discussing, debating, distinguishing black from
>   white.
> Asked to name the first principle of Divine Truth,
> Bodhidharma faced the emperor and said, "Who
>   knows?"
> Master, what business brings you to this place,
> Like a solitary moon suspended in the empty blue?
> When was this self that is like a floating cloud,
> Ever limited by the boundaries of north and south?
> If one leaves one's mountain having achieved no-
>   mind,
> Then when it rains, one will still be able to find
>   refuge.
> Long ago I made a promise to you by the Pearl
>   Stream,
> When will I return there to hang up my flask and
>   staff?[25]

Shan-pen had attracted many followers during his time in Hang-
chou, and when he left for the capital, there was a concern that they
would all disperse. Su, however, using his authority as prefect,
invited the elder monk Ch'u-ming of Yüeh-chou to come and take
over the leadership of the Ching-ssu temple. His choice proved to
be a good one, and the temple's membership increased significantly. Nor was this the only time that Su became involved in tem-

ple administration. During the time he was prefect of Hang-chou, the head monk of the Ching-shan temple died and left a vacancy, and Su made use of his official authority to sidestep the official procedure whereby the abbots of the temples would recommend a candidate. He appointed a new head monk himself, in this instance, Wei-lin (d. 1119), a disciple of his father's friend Huai-lien. Although this move aroused a considerable amount of controversy at first, Wei-lin soon managed to win the affection and admiration of the community, and all turned out well. Wei-lin was very grateful to Su and was one of two monks at his bedside when he died.

Throughout his life, Su Shih engaged in both Buddhist and Taoist practices (or a combination of both), although none with any great consistency. In a poem probably written during this second stay in Hang-chou, we can see that he still has not lost that detached quality evidenced in his earlier works. This poem describes a "meditation tower," a building designed for the express purpose of meditation, located in one of the temples in Hang-chou.

> In the three worlds there is no place to dwell,[26]
> But in this solitary tower a moment of inner peace.
> For worldly anxieties there is the bleached-bone
>   meditation
> In silent stillness the Yellow Court arises.
> A lingering echo sounds softly in the wind,
> The snow behind the solitary lamp looks blue.
> I must keep myself from playing around like the
>   chap,
> Who threw a tile and disturbed the clear, cold water.[27]

This poem begins with what is perhaps the most central of Su's Buddhist ideas, the idea of finding a moment, whether in the mind or in a meditation tower, of peace and tranquility in a world without a "dwelling place." In the next lines, although Su begins with a reference to the rather austere white-bone meditation, the eighth of a series of meditations on death and decay designed to curb desire, he is quickly distracted by the beauty of the deep silence and the blue pallor of the snow seen in the light of the altar lamp. Finally, in the last couplet the poet refers to the account of the contemplation of the water element in the *Śūraṃgama Sūtra*. This form of meditation involves looking at all the watery elements of the mind until one understands that "this element of water in the body does not differ from that of the fragrant oceans that surround the Pure Lands of Buddhas."[28] However, there are dangers involved. In the *Śūraṃgama Sūtra,* the bodhisattva who achieved his enlightenment in this way tells the Buddha how, although he succeeded in realizing the identity of the element of water, he failed to relinquish his view of the body. Thus one day when he was practicing, his disciple peeked into his room and saw that it was filled with nothing but clear water. Not knowing better, he threw a broken tile into the water and left. When the bodhisattva came out of his trance, he felt a terrible pain in his heart. When he found out what had happened during his meditation, he asked his disciple to remove the tile the next time he entered the meditative state. Su is identifying himself not with the bodhisattva but with the mischievous and ignorant disciple.

In 1091 Su was recalled to the capital only to find that the political backbiting had not abated very much. While in Hang-chou he had attempted to expedite famine relief. Now he found himself accused of exaggerating the famine conditions in order to do so. In addition, old accusations and rumors were dredged up—Su was accused of opportunism, nepotism, and trying to avoid facing his critics by retreating to provincial office. This last accusation did have some truth in it: Su quickly withdrew once more, departing for the scenic lake region of Ying-chou in Anhwei province. In the following poem (praised by Chi Yün for avoiding the tone of a religious hymn despite its use of Ch'an vocabulary), addressed to his friend Abbot Yüeh, a highly regarded monk from Ying-chou, Su again expresses his admiration for a man who has broken through the strictures of time and space. His tenuous position had made him once again acutely aware of the seemingly inescapable constrictions of his life.

> Heaven covers earth like a straw rain cape,
> While earth and sea spin like two wheels.[29]
> The entire domain of the Five Emperors,
> Is a grain of dust on the tip of a hair.[30]
> Success and fame are half a sheet of paper,
> Sons and daughters bring bitter hardship.
> But you have broken the shackles on your feet,
> And used them to cook your meal of stale rice.[31]

For ten years you have been living in this way,
And yet have become a truly distinguished man.
I am invited to take a seat by the earthen stove:
With gentle words of profound truth.
The pale ashes piled like drifts of snow
Around a *chi-lin*-shaped ember glowing red.
"Don't touch that *chi-lin*-shaped red ember.
If it turns to ash, the *karmadana* will be angry!"[32]
The Master nods but remains in seated silence,
And the very walls seem to preach the dharma.
This evening I regret there are so many visitors,
Your white felt monk's cap stained dark sweat.
I will make a point of coming alone another night,
When we can put aside the roles of host and guest.
If I sit on my cushion facing the paper curtain,
I will begin to see into the self's true nature.[33]

In the Buddhist context the image of the sojourner, traveler, or guest (which Su often used in reference to himself) is actually meant to symbolize the differentiating mind, forever moving from place to place, whereas the image of the host or innkeeper is used to symbolize the true mind that, to use the words of the *Śūraṃgama Sūtra,* "has nowhere else to go, for he owns the inn."[34] Nevertheless, one must ultimately go beyond distinctions of host and guest as well by seeing into one's true nature. Only then will the apparent duality between material form and emptiness, movement and quiescence, exile and home be resolved.

Su's respite in Ying-chou was brief. First he was transferred to Yang-chou, still in Anhwei province but closer to the coast. And in the fall of 1092 he was called back to the capital and promoted to the highest posts he had ever served in—those of minister of war and minister of rites. The slander did not stop, however, and Su again found a way to leave the capital, assuming the governorship of Ting-chou in Hopei province. It was there that Su's second wife passed away in 1093. Not long afterward, Su requested Ch'an Master Fa-yün Shan-pen to carry out the memorial services for the dead, the *shui-lu chai,* for his deceased wife. It was at this time that Su commissioned the great painter Li Kung-lin to paint a picture of Sakyamuni Buddha and his ten major disciples, which he dedicated to the memory of his wife and ordered installed in the Ch'ing-liang ssu in Nanking. To commemorate the occasion he wrote a hymn that reflects his understanding of the inherent Buddha-nature, the radiant original mind that is the ultimate goal from which true believers will never "turn back."

> I pray to the World-honored One, feet and hands
>   pressing the earth,
> That the sentient beings of the three thousand great
>   chiliocosms
> Pure and the color of crystal, will one and all find
>   liberation.
> Just as when the sun comes out, those that are sleep-
>   ing awake;
> Just as when there is thunder and lightning, hibernat-
>   ing insects stir.
> Together we acclaim the Peerless One and will never
>   turn back.[35]

Su also wrote a series of sixteen religious poems to accompany the *shui-lu* ceremony. These verses describe the set of sixteen paintings commonly used for this ceremony. They reflect the mixture of concepts and images from Ch'an, Hua-yen, Pure Land, and popular Buddhism-Taoism that characterized Su's (and many lay Buddhists' of the Northern Sung) understanding of Buddhism. In the preface to the series, he draws on images from the *Vimalakīrti Sūtra,* as well as the T'ien-t'ai "three thousand worlds in a single instant of thought," and the Hua-yen concept of the interpenetration of *shih* and *li.*

You have surely heard of the pure alms bowl that was able to feed ten thousand mouths [and the] precious parasol that extended over the ten directions. If one understands the *dharmadhatu,* then one can create [everything] within the mind. Thus, even the most ordinary things embody this principle *(li).* The former emperor Wu of Liang was the first to sponsor the feast for the souls of the land and sea *(shui-lu tao-ch'ang)* and to use [these] sixteen images to [represent] fully the three thousand worlds. By means of a limited [ceremony] one can extend [the merit] widely; although the [ritual] is simple, the principle is a comprehensive one.[36]

Su then goes on to note that he remembers that these sixteen paintings often were used for this ceremony in his home province of Szechuan. This comment would seem to indicate that he had seen this ceremony carried out when he was growing up in Mei-shan. In fact, in a miscellaneous piece Su wrote about his decision to give up butchering animals for food, he recalls seeing depictions of the six realms, including the animal realm, in these *shui-lu* paintings, which meant that animals were of the same nature as human beings.[37] Master Shan-pen, being himself from Szechuan, would also have known about this. Su also mentions that one of the reasons he wishes to sponsor this *shui-lu* feast is to preserve a ritual that, presumably, had been handed down orally and had not been printed.

The first eight verses in this sequence are descriptions of the major iconographical figures—Buddhas, bodhisattvas, and arhats as well as representations of the remaining two of the Three Jewels, the dharma and the *sangha*. The last of the eight are the Taoist immortals who have been absorbed into this Buddhist pantheon. The first one, while describing the portrait of the Buddha (or Buddhas, it is unclear which) discusses the interpenetration and inseparability of phenomenon or form *(shih)* and noumenon or principle *(li)*.

> If you say that this is the Buddha,
> That creates an obstacle between *shih* and *li*.
> If you say that this is not the Buddha
> Then it becomes a form of nihilism.
> But when *shih* and *li* meet each other,
> Then this nihilism is also empty.
> The Buddha appears spontaneously before us
> As if from the center of the sun.

The second poem describes the nature of the second of the Three Jewels, the dharma, in terms that are reminiscent of the *Śūraṃgama Sūtra*'s ideas that both the senses and their objects arise from a single source, the "uncreated and unending Tathāgata store," and that by turning the senses back onto themselves, returning them to their original source, one can attain liberation.

> If one takes consciousness as the root,
> This is called the dharma sense objects.
> If one takes the Buddha as the body,
> This is called the dharma body.
> When the wind stops, the waves are still,

> For they are not of a different water.
> When released, the water becomes rivers and lakes,
> When contained, it forms pools and islets.

The dynamic vision of the absolute reflected in this verse is in many ways close to that of the T'ien-t'ai school of Buddhism. As Junjirō Takakusu writes:

> The ultimate truth taught in the [Ti'en-t'ai] School is Thusness . . . the true state of things in themselves. . . . The true state of things cannot be seen directly or immediately. We must see it in the phenomena which are ever changing and becoming. Thus the true state is dynamic. The phenomena themselves are identical with the true state of things. The true state of things is Thusness, i.e., things as they are manifested, just as moving waves are not different from the still water. We generally contrast the still water with the moving waves, but moving and staying they are only the manifestation of one and the same water. What is being manifested or shown outwardly is nothing but the thing itself. There is no difference between the two. [38]

The next poem, describing the painting of the Hīnayāna Mahā-pratekeya-Buddhas or arhats who have realized enlightenment for themselves through arduous self-discipline and spiritual cultivation, shows once again Su's reluctance to discard the ideals of asceticism (which he often held up as standards for many of his Buddhist friends). It also shows his understanding that in this demoralized and darkened age, people need the various "remedies" for suffering offered by Mahāyāna Buddhism, the later or "Second" Vehicle.

> In these days without the Buddha
> We should cultivate the Second Vehicle.
> Just as when the sun goes down,
> We use oil and fire for light
> I say that the Second Vehicle,
> Is the medicine for our illnesses
> Respectfully I worship the Pratekeyas
> For their great and perfect realization.

A poem addressed to the great bodhisattvas reflects the ideas of the *Śūraṃgama Sūtra* and in particular the section in which the eighteen bodhisattvas describe the various means by which they were able to enter the state of *samādhi*.

> Divine wisdom has no boundaries,
> Final liberation has no obstacle.
> By means of which of the causes,
> Can one obtain the Great Ease?
> Obstacles disappear and vows are fulfilled,
> As one returns to the self-existent.
> From beginningless time until now,
> Those who have died will exist again.

The eight images of the lower series include such figures as officials, heavenly beings, and denizens of the various worlds, including the human world. They are illustrations not of spiritual achievement, but rather of spiritual struggle. Su's description of the second painting, depicting the heavenly beings or devas, explores the inseparability of joy and suffering, and how even the great bliss enjoyed by the gods eventually comes to an end.

> Pain at its limit rectifies itself,
> Joy at its limit dissipates.
> Calamity and good fortune are endless,
> Intertwined, they follow one the other,
> But if one transcends lust and desire,
> One can reach the realm of nonthought.
> There is nothing like a single thought
> The truth of which has no equal.

The *Śūraṃgama Sūtra* goes into considerable detail regarding the various hells that await those who indulge in habits of sexual desire, craving, and arrogance as well as the heavens that await those worldly beings who abstain from these things. And, although this point is somewhat lost in the graphic descriptions of cauldrons of boiling water and seas of molten copper, it also notes that, because in the end everything is Original Mind, which is luminously perfect, the worlds of hells, hungry ghosts, human beings, and gods have no inherent existence: "These states are brought on by the karma created by wrong thinking; if one were to awaken to *bodhi* (perfect wisdom), then [one would understand that] in the marvelous, complete luminosity [of the Original Mind] these [states] have never existed."[39] This idea is stated in the first four lines of Su's description of the painting of the human world:

> Underworld hells and heavenly palaces—
> Both are but a single thought.
> Nirvana or the world of samsara,
> Both are but one Buddha-nature.

It appears yet again in the verses that describe the denizens of the Buddhist hells, the fifth in this series:

> If you give rise to a single thought,
> The karmic fires will burst into flame.
> There is no one who is burning you,
> But rather you are burning yourself.
> Meditating on the *dharmadhatu* nature,
> Rising and disappearing like a lightning flash.
> Knowing that it is only a creation of the mind,
> Then all of these hells will be destroyed.

This idea that a single thought determines hell or heaven is reiterated again and again in the *Śūraṃgama Sūtra* and explains why this text was particularly popular with the Ch'an Buddhists. It intrigued Su Shih as well, and we find it in many of his writings.

Around this time, Su's youngest son, Su Kuo, made a copy of the *Suvarṇaprabhāsottama-sūtra* (Ching-kuang-ming ching), which he then bound and presented to the new library at the Ts'ung-ch'ing yüan in Wen-chou in memory of his departed mother. Su wrote a postscript for this sutra in which he describes how his son addressed him with tears in his eyes, saying:

> I cannot hope to attain generous merit from the scanty effort I have spent copying this sutra. Only if one recites it with both the heart and the mouth as one bends over to copy it out by hand will one be able to reach and move the Buddha and the patriarchs and obtain the succor of the gods. But [I, Su Kuo] am ignorant and dense and do not know whether the words of this sutra are all true or whether they are [just] metaphors. What is one supposed to perceive; what is one supposed to say?[40]

The *Suvarṇaprabhāsottama-sūtra* was a very popular sutra, and three Chinese versions exist. The version Su read was probably the complete third version in ten fascicles (*T* 665), which was translated in the late seventh or early eighth century by I-ching. This last version apparently added to the original versions certain things that had been left out, in particular numerous largely Tantric incantations, or *dharanis*, which explains why the text itself was considered to have magical powers. In fact, Sangharakshita calls this sutra "a medley of philosophy and devotion, legends and spells" that someone reading it for the first time might consider to be "a sort of ragbag, albeit a ragbag that contained wonderful scraps of jeweled brocade."[41] It is not surprising then that Su Kuo should ask his father whether the contents of this particular sutra should be taken as truth or metaphor. Su's reply reflects the concern with perception that lies at the heart of the *Śūraṃgama Sūtra* (which he quotes at length in this piece):

> That is a good question! I have often heard Master Chang An-tao [Fang-p'ing, 1007–1091] say: "The Buddha's vehicle is neither large nor small, [and His] words are neither empty nor true. It depends solely on how I perceive them. The ten thousand dharmas are all one. If I have [spiritual] insight, then the metaphorical language is factual language. If I have no insight, then both facts and metaphors are false.[42]

Later, Su will repeat much the same idea in his criticism of Wang An-shih's commentary on the *Avataṃsaka Sūtra*. Seeing that Wang's commentary was restricted to only one chapter of the eighty-chapter sutra, he asked a friend why this was. The friend explained to Su that Wang's idea was to separate the words of the Buddha, which he considered to be superior, from those of the bodhisattvas. Su then exclaimed that the two are combined together, and he could not understand how Wang, as insightful as he might be, could possibly distinguish between those that were true and those that were false. In illustration of his point, Su recounts how once he sent someone to buy some pork from a place known to raise a particularly tasty product. The man bought a pig, but on his way home stopped to have a drink at an inn and let the pig get away. The man then substituted another pig, and Su, who prided himself on being a connoisseur of food, in particular pork, was never the wiser. Su then goes on to say that if one is purified inwardly, then "even the walls and the tiles preach the peerless dharma," and for Wang to say that the words of the Buddha are profoundly marvelous while those of the bodhisattvas are inferior is "pure nonsense."[43]

The *Suvarṇaprabhāsottama-sūtra* is also known for its emphasis on the infinity of the life of the Buddha and contains numerous stories of the Buddha's past lives. In his postscript Su refers in particular to the story about how the Buddha in a previous life offered his own flesh to feed a hungry tiger who was too weak to feed her cubs. Curiously enough, he prefaces this with a paraphrase from a section of the *Śūraṃgama Sūtra* that discusses the mental inversions that lead away from a realization of one's absolute nature and to the existence of living beings and the world. Su notes how the various types of birth arise from the endless interplay between enmity and friendship, attraction and repulsion, subject and object. The *Śūraṃgama Sūtra* recommends engaging in self-discipline and spiritual cultivation designed to rid oneself of sensual desire of any kind in order to stop the growth of karma and return to the undivided, absolute perfection of the *tathāgata-garbha*. Su Shih's exposition of these ideas is somewhat confused, but his emphasis appears to be (like that of the *Śūraṃgama Sūtra*) on the necessity for morality, charity, and self-discipline during the first stages of the bodhisattva path.

> You will see that all the worlds, although they are very lovable *(k'o-ai)* are empty, illusory, and without substance and in the end do not belong to us. So if you [can] abandon and separate yourself from these [things] like the bodhisattva prince who offered his body, although it [appears] dreadful, yet the fact that it can eradicate karma shows deep commiseration and compassion. If you give charity, like the bodhisattva prince who gave [his flesh] to the tigers, if you carry out this kind of giving, feeding the hungry, giving drink to the thirsty, then the way can be attained, and Buddhahood can be realized, and evil can be uprooted.[44]

Both of these responses reflect Su Shih's openness to ideas and images of all kinds regardless of their provenance, an openness that stands in marked contrast to the obsessive concern with the "correct way" evidenced by a number of his better-known contemporaries. The dividing lines between "philosophical," "religious," and "superstitious," indeed between so-called popular and elite, were, in the case of Su Shih at least, often quite tenuous. Also tenuous are the lines between "gradual" and "sudden," between "Ch'an" and the doctrinal schools of Buddhism: Su Shih, although drawn to the spontaneity of the "sudden" school of Ch'an Buddhism, by no means rejected the need for more "gradual" types of spiritual cultivation, in particular the cultivation of moral qualities in this life, a process that would be of immediate benefit to society as a whole.

Su did not stay long in Ting-chou. The zeal of the newly empowered reformers followed Su out of the capital, and he was demoted and ordered to proceed to Ying-chou in the distant southern province of Kuangtung. However, that was not far enough away for the new leaders, and before he even reached Ying-chou, he received word that he had been banished to Hui-chou, even farther down the coast. On his way to Hui-chou, Su Shih stopped by Nan-hua ssu in Ts'ao-hsi on Mt. Nan-hua, a place associated with Hui-neng, the Sixth Patriarch of Ch'an Buddhism. The poem Su wrote at this time provides a glimpse into his state of mind when he visited this temple and the stupa said to contain the patriarch's remains:

> Why do I want to see the patriarch?
> I wanted to know my original face.
> The one in the high and lofty stupa,
> Asks me what it is that I have seen.
> Admirable, this enlightened elder,
> Myriad dharmas understood in a flash,
> Those who taste the water will realize their self-
>   nature,
> Finger pointing at the moon, their vision ever clear.
> I have ever been a seeker after enlightenment,
> Past, present, and future spent perfecting myself.
> Somewhere along the way, I lost a single thought,
> And so must suffer this hundred-year reprimand.
> Lifting my robe, I worship the patriarch's remains,
> My heart moved, tears pouring down like rain.
> I beg the use of water from the Master's Staff Tip
>   Spring,
> To wash this inkstone of its profane words.[45]

Here Su blames the misdemeanors of a previous life (perhaps as Ch'an Master Wu-tzu Chieh?) for his present troubles, a convenient and by this time widely accepted explanation. Su identifies with Hui-neng (known as the wandering layman Lu because he spent many years as a homeless lay practitioner before becoming a monk); elsewhere he goes so far as to claim he was a reincarnation of the Sixth Patriarch.

> Meals of wild greens, a cot of pigweed, a tattered monk's robe.
> Getting rid of old, stubborn attachments, no longer intoning poetry.
> In a previous life I was certainly the wandering layman Lu
> Although there are scholars who call me a Han T'ui-chih.[46]

Given Su's own situation and life in exile, it is not surprising that he might empathize with Hui-neng, who was forced to flee to the south to escape his enemies and who, according to some accounts, spent nearly sixteen years in obscurity before openly assuming his role of teacher. However, what is significant about this poem is that Su Shih once again expresses his desire to rid himself of the addiction of poetry and to take up the life of monastic seclusion he, presumably, once lived. Vincent Yang, in a recent study of Su Shih's poetry, comments on the rather pessimistic tone of these verses and concludes that, although Su did not stop writing poetry during this period, "he did renounce his former creative spirit, and therefore, his poetic genius never again reached the level that it had previously attained."[47] The Hui-chou period, in fact, was one of great productivity in terms of quantity if not always of quality. In the two years and seven months Su spent at Hui-chou, he wrote at least 170 poems, as compared to the 192 poems written during the four years and three months of his Huang-chou exile. His poetry also becomes increasingly philosophical and religious in character—more than a third of the poems written during the last period of his life are of this kind. Although I do not agree that Su Shih completely "renounced" his former creative spirit—there are still many examples of aesthetically successful poems from this period—it is clear that he became less interested in artistically weaving (or even disguising) his religious concerns and more apt to deal with them directly. In many ways this change parallels a gradual loss of interest in integrating his more transcendental religious concerns with the actuality of living in the world of society and politics. In other words, as his exile carried him farther and farther from the political center, he lost hope and eventually interest in ever returning to it again. Thus, when he speaks of return, as he does more and more often, it is the return to the absolute, of which the *Śūraṃgama Sūtra* speaks at length and with great eloquence. If anything is lost in this later writing, then, it is the tension, the sense of urgency created by the effort to reconcile two seemingly opposed things: the aesthetic and the religious, the world of the politician and that of the recluse and, ultimately, the transcendent and the immanent.

8. Like a Withered Tree

TRADITIONAL COMMENTATORS often mark the beginning of Su Shih's Hui-chou period with the poem titled "Passing Over Ta-yü Peak":

> In a moment, all my defilements have vanished,
> Leaving both body and soul transparently pure.
> So vast is it here between heaven and earth
> That even alone, all is well with me.
> Today as I travel along the mountain peaks
> Self and world are once and for all forgotten.
> The winds of the immortals seem to caress my head,
> As, tying up my hair, I receive their secrets.[1]

This poem reflects a desire not so much for integration as for transcendence, not for living in the world, but for leaving it all behind, forgetting it once and for all. It is not surprising, then, that much of Su Shih's time in Hui-chou was spent in Taoist practices that promised just such transcendence. If Hang-chou had been "Buddha country," Hui-chou was largely the province of the Taoists. One of its most famous scenic spots was Mt. Lo-fu, which was associated with the Taoist Ko Hung (283–363). Ko Hung was a practitioner of the alchemical arts, devoted to the search for physical immortality. Chung Lai-yin notes that Su Shih, who up to this point had been interested mainly in *nei-tan* exercises ("inner alchemy," or psychological and mental purification exercises exemplified by the *Huang t'ing ching,* or *Classic of the Yellow Emperor,* which Su Shih had read carefully) and the philosophic delights of Lao-tzu and Chuang-tzu, now spent much of his time engaging in Taoist *wai-tan* practices ("outer alchemy," or exercises more concerned with such things as the prolongation of physical life).[2] When Su arrived in Hui-chou in 1094, he found Taoist priests and practi-

tioners who were carrying on the spirit of Ko Hung, and he avidly
sought their company. For all his efforts at achieving transcendence
and immortality, however, in practice Su continued to seek ways to
accommodate himself to the situation in which he found himself, as
seen from the preface to a poem written shortly after his arrival in
Hui-chou:

> On the second day of the tenth month of the first year of Shao-
> sheng (1094), I arrived in Hui-chou and took up residence in Ho-
> chiang Tower. On the eighteenth day of that month, I moved to
> Chia-yu ssu. On the nineteenth day of the third month of the sec-
> ond year [of Shao-sheng] I moved again back to Ho-chiang Tower,
> and on the twentieth day of the fourth month of the third year I
> returned again to Chia-yu ssu. By that time, I had found a place to
> build on Pai-ho [White Crane] Peak; now that my new residence
> is completed, I may be able to get some small measure of peace!

> The year before last I lived east of the river;
> Where one could look back at the fine evening light.
> Last year I lived west of the river;
> Where the light spring rain dampened one's face.
> West or east, it was not for me to choose.
> When my time at one place was up, I was moved on.
> This year I've been moved back again to the east:
> Back to my old quarters, where I can rest for a while.
> Now I've already bought some land on White Crane
>   Peak,
> And made my plans for a spot to live out my years.
> The Yangtze lies at the northern entrance,
> And my "snow wave" stone dances on the stairway.
> The blue-green mountains fill my windows,
> Along with a few lovely tresses of cloud.
> I am ashamed that I am not like Pao P'u-tzu,
> Who left the world the way a cicada leaves his skin,
> Nor do I aspire to be like the sagely Liu of Liu-chou,
> At whose shrine people leave dishes of red lichee.
> In my lifetime I've never been allowed to stay put.
> Looking up and down, I finally understand this
>   world.
> Instant after instant, naturally forming kalpas,
> Dust particle after dust particle, each one a world.
> If you look down from above at all living things,
> They are but gnats blowing each other about.[3]

The last line of this poem is a reference to the first chapter of *Chuang-tzu,* which describes the great bird P'eng. During its journey to the South Ocean, it soars higher and higher into the heavens until "everything below looks the same as above (heat hazes, duststorms, the breath that living things blow at each other)."[4] Not surprisingly the same image occurs in Buddhist texts. In the *Śūraṃgama Sūtra,* the Bodhisattva of Crystal Light, explaining how he achieved enlightenment by meditating on the nature of boundless space, describes the change of perspective that accompanied this experience: "All the sentient beings within every world were like mosquitoes trapped in a jar buzzing and humming in confusion."[5] Su juxtaposes this expanded spatial perspective with Buddhist concepts of time (measured by the flow of thoughts, each of which lasts ninety moments, or *kṣana*s, each of which encompasses nine hundred births and deaths) and space, the innumerable worlds that the *Avataṃsaka Sūtra* describes as existing "on every single point throughout the whole of space." Su does not use these vast cosmic perspectives to escape the world or even to transcend it: in fact, he is quick to extend his apologies to Liu Ts'ung-yüan, who died in exile but was venerated by the people of the area after his death,[6] and also to Ko Hung, who in his *Pao p'u-tzu* described the hierarchy of immortals, the superior ones being those able to ascend to the heavens in their human bodies and the inferior those who became immortals only after death, shedding their bodies like cicadas shedding their skins.[7] Su's ambitions are both more modest and more practical: these perspectives on time and space help him to appreciate more fully what he does have—the blue-green mountains that fill his window and the snow-wave stone (an oddly marked stone that Su had found in Ting-chou and brought with him to Hui-chou) that lay by the steps of his courtyard.

> Once when I was staying at Chia-yu ssu in Hui-chou, I took a stroll below Pine Wind Pavilion. Exhausted and with tired feet, all I could think of was lying down in bed to rest. I looked up toward the roof of the pavilion, which was still at tree-top level, and I thought, "How will I ever get there?" After a while, I suddenly said, "Why should I not rest right here where I am now?" Thereupon my mind felt like a fish who suddenly slips free of the hook. If a person understands [*wu,* "enlightened"] this, then even [if one finds oneself caught between] two armies facing each other in

battle, the drums rolling like thunder, where to advance is to die at
the hands of the enemy, to retreat is to die at the hands of the law
—even at a moment like this, there is nothing to keep one from
[remaining in a state of] profound repose.[8]

This piece in a way epitomizes Su Shih's "spiritual problem": he
was constantly aiming toward extremely lofty and transcendent
goals, toward the undefiled "absolute" described in luminous
terms in texts like the *Śūraṃgama Sūtra,* and constantly finding
these goals unattainable. However, this lack of success was not due
merely to his own shortage of interest or motivation, but also to the
nature of the goals themselves, the "leap to the absolute" seemingly
required by the very schools and texts of Buddhism he was most
attracted to, in particular Ch'an and the *Śūraṃgama Sūtra.* Thus
his profound sense of relief when he realizes that he need not attain
the absolute, since he carries it within him wherever he goes.

For all Su's interest in these so-called *wai-tan* practices, the old
concerns for integration still appear time and again in the writings
of the period. They are particularly evident in his numerous written
exchanges with a Taoist by the name of Wu Tzu-yeh (d. 1100),
whom he had met many years before in the capital. Lin Yutang
calls Wu an "eccentric Taoist," but to Su he appears to have represented the life of untrammeled inner freedom that so many talked
about but so few achieved. Interestingly enough, the poem Su
writes to him makes liberal use of Buddhist terminology, yet
another indication of the disregard Su had for such apparent incon-
sistencies.

> Back in the days when you were young,
> You aspired to be an imperial knight-errant.
> You yourself said you were like Chü Meng,
> Who could tell an emergency by a knock on the door.[9]
> Now your thousand gold pieces are all spent,
> Your hair is white and your house is bare.
> The war hero sighs at the coming of old age,
> The old warhorse crouches sadly in the stable.
> Wife and children just like a pair of old shoes,
> No need to grieve at tossing them away.
> If the Four Elements are but an illusion,
> How much more so official caps and robes?
> One morning you made a vow to the Supreme Buddha,

To live your last years on sacred Eagle Peak.[10]
But when have you ever cared about worldly affairs?
Your Ch'an mind has long dwelt in empty tranquility.
Whether one remains in the world or leaves it,
There is only a single Way to be followed.
One must make one's mind like a withered tree,
And rid oneself of all worldly attachments.
The life of a true disciple is not easy:
And one's resolve must be firm as stone.
You must wake the world with a lion's roar,
For the dharma knows neither north nor south.[11]

In a piece written earlier in Hsü-chou titled "Asking [about the Principle of] Nourishing Life," Su Shih credits Wu with having introduced him to two important ideas—that of "tranquility" and that of "harmony." Wu, Su writes, claimed that his only technique is "being light on the outside and accommodating on the inside."[12] He then defines tranquility as being only lightly *(ch'ing)* moved by external phenomena and harmony as responding to external phenomena in a smooth and unobstructed *(shun)* manner. Thus, the nourishment of life depends no longer on externals but rather on oneself—the old concern of how to live in the world without being completely of it. As Su writes in the following poem addressed to Wu Tzu-yeh, "Whether one remains in the world or leaves it / There is only a single Way to be followed." For Su Shih although the means (Taoist and Buddhist) might have differed, the ends were much the same.

He also admires men such as the Taoist Wu Tzu-yeh who neither are Buddhist nor have left home but who have achieved the same state of mind. In fact, Su may have reserved his greatest admiration for men like this, who were able to dwell in empty tranquility, whether living in the world of men or not, as he himself greatly aspired to. In describing his friend Wu Tzu-yeh as one who has made his mind "like a withered tree" and dwells in empty tranquility, Su shows his awareness of what makes this sort of wandering possible. In a piece written many years earlier in Hang-chou, Su Shih echoes an idea to be found, in one form or another, in almost every major Buddhist text: "If one can perceive the *dharmakāya,* then one can perceive that the waking state and the sleeping state are both empty. If one knows that they are both empty, then whether sleeping or waking, it doesn't matter. One can travel and wander about the four directions without moving one's residence. South, north, east, west; the *dharmakāya* is everywhere.[13]

Here is yet another poem addressed to the Taoist Wu Tzu-yeh, presented along with a folding pillow screen on which a landscape of mountains and rivers has been deftly and beautifully painted. One of the reasons this screen can contain the myriad delights of the natural world is that it was painted by an artist who himself contained "a thousand peaks" within his heart:

> Towering and lofty are the mountains on this screen,
> Their sheer cliffs clearly hewn by Heaven itself.
> Who understands the Great Perfect Mirror Wisdom?
> It is as if the Heng Huo mountains had come in the
>   door.
> The one I got it from was Elder Master Yüeh,
> The one who painted it was the Drunk Old Fellow.
> I have often wondered whether within this artist's
>   breast,
> There was not an actual Cloud-Dream Lake?[14]
> A thousand peaks lay in the palm of his hand,
> For him to use or not in a snap of the fingers,
> Although not all their summits and valleys are clear,
> It would be a pity to leave them to my children.
> This low-lying screen, although it twists and folds,
> Can still help keep you above the madding crowd.
> Your leaving home happened long before this day,
> With the dharma waters you have cleansed your
>   imperfections.
> Peacefully wandering, you walk the clouds and
>   peaks,
> Sitting in meditation, willows sprout from your
>   elbows.
> You can lose yourself in these purples and greens,
> Which will be your companions till your hair turns
>   white![15]

A number of Su's Buddhist friends came to visit him in Hui-chou. One of these visitors was a poet-monk by the name of T'an-hsiu from Mt. Lu. In a poem Su wrote for T'an-hsiu, he expresses more than a touch of envy at the apparent freedom of this monk who does not travel because he is in exile, but because he enjoys it.

Although he may "feel no longing for the woods of home," he can, unlike Su, leave and return there whenever he pleases. Su had admired the same quality many years previously in monks like Master Pien-ts'ai, and he still felt it lacking in himself.

> He is like white clouds rising from the mountains—
> No-mind from the start,
> He is like the roosting bird who feels no longing
> For the woods of home.
> But because this man of the Way happens to enjoy
> The mountains and streams
> He wanders among them unconcerned about how
>   deep
> Into the lakeside mountain peaks he goes.
> He has gone to the empty cliffs to worship
> The hundred thousand forms of the Buddha,
> And now wishes to visit Ts'ao-hsi and pay his
>   respects
> To the relics of the Sixth Patriarch.
> If you want to know whether the water is hot or cold,
> You must taste it for yourself.
> I am beginning to think the dream I had of you
> Was not an illusion after all!
> In that dream you suddenly pulled from your sleeve
> A sutra written on papyrus leaves,
> Its lines and phrases jade-pure as the moon,
> And stars strung together like pearls.
> There are many beautiful spots in this world,
> And he has just about seen them all:
> From the southern peaks of Mount Lu
> All the way to West Lake—
> West Lake, which, if one looks to the north,
> Lies three thousand *li* away,
> Its great dike stretching out unbroken
> Across the autumn waters.
> As I chant the verses the master wrote
> Describing the beauty of Mount Nan-p'ing,
> The miasmic summer airs of Hui-chou
> Seem to vanish in an autumn breeze.
> Is it possible that the pleasure of your company
> Will end in but ten short days?
> Cutting through the brambles, it won't be easy

To find the road home again.
The wild greens I use to entice the master to stay
Are not much to speak of:
Oh how I look forward to the season
When the lichees turn red.[16]

Su also received a visit from a disciple of Abbot Shou-ch'in of
Ting-hui Monastery in Su-chou, who stopped by with a message
and a sheaf of poems written by the abbot in imitation of the poems
of Han Shan, the famous lay Buddhist poet of the early T'ang.[17] Su
liked these poems very much and wrote that they showed the "[spir-
itual] insight of the Third and Fifth patriarchs, yet did not suffer
from the chilliness of [the poetry] of Chia Tao and K'o ming."[18] He
then used the rhymes of Shou-ch'in's poems to compose a series of
eight remarkable poems that demonstrate the extent to which he
could successfully integrate Ch'an and Taoist ideas, language, and
legend along with allusions to the places he visited during this
period, in particular Mt. Lo-fu. In the second poem in this series,
for example, what appear to be paradoxical koans are actually not:
on Mt. Lo-fu there was a doorless pagoda called the Iron Bridge
Stone Pagoda; while the "barking" thousand-year root is the name
of a species of aspen tree whose roots take the shape of a dog.

If the iron bridge was never supported by piers,
Then how could the stone tower have had a door?
Dancing in the void, five-colored feathers,[19]
Barking in the clouds, thousand-year roots.[20]
Using pine blossoms to brew a divine ambrosia,
The woodcutters sup on mountain fare alone.
After I get drunk and my guests have gone,
What T'ao Yüan-ming once said I will say too.

In the third poem of this series, Su describes himself as seated in
the Vermilion Bright Cave, more familiarly known as the seventh
cave of P'eng-lai, which was also located on Mt. Lo-fu and where
Ko Hung himself is reputed to have spent some time. From this
cave high on the mountaintop, it was said one could see the sunrise
at midnight—thus Su's reference to the legendary Fu-sang tree out
of which the sun was supposed to rise every day. The Jade Pool,
also located on Mt. Lo-fu, probably refers to a Taoist technique of
meditation and breath control. The physical sign of effective prac-

tice is the "pooling" of saliva in the mouth, while the psychological or spiritual sign is the forgetting of one's "self."

> Mt. Lo-fu is twenty-four thousand feet high,
> From it can be seen the sun rising from the Fu-sang
>   tree.
> Silently I sit in the Vermilion Bright Cave,
> As the Jade Pool produces a natural fecundity.
> My nature has always been candid and straight-
>   forward,
> My drunken words revealing my innermost thoughts.
> Later we will meet without greeting,
> For I no longer remember who it is I am.

In the next poem, Su alludes to the *Śūraṃgama Sūtra,* where the Bodhisattva Upaniṣad describes how he attained enlightenment by means of a meditation on the impurity of all conditioned things, including the "bleached bones" of human beings that would eventually disintegrate into dust and "return to emptiness."[21] Here Su once again laments that he is so far from having purified himself and that, despite all he has learned, he still feels the "tug" of the world:

> The hermit practices the Bleached Bones Meditation,
> The Mahāsattva vanishes into the void like sweet dew.
> Each of the six senses is completely clean and pure,
> Both the mind and the world are out of the ordinary.
> For me, the True Source has not yet completely
>   matured,
> And the residue of unrooted habits still lingers on.
> It is like the falcon who although set free,
> Still feels the tug of the midnight leash.

During his time in Hui-chou Su Shih spent much time practicing some form of meditation, whether Buddhist, Taoist, or a combination of the two. In a piece written in 1096, toward the end of his time in Hui-chou, he once again tries to provide a Confucian justification for his meditation practice:

Layman Tung-p'o asked Tzu-yu (Su Ch'e) about the Way. Tzu-yu replied using Buddhist terminology; he said: "[When the] Original Mind is illuminated, [then] ignorance will be be illumined." The layman was delighted and, quoting from the words of Confucius,

said: "[The one phrase that embraces the spirit of] the three hundred poems of the *Book of Poetry* is 'Having no depraved
thoughts.' "[22] Now, [as soon as one] has thoughts, there is [the
possibility] of their being depraved; [but if] one has no thoughts,
then [one might as well be a clod of] dirt or [a piece of] wood. Is
there not then only one way of achieving the way: by having
thoughts without there being an object of those thoughts? Thus,
one wraps one's head [in a piece of cloth] and sits upright, and
passes the entire day in silence. With clear eyes gazing straight
ahead without focusing on anything [in particular], one collects
one's mind and orders one's thoughts and has no [particular] feelings. In this way [one may] attain the way; so I named my studio
"Having No Depraved Thoughts" and wrote an inscription for it
as follows:

> Great calamities stem from the possession of a body,
> If one had no body, then one would never fall ill.
> In stillness naturally comes complete illumination,
> A mirror facing a mirror—the mirror of non-self.
> It is like using water to cleanse water:
> The two waters in fact share the same purity.
> Spacious and at ease between heaven and earth
> Completely alone with myself, I sit upright.[23]

The first two lines come from the thirteenth chapter of the *Tao-
te-ching,* reflecting the strong Taoist tone of Su's Hui-chou period.
Su once again searches for a "middle way" between the Confucian
dictum that one must live in the world with "undepraved" thoughts
and its opposite, which is to leave the world and cleanse one's mind
of all thoughts whatsoever. Su looks instead for a method by which
one's thoughts are detached from any "particular" object and thus
free ("spacious and at ease between heaven and earth") to respond
fully to the world around it. This idea in many ways represents the
heart of Su Shih's transcendent ideal.

I have noted that Su, like many of his fellow literati, readily combined philosophical ideals (i.e., Ch'an Buddhist ideas) with more
traditionally religious ones (i.e., Pure Land devotions). Another
expression of this is seen in a piece Su wrote to commemorate the
death of Wang Chao-yün, who had once been a lovely and talented
courtesan in Hang-chou and who had accompanied Su Shih for
over twenty years. Her life had not been easy; she had lost a child
and had served as Su's wife and helpmate under very trying circum-

stances in the years following the death of his wife. Lonely and in ill health, Chao-yün spent much of her time in Hui-chou reciting Buddhist sutras; she died in the spring of 1096 while reciting the *gāthā* on impermanence from the *Diamond Sūtra*. In a commemorative essay, Su writes: "Because of my karmic debt, I was exiled to this southern wasteland with my concubine companion, Wang Chao-yün, who has suffered bitterly all her life. [She] followed me over ten thousand *li* [until] she was struck down by a disease caused by the pestilential [weather] and fell ill and passed away."[24] Su then recounts how three days after Chao-yün was buried on the grounds of the local Ch'an Buddhist temple, there was a great storm. When the storm died down, "five miraculous footprints [of the Buddha appeared] on the road to be seen by all."[25] This, he continues was a sign of

> the breadth of the Buddha's compassion, [which] does not abandon even the most inconsequential of sentient beings. Therefore I carry out to the fullest this dharma ceremony. Humbly I pray that every single blade of grass and every single tree in these mountains will be clothed in the Buddha's radiance. On this night, may [the fragrance of] this bit of incense, these few flowers, spread throughout the *dharmadhatu*. [May] the lakes and mountains be [filled with] peace and tranquility [auspiciousness], and [may] this tombstone stand forever, [there to] receive the soul of the departed that may soon be reborn in the Pure Land. We will not speak of the deep and dark [underworld]. . . . Together we will vow before the peerless *bodhi* that we will forever liberate ourselves from the fiery dwelling place of the Ten Realms.[26]

In Hui-chou Su continued with a project begun earlier in Huang-chou. At that time he had begun to make a copy of the *Diamond Sūtra*. However, he had only gotten to the fifteenth section when he was called out of exile. During the move part of the manuscript was lost. Many years later in Hui-chou Su would complete what he had begun and present it to a local temple.

By 1097 the reformist clique had achieved a firm grip on the reins of power, but they nevertheless wanted their conservative rivals as far away as possible. And so the ailing Su was banished far away to the southernmost island of Hai-nan. He received word of this new banishment through the magistrate of Hui-chou, who, in an effort to comfort his friend, related a dream his wife had had. Apparently

Wang's wife was a devotee of Sangha (628–710), a monk of Indian
or Central Asian origin who had come to China during the T'ang
dynasty, traveling along the Yangtze River valley and finally building a temple in Ssu-chou in eastern China. He is said to have performed many miracles and to have once revealed his identity as the
eleven-headed form of the bodhisattva Avalokiteśvara. Su's fascination with him shows that the popularity of his cult, which was
extremely widespread during the Sung, had extended to the
literati.[27] More than twenty years previously (in 1071), Su Shih had
passed by Sangha's stupa in Ssu-chou on his way to Mi-chou and
commemorated the visit with an appreciation and a poem.[28] When
Sangha appeared to Wang's wife in a dream, he told her he had
come to bid her farewell, because in seventy-two days he would be
departing with Su Shih. Wang's purpose was to console Su by
assuring him that this new journey was fated to be. Su replied that
he already knew that it was fated and did not need a dream to tell
him so, but nonetheless he was grateful for the good karma to have
a bodhisattva to accompany him personally!

As mentioned earlier, Su took with him into this last exile a scroll
painting of Amitābha Buddha. When someone asked him why, he
replied that it would serve as his ticket to the Western Paradise
should he die en route.[29] It seems that Su had little expectation of
ever returning to the mainland and that he felt death was a real possibility. He left his remaining family in Hui-chou and proceeded to
Tan-chou in Hai-nan accompanied only by his son Su Kuo. On his
way to Hai-nan, he stopped by the Ch'ing-liang Kuang-hui Ch'an
temple in Nanking and wrote the following poem for the abbot in
residence.

> Crossing the Huai and entering the Lo,
> The terrain becomes so dusty;
> As I lift my fan against a west wind
> Intent on covering me with dirt.
> I can only marvel at the cloud-shrouded mountain
> That never changes color:
> But of course he knows that it is a single moon
> That is reflected in a thousand rivers.
> If one has a peaceful mind and the Way,
> Then old age can be good.
> If one responds to objects without emotion

> Then one's phrasing will be fresh.
> He sends me off in a long boat
> Fashioned from a single reed,
> And laughs at how the snowy waves,
> Fill the collars of my robe.[30]

In this poem, Su Shih is expressing his characteristic admiration for men like this abbot who are able to remain aloof and unaffected by the dirt and dust of daily life. According to Wang Wen-kao, the moon that divides itself into many reflections is an allusion to a statement in the *Ching-te ch'uan-teng lu,* "a thousand rivers share a single moon; ten thousand homes all greet the spring," and the long reed boat is a reference to the mode of travel tradition has it was favored by Bodhidharma. More important is the aging poet's assertion that as long as one's heart is at peace, old age will not come as a burden and that transcending one's personal emotions will result in "fresh" poetry. This is not to say that he has achieved this state—he is still fighting off the dust with his uplifted fan—but it remains his ideal.

In Tan-chou, Su lived at first in a leaky magistrate's compound but later was ordered to leave. He built himself a small house south of the city and spent the next few years familiarizing himself with the language, diet, and customs of the local Li tribespeople. Despite the inevitable loneliness and hardships, it seems his natural optimism and his practice of Buddhist-Taoist breathing and meditation exercises helped him attain a degree of contentment. In a letter to a friend he writes,

> When I was young, I longed to run away into the mountain forests. However, my father and brothers would not allow it and instead forced me to marry. So it is that I have been tossed to and fro ever since. Since being banished to the south, I have been able to arrange the affairs of my life; there is no longer anything that worries me. My life can be compared, in a general way, to that of an itinerant monk.[31]

Here the process of self-invention results from the necessity of adapting to a hostile environment. There is not the slightest evidence that Su's family forced him to marry against his will, but the self-image of an itinerant monk was one he found appealing. In a letter to his friend Ts'an-liao, he also compares his new life-style, in

cramped quarters and with nothing but coarse food to eat, to that
of the lowliest of monks in a temple compound. If there is a touch
of self-pity here, there is also a note of truth.

Su's Hai-nan writings, although they may not number among his
greatest, do attest to a certain serenity of mind and acceptance of
the impermanent nature of life. In the following poem he describes
how, in the absence of water for bathing, he indulged in a "dry
bath," a Taoist practice of breathing and massage.

> A thousand brush strokes and my hair is clean,
> The wind does a better job than a hot bath.
> Holding one's breath unclogs the myriad pores,
> And a dry bath dispels any noxious vapors.
> If then one relaxes and abstains from conversation,
> In tranquility one sees heaven and earth return.[32]
> Now and then I gather kindling and fresh water,
> In hopes of leisurely soaking my limbs.
> However, I cannot find anyone to build me a tub,
> And how can a tiny basin do the trick?
> The old chicken lies in the dust and dung,
> The weary nag rolls in the mud and sand,
> And then shakes its mane with a spray of saliva.
> Defilement and purity, each has its particular nature,[33]
> Living in the moment, I bathe in whatever way I can.
> Cloud-mother gems are as transparent as Szechuan
>   silk,
> And Ch'i bamboo is as glossy as painted glass.
> Sometimes one can come to realization in dreams,
> And thus gradually the unripe can become mature.
> The *Śūraṃgama Sūtra* lies at the foot of my bed,
> Often I sit up to read its marvelous words.
> Reversing the stream, return to the luminous Buddha-
>   nature,
> And renounce that which I once looked forward to.
> I still do not understand the Ch'an of Yang-shan,[34]
> But I know a little about the predictions of Chi-chu.
> A serene mind will be achieved naturally,
> By nourishing it rather than strictly overseeing it.[35]

According to Heinrich Dumoulin, by the Sung there was a clear
differentiation between the Ch'an of the Patriarchs, which did not
depend on the sutras, and the Ch'an of the Tathāgatas (generally

considered inferior) which relied on the meditational doctrines of
texts like the *Śūraṃgama Sūtra* and the *Laṅkāvatāra Sūtra*.[36] Su
Shih claims here that he prefers the practical "predictions of [Ssu-
ma] Chi-chu," a Han dynasty fortuneteller who practiced his art in
the East Market of Ch'ang-an, to the demanding Ch'an of Yang-
shan.

Su Shih's earliest contact with Buddhism was with the pictures of
arhats hanging in his home. In 1098 he writes of these childhood
memories. While in exile on Hai-nan, Su happened to come across
a painting of the eighteen *lohan* by a Szechuan artist of the late
T'ang named Chang Hsüan. He records his discovery as follows:

> While living in exile in Tan'erh, I came upon [this painting] in the
> home of a local farmer. Hai-nan being a remote and provincial
> place, very unlike the rest of the world, I was [as startled] to find
> them there as if I had suddenly met my teachers and friends in an
> empty valley! Although I was living in very difficult circum-
> stances, I had it mounted and placed lamps, incense, and flowers
> before it in order to express my reverence.[37]

Later, Su sent the painting to his brother, who had it restored and
offered it to a temple in memory of their parents.

In 1101, on his way back north, he stopped at the Pao-lin ssu
(located on Mt. Hsia in Ch'ing-yüan in what is today Kuangtung
province), where he saw a painting of eighteen *lohan* by the famous
Szechuan Ch'an monk poet and painter Kuan-hsiu that was much
like the one he remembered from his own childhood. He wrote a
series of eighteen *gāthā*s in commemoration of this event. In a
much earlier piece written for Ou-yang Hsiu, who had another
Kuan-hsiu painting of *lohan* remounted and offered to a temple in
memory of his departed wife, Su says of Kuan-hsiu:

> The manifestation form of the [state of] Great Awakening is by
> nature intangible; [however] in response to the truth and moved
> by [the needs of sentient beings], it divides itself and [appears in]
> many places, [thus] pointing out the road that leads back to [the
> state of] tranquility and nourishment, and shatters the terrible bit-
> terness of the Avici [hells]. The great master Ch'an-yüeh [Kuan-
> hsiu] of the late Five Dynasties period carried out his Buddhist
> work by means of poetry and preached by means of painting.[38]

The first verse describes Piṇḍola Bhāradvāja, an enlightened being who in his samadhic state had "forgotten both scripture and man," meaning that he had transcended the duality between the religious and the secular in his vision of the infinite.[39]

> A fine white cotton robe across his knees;
> The palm-leaf scriptures on the mat.
> His eyes gaze into the infinite,
> Forgetting both scripture and man.
>
> Face and skull covered with wrinkles,
> Untouched by the razor's blade;
> He has no mind to sweep away;
> Only a bit of leftover snow.

Su's description of the second *lohan* would seem to confirm Yoshikawa Kōjirō's contention that the poetry of the Sung period, and especially Su Shih's, differs from that of the T'ang in seeking to transcend sorrow even while acutely aware of the ephemerality of all things human. It also reflects the Ch'an emphasis on being-in-the world, the "everydayness" of the Ch'an experience, which is characterized by spontaneity, joy, and humor rather than by dour resignation or nihilism.

> He has lived long, but is he old?
> Smiling broadly, he is young again!
> I know that deep in his heart,
> The Buddha does not begrudge laughter.
>
> Anger and joy are both illusions;
> Still a smile differs from a glare.
> He spreads this Way of nonsorrow,
> Bestowing it on countless beings.

The next verse, a description of the painting of the fifth *lohan*, Panoka, stresses the need to respond spontaneously, as a child would, to all things without making artificial distinctions between high and low, important and trivial. (Panoka is said to have converted to Buddhism at the age of 120, after which he became youthful and full of joy.) It also mirrors the concern for "response" of the hymn to the Thousand-Armed Bodhisattva. Finally, it touches on the idea of "nonabiding," that is, establishing one's home in the dharma rather than any geographic location. Not surprisingly, this idea was especially attractive to Su Shih, who so often found himself in exile.

> A kindly heart instead of sons,
> The dharma instead of a home.
> Who will scratch his back?
> A little child made of wood.

> High and low, all is as it should be,
> Important and unimportant all fittingly met.
> If you really want to become like a child,
> You have to become like this.

The next verse, a description of the third *lohan*, Kanaka the Bhāradvāja, touches on the paradox of language, a theme that greatly intrigued the poet in Su Shih.

> Brows raised, he stares ahead,
> Across his knee he holds a whisk.
> Ask a question of this great man;
> He either speaks or remains silent.

> His silence like a clap of thunder,
> His words like a wall of stone.
> There are no words, there is no silence,
> The hundred patriarchs have passed this test.

This paradox is also raised in Su's description of the sixteenth *lohan,* Chote-Panthaka, or Pantha the Younger, who is traditionally depicted as an old man sitting under a withered tree, one hand holding a fan and the other raised in the gesture of teaching.

> Although he speaks of the dharma,
> The dharma cannot be spoken of.
> With his hands he teaches people,
> Take away the hands, the dharma disappears.

> In the midst of life and extinction,
> Nature and truth persist.
> It is for this reason that my Way
> Does not separate from form and sound.

In 1100 Emperor Che-tsung died, and the political pendulum once again began to swing back toward the conservatives. Much to his delight, Su Shih received permission to leave Hai-nan and return home. He set out in the sixth month of that year on the journey that would be his last. The trip was beset with difficulties and obstacles. However, as usual, he made frequent stops along the way to visit old friends. One of his first stops was Nan-hua ssu at Ts'ao-hsi, which he reached at the close of 1100. The two pieces Su wrote at this time explored the relationship between Confucianism and Buddhism. The first of these was written at the request of the abbot of Nan-hua ssu, a man who had started out as a Confucian scholar before becoming a Buddhist monk. Su quotes with approval the abbot's firm belief that "statesmen and officials carry out the way of the world *(shih-chien fa);* monks carry out the way of leaving the world *(ch'u shih-chien fa).* Living in the world and leaving the world are the same and not different."[40]

This view is a direct refutation of the Neo-Confucian claim that these two ways of life are diametrically opposed to each other. However, Su Shih does not simply leave it at that. He goes on to explore other points of analogy between the Buddhist and Confucian experience. He begins with his perception of the Buddhist way, a view largely shaped by the Southern Ch'an emphasis on the importance of mind and instantaneous enlightenment:

> Do scholars think it is difficult to become a Buddha? Making sand piles and drawing in the sand, although [these things are like] child's play, are all one needs to become a Buddha.[41] They think it is easy? [Among] those destined to achieve enlightenment, the bodhisattvas and the great disciples, [there are those who] dare not [face the great sage Vimalakīrti] and inquire after his health. What is the meaning of this? Just when one is confused and lost, turned upside down and floating in the bitter sea [of suffering], in a single thought-instant *(nien)* all can be put right and the ten thousand dharmas all brought together. [However,] even if one labors diligently and piles up merits into a mountain nine *chieh* high, if one slips by a single hairbreadth, one will be unable [to return to where one was] for another thousand kalpas. The Way is just like this, and not only in Buddhism![42]

Here Su Shih is commenting on the greatness of the Way, which is simple enough for children to understand and yet so profound that even the great bodhisattvas are reluctant to engage the great layman-sage Vimalakīrti in a discussion of essential Buddhist doctrines.[43] He then notes that even if one is in a state of complete confusion, if one manages to get at the root of this confusion with a glimpse of one's Buddha-nature, the no-mind, one can achieve enlightenment. By the same token, even if one has spent years and even lifetimes accumulating religious merit, if one fails to attain that essential insight, then that merit becomes meaningless. He makes a clear distinction between the outward state, which can be completely confused or clearly saintly, and the inward state of mind, which is of the essence.

Su then turns to the important Chinese Confucian classic the *Chung yung* (which Tu Wei-ming translates "Centrality and Commonality"). Su Shih had written a careful commentary on the *Chung yung* for his examination forty years earlier; in fact, it was the only Confucian classic he dealt with at any length in his portfolio. Although solidly situated in the Confucian canon, The *Chung yung* is known for its comparatively metaphysical and even religious approach to the usual Confucian concerns and as such "formed a bridge between Taoism and Buddhism and the Confucian school and in this way prepared for the influence of Buddhism and Taoism on Confucianism, thus ushering in the Neo-Confucian movement."[44] It is not surprising, then, that Su should turn to the *Chung yung* in his search for parallel analogies.

Su begins with Tzu-ssu's (492–431 B.C., the grandson of Confucius and the reputed author of the *Chung yung*) description of the Confucian Way: "Men and women of simple intelligence can share its knowledge; and yet in its utmost reaches, there is something which even the sage does not know. Men and women of simple intelligence can put it into practice; and yet in its utmost reaches there is something which even the sage is not able to put into practice."[45] In other words, the Way is both common (such that children and men and women of simple understanding can understand it) and profound (such that even Confucian sages and Buddhist bodhisattvas cannot fully understand its profundity). There are other implications as well. As Tu Wei-ming notes:

> For one thing, the Way can never be specified in terms of objective doctrines. It is absolutely impossible to establish a fixed model by which all people can learn to become profound persons. The way can neither be determined by a limited set of rules nor be divided into discrete stages in a unilinear procedure. The multiplicity of models as well as the complexity of its rules and procedures renders it unrealistic even to attempt to formulate an all-embracing

pattern of behavior universally applicable to those aspiring to become profound persons.[46]

Su Shih seems to be implying that, given the profound mystery of the Way, there may well be more than a single model by which one can attain enlightenment. In fact, Buddhism, the way of the monk, may be simply another model, another pattern of behavior, for what are ultimately similar goals. Thus, he continues, it is not the patterns of behavior one should look at, but rather the motivation that lies behind those patterns of behavior. This time he turns to Mencius for confirmation: "Thus Mencius believed that the Way of the Sages commenced with [the basic moral decision] not to engage in petty thievery;[47] the improbity of petty thievery is the same as that of not speaking [to someone] when one should speak [to him]."[48]

Su reminds his readers that Mencius (expanding on an early comment by Confucius) equates robbers who steal from their neighbors with "gentlemen" who, because of some ulterior motive, commit the fault of not speaking to those who should be spoken to. In other words, although superficially there is a great difference between the robber and the sage, just as there is between the deluded man and the bodhisattva, the dividing line between them is a precarious one. Su carries this argument a little further:

[There are] those who steal things without having the intention [of doing so]: although they steal, they do not mean to. Thus, if he seeks [the Way] with this purity of intention, then [even] the petty thief is capable of becoming a sage. To not speak to [one who] can be spoken to, to speak to [one] who cannot be spoken to: these are [forms of behavior] that even the sage and the superior man cannot avoid. If [knowing] how these mistakes are difficult to avoid, one [lets them go], then even the sage or the superior man is at times a thief.[49]

Su Shih seems to be saying here that, judging solely on their "labels" and their actions, as indeed Ch'eng I urged his followers to do as regards the Buddhists, it is indeed easy to differentiate between the thief and the sage. However, if one looks instead at the motivation behind their actions, then the difference may be considerably less. Thus the thief, like the person caught in the sea of delusion, is still capable of achieving the Way if his mind is pure and centered. And the sage, like the Buddhist bodhisattva, is still capable of missing the Way if his mind is not completely pure. Su seems to be equating the Buddhist emphasis on "original mind" with the state of "centrality" (defined by Tu Wei-ming as "the ultimate ground of existence") described in the *Chung yung*. Thus, he concludes, "these two ways seem mutually opposed, and yet [they are] mutually useful. Confucianism and Buddhism are like this."

This apparent willingness to include Buddhism in the definition of the Way did not sit well with contemporaries such as Ch'eng I and later Chu Hsi, who felt strongly that, although diversity was to be tolerated, in the end there was only one true, Confucian, way. Chu Hsi often accused Su Shih of being a Buddhist or a Taoist. Judging from the tone of this piece of Su's, his accusation may have been justified.

The second piece written in 1101 is even more radical in its implications. On his way home, Su visited the Chung-yen Ch'an temple in Nanking where he had stopped several years earlier on his way to Hai-nan. At that time, he had admired a statue of Kuan-yin that the abbot of the monastery had personally collected funds for and vowed that if he were to return from exile, he would write a special hymn in its honor. True to his word, in 1101 he wrote a hymn in which he explores the similarities between Buddhism and Confucianism.

> [Buddhist] friendliness approaches [Confucian]
>   humanheartedness;
> [Buddhist] compassion approaches [Confucian] righ-
>   teousness;
> [Buddhist] endurance approaches [Confucian] courage;
> [Buddhist] equanimity approaches [Confucian] wisdom.
> These four [virtues] are similar
> But in the end not the same.
> In the state of the Great Perfect Awakening,
> Everything is equal and nondual.
> Because there is no enmity, there is humanheartedness;
> Because there is no partiality, there is righteousness;
> Because there is no "other," there is courage;
> Because there is no "I," there is wisdom.
> If [one perceives] these four virtues as similar,
> Then there will be action and refraining from action.
> If [one perceives] these four virtues as nonbeing,

One will be able to draw from them without exhaustion.
There were once two elders
Both of whom delighted in giving alms.
One of them was very wealthy,
And gave a thousand gold coins a day;
The other was extremely poor,
And could only afford a hundred.
I say that these two men
Were equal and do not differ.
Ah, Kuan-shih-yin,
Pure and saintly bodhisattva,
Who pervades the realms of emptiness,
Lending a hand to heaven and earth,
With her great powers of salvation.
It is not for me to dare doubt:
If these four virtues are empty,
I too am also thus.[50]

Men like Chang Tsai were very worried that the apparent similarities between Buddhism and Confucianism would lead people to think that they were, in fact, the same. In this hymn, Su Shih agrees that actually the two are *not* the same. However, he does not, as Chang Tsai did, thereby assert the primacy of the Confucian virtues. Rather, he seems to imply that all of these virtues, Confucian and Buddhist alike, are nothing more than skillful means, rather than ends unto themselves.

In a colophon written in 1101 on the anniversary of the death of his mother, Su laments that in Hai-nan he was unable to offer the proper Buddhist ceremonies on the anniversaries of his departed kin, and now is looking forward to doing so. Although on the actual anniversary his boat was delayed by bad weather that prevented him from reaching a temple in time, Su wrote out "Mañjuśrī's *Gāthā* on Complete and All-pervading [Understanding]" from the *Śūraṃgama Sūtra* in his own hand, and several days later he presented it to the monks on Mt. Lu. Shortly after, Su stopped at nearby Ch'ien-chou (also located in present-day Kiangsi province), where he remained for over a month. Interestingly, a significant number of the poems written during this period concern the question of nonduality and reflect the influence of the *Śūraṃgama Sūtra:* "The body is [hollow] like a plantain; the mind is like a lotus. The hundred sections all interconnected, the ten thousand

holes elegant and fine. When it comes it is but one; when it goes it is
eighty-four thousand. These ideas come from the *Śūraṃgama
Sūtra*, but there are few in this world who understand it."[51] These
same images recur in another poem written during this time. The
long title relates the circumstances in which it was written:

> Several days ago, a monk appeared to me in a dream and offered
> me two mirrors in exchange for a poem. Taking the mirrors, he set
> them in the sun. The shadows [they cast] were truly unusual: one
> was the shape of a plaintain, the other that of a lotus. In my
> dream I composed this poem for him.

> > In your household there are two mirrors,
> > Their surfaces shiny like fine swords.
> > One is long like a plaintain leaf,
> > The other round like a lotus flower.
> > The flashing lightning inscribes your wall,
> > The bright moon comes inside my hut.
> > Beneath the moon, the three jades join,
> > Sun and moon dance like bright pearls.
> > I ask whether this is I or not?
> > It is I, it is not Mañjuśrī.[52]

The last lines of this poem refer to a section of the *Śūraṃgama
Sūtra* in which the Buddha responds to an inquiry posed by Mañjuśrī concerning the nature of nonduality. The Buddha first notes
that seeing, the causes of seeing, and the objects that are seen are,
"like flowers in the sky," fundamentally nonexistent. However, this
does not mean that they do not exist, but rather that they are
the essentially "marvelous, pure, and luminous body of wisdom
(bodhi)" that transcends existence and nonexistence. The Buddha
then asks the bodhisattva: "If, apart from yourself, there were
another Mañjuśrī, would this Mañjuśrī be a not-Mañjuśrī?" "No,
World-honored One," replies Mañjuśrī, "I am the real Mañjuśrī,
and there cannot be another. Why? Because if there were, then
there would be two Mañjuśrīs. However, the fact that today there is
no non-Mañjuśrī here has nothing to do with "to exist" and "not to
exist."[53]

Su Shih had been pondering these ideas for much of his life. As
he sensed his life coming to a close, the urgency and—perhaps even
more noteworthy—the frustration became intensified. An air of

melancholy and even frustration pervades poems such as the following, addressed to Abbot Wei-shih of the Ch'ung-ch'ing Ch'an temple in Ch'ien-chou. These poems, also replete with mixed Buddhist and Taoist language, reveal a deepening despair of ever achieving peace in this life. After all his study of Buddhist texts and practice of Taoist exercises, he seems to have given up hope of ever mastering them, of ever attaining his goal of "tranquility."

> Wishing to request a rosary from you sir,
> I take the opportunity for an excursion late in life.
> I am still unable to teach about the thousand Buddhas,
> So I must continue being taught by the thousand Buddhas.
> Confucians base their predictions on the principle of
>   change.
> Its many hexagrams like the peaks of the T'ai-heng
>   mountains.
> Taoists preserve within them the male and the female,
> As they watch the metal dragon and wood tiger unfold.
> I am old and am unable to do these things,
> Countless, all lost in a single breath.
> Quietly sitting, I observe the changing of this dusty world,
> Coming and going, created and destroyed eighty times.[54]
> How tiny and insignificant this place I inhabit,
> So shrunken and small as if within a cocoon.
> If I should ever return from my exile on the sea,
> The waters of P'eng-lai will seem limpid and shallow.[55]

Lines 3 and 4 of this poem seem to refer to the story in the *Ching-te ch'uan-teng lu* about the Ch'an master who in his zeal recited the entire *Lotus Sūtra* over three thousand times. The Sixth Patriarch, Hui-neng, then said to him, "If your mind is confused, the *Lotus Sūtra* will transform you; if your mind is enlightened, you will transform the *Lotus Sūtra*."[56] Here Su is again insisting that he still has not reached the point of being able to go beyond the sutras— that is, beyond the Ch'an of the Tathāgatas—and that he still needs help. By the same token, however, he claims also to have been unable to master the techniques of the Confucians or the Taoists. Su has all along confessed his inability to understand these things, but in this poem the tone is of disappointment rather than the usual false modesty: he feels trapped, and the usual outlets for his transcendent urge seem closed to him. This same profession of spiritual inadequacy appears in yet another poem written during this time:

> I arrive south of the river to meet with the man in the
>   clouds,
> He asks me about Ch'an, but I confess ignorance as to the
>   "Three,"
> I did offer a six-foot Amitabha to be placed in his temple.
> When the teacher departs the monastery, his disciples
>   dream of him;
> After the rain, the bells and drums sound even more
>   clearly.
> It should be enough to clear away this sickly late summer
>   air.
> No need as yet to wrap the head in a tight white turban.[57]

This poem shows that, for all his admiration of the Ch'an way, Su often found such tangibly religious activities as sutra study, alms giving, and analytical meditation (Tathāgata meditation) more understandable than the Ch'an Buddhist demands for a sudden spiritual transformation of consciousness supposedly transferred from mind to mind (patriarchal meditation) unmediated by either texts or good works.[58] The "Three" refers to the story from the *Ching-te ch'uan-teng lu* about the monk Wu-cho, who upon arriving at a temple on Mt. Wu-t'ai, asked how many monks were living there. "In front there are three and three and behind there are three and three," answered the head monk. Wu-cho, not understanding what this meant, made no reply. Then the head monk said, "Since you do not understand my words, you had better leave." So Wu-cho turned around and left.[59]

One other person Su visited during this time was the *fang-shih* (diviner) Hsieh Chin-ch'en.

> I have just recently returned from beyond the seas,
> And so, Chün-p'ing, do not lower your curtain on me.
> In my previous life I was the wanderer called Lu,
> Although later students call me Han T'ui-chih.
> After I die, they will say I practiced discipline, medita-
>   tion, and wisdom;
> But while alive, my stars are between the constellations
>   of *tou* and *niu.*

I am relying on you, sir, to read my life's chart,
And number the years until I die.[60]

In this poem, Su Shih once again claims to be a reincarnation of
Hui-neng, the Sixth Patriarch, even though later students are
inclined to think him a manifestation of Han Yü. Here Su is identifying with Han Yü, who in a poem laments that his great sufferings
in exile were a result of having been born under unfavorable stars.[61]
He also addresses Hsieh as Yen Chün-p'ing, a Han dynasty diviner
and scholar from Szechuan, who as soon as he had earned enough
money for one day, closed shop and devoted himself to the study
and instruction of the teachings of Lao-tzu. Then, with a touch of
irony and some precognition of his own, Su comments that later
men will see him as having been a realized individual ("The Buddha
said: 'Ananda, you have always heard me teach about discipline
[vinaya] that consists in the practice of three decisive steps. The
concentration of the mind is called moral discipline [Skt. sīla; Ch.
chieh]. Moral discipline then gives rise to meditation [Skt. dhyāna;
Ch. ting], and meditation leads to wisdom [Skt. prajñā; Ch. hui].
These are what are known as the three pure studies.' "),[62] although
his life was fated by the stars to be one of continual turmoil and
change. And finally, with a note of resignation to fate, he asks
Hsieh to tell him how many years he has left to live. Whether or not
Hsieh told him, he had very little time left. Su left Ch'ien-chou and
continued his journey, first to Lien-chou and then to Yung-chou in
Hunan province, where he was given an honorary post. Too ill to
return to Mei-shan as he would have liked, he journeyed on toward
his property in Ch'ang-chou. However, he fell ill along the way and
not long after found himself lying on his deathbed. When they
heard of his failing health, many friends, Buddhist and Taoist
alike, wrote to him inquiring after his health and suggesting various
medicinal herbs and special incantations. Wei-lin, the abbot of
Ching-shan ssu in Hang-chou, sent him a short verse in which he
urged Su to recite special prayers. Su replied with what was likely
his final poem:

Like you, I was born in the year ping-tzu [1037];
We've each had thirty thousand days so far.
Even if we recited a thousand hymns a day,
No place is safe from the lightning bolt.

> Great calamities stem from possessing a body;
> If there were no body, there would no illness.
> All my life I have laughed at old Kumārajīva
> Trying to prolong his life with magic spells![63]

Legend has it that when Kumārajīva, the great Indian preacher and translator, was about to die, he tried reciting all kinds of mantras in an effort to prolong his life, all to no avail. Su Shih, in contrast, appears to have preserved his dignity at the end, realistically and tranquilly facing the inevitability of bodily decay with neither bitterness nor fear. It is said that when Su was at the point of death, the Buddhist monk Wei-lin, who had come to be with his friend, bent over close to his ear and shouted, "Sir, you should not forget!" "It is not that the Pure Land does not exist," Su Shih is said to have replied, "it is simply that I haven't the energy [to aspire to it]." When reminded by another friend that this was precisely the time when one should redouble one's efforts, Su sighed and said, "I don't have what it takes." Yet another account relates how, when a friend tried to console Su Shih by reminding him he had studied Buddhism all his life and therefore (assured of a good future life) should rejoice, Su is said to have replied simply, "I cannot be sure of that," and passed away.[64] Not surprisingly, Su's failure to summon his religious zeal at the critical juncture between life and death was a source of great disappointment to later Pure Land Buddhist commentators. In an 1826 text by the monk Wu-k'ai (?–1830) titled *Nien-fo pai-wen* [One hundred questions about Buddha-recitation], one of the questions posed is why Su Tung-p'o failed to achieve rebirth in the Pure Land *(pu wang sheng)*. The reply is that Su, for all his spiritual potential, was too much of a genius for his own good. In fact, he was an example of someone who "tried to be clever and ended up stupid" *(nung ch'iao ch'eng cho)*.[65] However, one is also tempted to recall a literary figure from a very different time and place, Henry David Thoreau, who, when on his deathbed he was urged to make his peace with God, was said to have remarked that he could not recall there ever having been a quarrel.

9. Epilogue

GEORGE HATCH contends that Buddhism, unlike Taoism, is a religion of salvation: it is "about absolutes, not relativities; it seeks deliverance, not accommodation."[1] He then goes on to suggest that Su Shih, unwilling to renounce the relative for the absolute, tried to avoid a true religious commitment by simply equating samsara and nirvana: "If *samsara* and *nirvana* are ultimately the same, best to appreciate its meaning within the world of men and nature, avoiding then the uncertainties of understanding which so torture the supplicant. Ambiguities of meaning in Su Shih's Buddhism are simply dissolved in the larger and entirely receptive pantheism of his literary mind."[2]

I would argue, however, that this represents far too simplistic and reductive a characterization of Su Shih's Buddhism. In fact, I would suggest that at the heart of Su's creative life was the struggle to locate a middle ground that not only could contain (rather than simply dissolve) uncertainty and ambiguity, but would make it possible for the individual to experience the abstract within the particular, the absolute within the relative, nirvana within samsara. If Su does tend to appreciate the meaning of Buddhism largely "within the world of men and nature," it is because he believed that the only way human beings could truly come to know and realize the transcendent (whether the Confucian *tao* or the Buddhist nirvana) was through the immanent, through the things and affairs in which the transcendent made itself known. As Peter Bol persuasively argues, Su Shih was a man "opposed to dogmatism in any form, who treasure[d] flexibility, diversity, and individuality, yet [was] consumed by the search for unifying values."[3] Bol's discussion of "Su Shih's [Confucian] Tao" offers an illuminating parallel to what this study has revealed about Su Shih's understanding of Buddhism. A great number of Su Shih scholars have come to agree with Bol that one of the most outstanding characteristics of Su Shih's thought is its concern with learning "how to respond creatively yet responsibly to a changing world."[4] Unlike his Neo-Confucian contemporaries, many of whom were obsessed with the "one, correct way," for Su there could not be a single, constant method or "a single moral human nature, a single moral politics, or a single doctrine as the *tao* of the sage."[5] Nevertheless, this diversity of possible responses was possible only if it was fully grounded in the unifying "*tao* of the sage," which was "universal, all-embracing, and irreducible," a "unitary, inexhaustible source . . . whence all things come into being."[6] The ideal sage was one who was able to use this all-embracing, if undefined, ground of *tao* to respond flexibly, creatively, spontaneously, and above all appropriately to all situations. Although Bol discusses this idea primarily in terms of Su's conception of the Confucian sage, it is applicable to Su's conception of the Buddhist bodhisattva as well. The best illustration is Su's famous description of the Great Bodhisattva of Compassion of Ch'eng-tu, who is able to respond perfectly to the varied needs of suffering sentient beings—unlike ordinary human beings for whom it is almost impossible to do more than two different things at once without becoming completely disoriented and confused. The bodhisattva is able to respond this way because he is fully grounded in the ultimate, nondualistic one mind or no-mind, or, as Su puts it, "because these thousand hands [emerge from] no-mind, each is able to find its own place." This idea in turn is echoed in chapter 30 of the *Chung yung:* "The myriad things are nurtured at the same time yet do not harm each other, and [the various] *tao* are practiced at the same time yet do not conflict with each other."[7] This celebration of a dynamic diversity grounded in an underlying unity also explains Su's distaste for sectarian divisions both within Buddhism and Confucianism and between them. He writes: "To point at robes and cap and call that Confucianism is surely a sign of Confucianism's decay. To consider that Ch'an and Vinaya are what is Buddhism is a [gross] simplification of Buddhism. How can that which is originally clear and pure be termed 'Vinaya?' If everything is ultimately liberated, how can there still be such a thing as 'Ch'an'?"[8]

This idea appears in many of the poems in which Su describes monk friends like Pien-ts'ai, for whom "practice and theory are one," and Hui-pien, who was "neither defiled, nor pure; neither Vinaya, nor Ch'an." What he admires about these men is that they have found "a middle way" between the secular world and the religious world. Even more important, grounded as they are in that which is "originally clear and pure," they are able to respond appropriately to any particular person or to any situation in which they find themselves.

Peter Bol summarizes Su Shih's conception of the *tao* of the sage as follows:

> Men generally lack an inclusive perspective. They live in a world of dualities, cut off from the source, and are always being carried "downstream" into a world that is becoming ever more complex and diverse with the creation of new things. Were a man able to tap into the common source and respond to particular events from the common basis, his responses would have real value. Thus he must work his way "upstream," as Su puts it. He can do this, as Su argues with reference to things as diverse as swimming, music, and the desires, by understanding intellectually the inherent patterns by which the thing or affair came into being. He can study the *li* of water (how one sinks or floats) and learn to swim; he can reflect on his feelings and see that there is something beyond desire whence desire comes. But in the end he makes a leap into an intuitive unity with the source or oneness with the thing. At this point he achieves spontaneity, and being one with water or with his own character, he can respond to it (or from it) without calculation.[9]

This summary, the language of which in some ways echoes the important idea of reversing the stream of ignorance and returning to the Ultimate Source, found in the *Śuraṃgama Sūtra,* suggests several different ways of understanding Su's attitude toward Buddhist ideas. In particular, it helps illuminate Su Shih's feelings about the differing views within Buddhism regarding "sudden" and "gradual" enlightenment. Su Shih was primarily attracted to the Southern school's doctrine of "sudden enlightenment," with its associations of spontaneity, originality, and untrammeled freedom. Nevertheless, his writings contain both strong criticisms of Ch'an monks who engage in "spontaneous" activities with no regard for social values and high praise for those who build religious statues, repair bridges, and feed the poor. In the same way, he admits that he does not quite understand the Patriarchal meditation of the Southern school of Ch'an Buddhism, as opposed to the Tathāgata meditation of schools such as the T'ien-t'ai, with its emphasis on a gradual cultivation based on discipline, meditation, and wisdom. From Bol's discussion of Su Shih's lifelong interest in finding a middle position between extremes, it becomes clear that Su is trying to do the same in the case of Buddhism. One of Su's strongest arguments for a Confucian middle way, in fact, is found in a piece written for a Buddhist temple in 1075. In this writing, Su uses a cooking analogy to argue that even if everyone makes use of the same ingredients and the same recipe, the quality of the results depends on the cook. But, says Su, if they simply ignore "the proportions, set aside the quantities, thinking that [quality] does not depend on them . . . [and] create everything alike according to their own whim, then little [of what they create] will not be spit out by others."[10] The answer to this dilemma, as Bol suggests, is to "learn how to create recipes by learning from past experience. . . . Received knowledge is useful—it enables men to roughly approximate the achievements of others—but the quality of the result depends on what individuals bring to it."[11] In other words, although the ultimate goal may entail "a leap into an intuitive unity with the source or oneness," the process by which one prepares oneself for this leap is in fact gradual, a matter of "working one's way upstream." Here I think there is a clear parallel to the reaction of certain Sung Buddhists to the more extreme forms of antinomian Ch'an Buddhism as well as to the call for a unification of doctrine and practice issued not only by certain schools of T'ien-t'ai Buddhism but also by the growing number of advocates of *wen-tzu Ch'an.*

However, if Su emphasized the importance of "working one's way upstream," he was equally adamant that there was no such thing as a single, correct way of doing so that applied to all individuals without exception. Rather, it was "better to encourage a broad range of learning from many sources than to teach a single model."[12] The closest parallel to this idea in the Buddhist context would seem to be the idea of *upāya,* or skillful means. A good illustration in the *Śūraṃgama Sūtra* finds eighteen Bodhisattvas describing how they attained enlightenment through the various senses of taste, touch, smell, and so forth, culminating with the bodhisattva Avalokiteśvara's description of what is held up as the most effective (although not the only) means, the sense of hearing. Most significant is that the six senses (and, by extension, the world of phenomena) are not simply repressed or abandoned in the search for transcendence, but rather are utilized as an important means of acquiring insight and achieving enlightenment. The idea is even more clear in the following poem by Su Shih:

> When I observe the Buddhas and bodhisattvas,
> I see how they carry out their work by means of
>   the six senses.
> Even those with marvelous wisdom like Avalo-
>   kiteśvara,
> Return by means of hearing and thought to the
>   Source.
> The Buddhas have wandered for beginningless
>   kalpas,
> Without emptying themselves of words and
>   language.[13]

Su then goes on to use the analogy of a wealthy man who, although fully aware of the dangers of attachment, also knows that it is better to get rid of his wealth by distributing it to the poor and sick rather than by simply flinging it away into the rivers and ravines. Elsewhere, Su complains that certain scholars are all too ready to toss away the study of such things as "astronomy and geography, the calendar and music, building and clothing, the rules of capping marriage, mourning, and sacrificing, what the Spring and Autumn Annals rejected and adopted, what ritual allows and the law forbids, why the successive dynasties rose and fell, and why some men are wise and others worthless."[14] Su's argument is that all of these things, like the rich man's money, although they must not be considered ends in and of themselves, should be used skillfully rather than abandoned altogether. Thus, he criticizes scholars (and here, one can also read "Ch'an Buddhists") who say, "None of these are worth learning; learn what cannot be transmitted through speech and conveyed through books."[15]

This emphasis on the usefulness of learning holds true for almost every area of human endeavor, including the literary arts. Thus, Ts'an-liao, because he "has a heart as clear as water / His vision a spotless void with nothing to sweep away," is able to "use marvel-

ous language to express the various emotions."[16] And, as Su writes
in another poem addressed to Ts'an-liao: "If you wish to make
your poems marvelous / You must not despise emptiness or stillness
/ For it is in stillness that all movements are completed / And it is in
emptiness that all worlds are contained."[17] Su expresses the same
idea in the following piece addressed to a Buddhist monk:

> The sea of dharma of the [*Avataṃsaka Sūtra*] is in the end [as
> insubstantial as] a "grass hut"; how much more so poetry, callig-
> raphy, and the zither. However, among those of antiquity who
> learned the *tao*, none began from emptiness: Wheelwright Pien
> chiseled wheels, and the hunchback caught cicadas. As long as
> one can develop one's cleverness and skill with it, nothing is too
> humble. If [Monk] Tsung apprehends the *tao*, then both his lute
> playing and his calligraphy will gain in strength, and his poetry
> even more. If Tsung is able to be like a mirror in that the one con-
> tains the ten thousand, then his calligraphy and poetry ought to be
> even more unique. I shall peruse them, taking them as an indicator
> of the degree to which Tsung has apprehended the *tao*.[18]

As Bol points out, "For Su the cultural enterprise represents one
possible way of practicing his vision of morally engaged learning. It
is not the only way, and the prose, poetry, calligraphy, and painting
that result are not of vital importance to human welfare or the most
important qualities of an individual. But they do offer a terrain in
which a student can learn to practice *tao*, and anyone who can learn
to practice the *tao* in the area of *wen* can do it in other areas as
well."[19] Bol further notes that "the irony of Su Shih's position is
that in order to explain how what an individual writes can have real
value, he settles on a way of thinking about values that does not in
theory privilege the literary enterprise."[20] In other words, skillful
means are ultimately just fingers pointing at the moon (and for Su
there are a great number of possible fingers), but they are not the
moon itself. Although in many of his Buddhist-related writings Su
laments being caught in a "karma of words" and longs to realize
Vimalakīrti's "thunderous silence," in the meantime there is a
delight in the creative and playful possibilities of language. Justification (if justification be needed) was readily available in places
like chapter 2 of the *Lotus Sūtra,* which describes the various
means by which people may express their attainment of the Buddha
path, including "the art of creating Buddha images" and "beating

drums and blowing horns and conchs." For instance, he envies the
way Pien-ts'ai "playfully roams amid the froth of the floating
world / He laughs at me: 'Glory and decay both reside in the snap
of a finger' / Neither tasting tea nor appreciating paintings is
wrong / Asking about the dharma and asking for a poem / These, I
see now, are not mutually opposed!"[21] Su Shih would have agreed
heartily with Yoshitaka Iriya's description of truly successful religious poetry. It is not works that "attempt religious statement, but
those in which the poet disports himself in a free, effortless revel-
ling in the Way—the joyful outpouring of a 'sportful samādhi.' "[22]
Although Su by no means attained this in all or even most of his
Buddhist-related poetry, it became an important aesthetic ideal
for him.

> Five syllables, seven syllables—truly child's play;
> Three lines, two lines—just a silly game.
> I've always been able to get drunk without drinking;
> Like the spring wind that flirts with the flowers!
> These forty years have gone by as if in a dream,
> Older now, I need not choose between foolish and wise.
> The ancients are no longer here, but neither are they gone.
> And now, neither am I acting, nor am I ceasing to act.
> Lodging distant words to all the dwellers of the earth;
> A wave of life, a wave of death, all on a grain of sand.
> I have no pond to wash my brush, its tip worn to the nub,
> So for now I'll simply amuse myself and cheer myself up![23]

The question of whether to write poetry or to disengage from it
was another formulation of the perennial question around which
Su Shih's life—and to a large extent his writings as well—revolved.
Since it was apparently impossible to leave the world of politics and
pain, how might one accommodate oneself to them without com-
promising one's integrity too much. Toward the end of his life, Su
Shih came up with answers that found positive confirmation in
Buddhist concepts of nonduality and Taoist ideas of relativity, both
of which insisted on the importance of going beyond the conventional distinctions between sacred and secular, mundane and transcendent, foolish and wise, and perhaps between the artist and the
mystic. Su's approach to Buddhist ideas was, in the end, not all that
different from his approach to Confucian ones. Su Shih did not, as
Hatch implies, simply "dissolve" his "uncertainties of understand-

ing" and "ambiguities of meaning" in the "receptive pantheism of his literary mind." Rather, as Bol writes, "in a world where not a few found teachers of dogmas, Su was unwilling to promise absolute certainty or an unreflective spontaneity. Living with uncertainty was hard work; spontaneity required study and thought. In place of certain total knowledge, he offered deeper, broader, and more nuanced awareness."[24] I would suggest that Su Shih did more than assume the equivalence of samsara and nirvana. Rather, he actively sought a middle way between transcendence and immanence, the absolute and the relative, the sudden and the gradual. Above all, he sought a middle path that one could actually travel on. Or, to use his own analogies, he was interested not in the pearls and jades of abstract ideas, but rather in food and clothing that could be used readily; he chose the nourishing reality of plain pork rather than the theoretical delights of dragon's flesh.

ABBREVIATIONS

CLSPC *Ch'an-lin seng pao-chüan* [Chronicles of the Ch'an order]. 30 chüan. By Chüeh-fan Hui-hung (1071–1128), completed in 1101. In *HTC* 137:1–414.

FTTC *Fo-tsu t'ung-chi* [A chronicle of the Buddhas and the Patriarchs]. 54 chüan. Compiled by Ch'ih-p'an (1220–1275), completed in 1269. In *T* 49:129–475.

FTLTTT *Fo-tsu li-tai t'ung-tsai* [A comprehensive registry of the successive ages of the Buddhas and the Patriarchs]. 32 chüan. By Nien Ch'ang (1282–1323), completed in 1341). In *T* 49:477–735.

HTC *Hsü tsang-ching* [Tripiṭaka supplement]. 150 vols. Taipei: Hsin-wen-feng ch'u-pan-she, 1977; originally published as *Dainihon zokuzōkyō,* 750 vols. Kyoto: Zōkyō Shoin, 1905–1912.

SPPY *Ssu-pu pei-yao.* Taipei: Taiwan Chung-hua shu-chü, 1965–1966.

SPTK *Ssu-pu ts'ung-k'an.* Shanghai: Commercial Press, 1919–1937.

SS *Śūraṃgama Sūtra (Ta Fo ting ju-lai wan-hsing shou leng-yen ching).* Attributed to Paramiti (T'ang dynasty, exact dates unknown), but probably of Chinese origin. In *T* 19:105–155.

SSSC *Su Shih shih-chi* [Collected poetry of Su Shih]. 8 volumes. Annotated by Wang Wen-kao. Peking: Chung-hua shu-chü, 1982.

SSWC *Su Shih wen-chi* [Collected prose of Su Shih]. 6 volumes. Compiled and edited by K'ung Fan-li. Peking: Chung-hua shu-chü, 1986.

T *Taishō shinshū daizōkyō* [The Tripiṭaka newly compiled during the Taishō era]. 100 vols. Edited by Takakusu Junjirō, Watanabe Kaigyoku, and Ono Gemmyō. Tokyo: Daizō shuppansha, 1924–1932.

WTHY *Wu-teng hui-yüan* [The collated essentials of the five lamps]. 20 chüan. Compiled by P'u-ch'i (1179–1253), completed in 1252. Modern edition edited by Su Yüan-lei. Peking: Chung-hua shu-chü, 1984.

NOTES

1. George Hatch, "Su Shih," in Herbert Franke, ed., *Sung Biographies,* (Wiesbaden: Franz Steiner Verlag, 1976), p. 901. This concise but insightful piece is one of the best biographies of Su Shih available in English.

2. "T'i Hsi-lin pi" [Written on the wall at Hsi-lin Temple], in *SSSC* 4:1219. I found it difficult to improve on this translation by Burton Watson. See *Su Tung-p'o: Selections from a Sung Dynasty Poet* (New York: Columbia University Press, 1965), p. 101.

3. Much of Su's religious writings, especially the hymns and *gāthās,* are untranslated and unannotated. However, although not always directly acknowledged, many of my translations of Su's poetry would have been impossible without the aid of the meticulous annotations of Japanese scholars such as Ogawa Tamaki. I have relied heavily on his *So Shoku* [Su Shih] in two volumes (*Chūgoku shijin senshū,* 2d series, vols. 5–6 [Tokyo: Iwanami, 1973]) along with the anthology translated with Yamamoto Kazuyoshi entitled *So Tōba shishū* [The collected poetry of Su Tung-p'o] in three volumes (Tokyo: Chikuma, 1983, 1984, 1986). Another very useful annotation is *So Tōba shishū* [The collected poetry of Su Tung-p'o], thoroughly annotated and translated into Japanese by Iwamizu Kentoku, Seitan, and Kubo Tenzui. This collection in six volumes is part of the Zokkoku yaku kanban taisei series (Tokyo: Kokumin bunko kankōkai, 1936 reprint of 1931 publication). Interestingly enough, volumes 3 and 4 are edited by Seitan, a Buddhist priest.

4. For many years, the only readily available full-length study of Su Shih was Lin Yutang's *The Gay Genius* (New York: John Day, 1947), a fascinating information-filled biography that lacked, however, a critical and analytical edge. This was followed by two important doctoral dissertations that offered a more critical if narrower perspective: Andrew L. March's "Landscape in the Thought of Su Shih" (University of Washington, 1964) and, ten years later, Stanley Ginsberg's "Alienation and Reconciliation of a Chinese Poet: The Huang-chou Exile of Su Shih" (University of Wiscon-

sin, 1974). During this time there were only a few translated collections of Su's writings: Cyril Drummond Le Gros Clark's *Selections from the Works of Su Tung-p'o* (London: Jonathan Cape, 1931) and *The Prose-Poetry of Su Tung-p'o,* 2d ed. (New York: Paragon Book Reprint Corp., 1964), and Burton Watson's *Su Tung-p'o: Selections from a Sung Dynasty Poet.* In the last decade things have changed considerably as Sung intellectual historians have found Su Shih an endless source of inspiration and information. See Peter Bol, *"This Culture of Ours": Intellectual Transitions in T'ang and Sung China* (Stanford: Stanford University Press, 1992), and Kidder Smith, Jr., Peter K. Bol, Joseph A. Adler, and Don Wyatt, *Sung Dynasty Uses of the I Ching* (Princeton: Princeton University Press, 1990). Art historians have always been aware of Su's pivotal role in the formation of the new aesthetics of this period, a fact reflected in the title of Susan Bush's well-known book *The Literati and the Art of Painting: Su Shih (1036–1101) to Tung Chi-chang (1555–1636)* (Cambridge: Harvard University Press, 1971). Michael Fuller's *The Road to East Slope: The Development of Su Shi's Poetic Voice* (Stanford: Stanford University Press, 1990) has helped to fill an important gap in our understanding of Su's poetry and poetics. In addition, we now have Ronald Egan's much-needed study *Word, Image and Deed in the Life of Su Shi* (Cambridge, Mass: Harvard-Yenching Institute Monograph Series, 1994), which provides a clear and critical overview of Su Shih's life and writings. There are also two excellent recent dissertations, "The Way and the Self in the Poetry of Su Shih (1037–1101)," by Alice Cheang (Harvard University, 1991) and "Poetry of Exile and Return: A Study of Su Shi (1037–1101)," by Kathleen Tomlonovic (University of Washington, 1989).

5. Su Shih's interest in Buddhism has often been noted by Chinese and Japanese scholars, past and present: examples of relatively recent studies are Yoshikawa Kōjirō's "So Tōba no bungaku to bukkyō" [Su Tung-p'o's writings and Buddhism], in *Tsukamoto hakushi shōju kinen Bukkyō shigaku ronshū* (Kyoto: Research Institute for Humanistic Studies, 1961), pp. 939–950; and Chikusa Masaaki's "So Shoku to bukkyō" [Su Shih and Buddhism], *Tōhō gakuhō,* no. 36 (October 1964), pp. 457–480. See also Chinese scholar Ts'ao Shu-min's "Su Tung-p'o yü Tao Fo chih kuan-hsi" [The relationship between Su Tung-p'o and Taoism and Buddhism], in *Kuo-li chung-li t'u-shu-kuan kuan-k'an* 3, nos. 3 and 4 (October 1970), pp. 34–55. In the West, although nearly every scholar has made at least passing reference to Su Shih's Buddhism, George Hatch in his 1976 biography of Su Shih is one of the few to engage critically the question of its importance in the poet's life, and Ronald Egan has devoted a chapter to this question in his new study. It remains, however, a question that deserves to be explored in much greater detail, not only for the light it sheds on what one

might term the "religious" dimensions of Su Shih the man and the artist, but also for what it can tell us about the religious climate of the Northern Sung dynasty.

6. See Norman Girardot, "Chinese Religion and Western Scholarship," in *China and Christianity: Historical and Future Encounters,* ed. James D. Whitehead, Yu-ming Shaw, and Norman J. Girardot (Notre Dame: University of Notre Dame Press, 1979), p. 94. See also Bernard Faure's discussion of how the early Western (and particularly Jesuit) interpretations of Chinese Buddhism have contributed to a tendency on the part of Western sinology to focus almost exclusively on Confucianism. *Chan Insights and Oversights: An Epistemological Critique of the Chan Tradition* (Princeton: Princeton University Press, 1993), pp. 18–51.

7. See, for example, T. Griffith Foulk, "Myth, Ritual, and Monastic Practice in Sung Ch'an Buddhism," in Patricia Buckley Ebrey and Peter N. Gregory, eds., *Religion and Society in T'ang and Sung China* (Honolulu: University of Hawaii Press, 1993), pp. 147–208; Ronald Egan, "Looking on Curiously: Poet-Monks' Perceptions of Literati Culture" (unpublished paper, 1992); Robert M. Gimello, "Mārga and Culture: Learning, Letters, and Liberation in Northern Sung Ch'an" in *Paths to Liberation: the Mārgā and Its Transformations in Buddhist Thought,* ed. Robert E. Buswell, Jr., and Robert M. Gimello (Honolulu: University of Hawaii Press, 1992); Miriam Levering, "Ch'an Enlightenment for Laymen: Ta-hui and the New Religious Culture of the Sung" (Ph.D. dissertation, Harvard University, 1978); and Chou I-kan, "Pei Sung di Ch'an tsung yü wen-hsüeh" [Northern Sung Ch'an sect and literature], in *Wenhsüeh i-ch'an* 1983, no. 3, pp. 44–50.

8. See Araki Toshikazu's entry on Yeh's *Pi-shu lu hua* [Notes taken in my summer resort], in Yves Hervouet, ed., *A Sung Bibliography* (Hong Kong: The Chinese University Press, 1978), p. 291.

9. This remark is included in the prefatory comments to complete Ming (1621) collection of Su's Buddhist-related poetry, *Tung-p'o Ch'an-hsi chi,* annotated by Ling Meng-ch'u (1580–1644), in the Peking University Library. Unfortunately, I have been unable to locate it in any of the collections of Yeh Meng-te's writings.

10. There is an edition of Hsü Chang-ju's 1590 anthology in the Fu-ssu-nien Library of the Academia Sinica in Taipei. The modern reprints have been published in 1982, 1988, and 1991 by the Lao-ku wen-hua shih-yeh kung-ssu in Taipei. There are, as far as I know, three extant editions of Ling Meng-ch'u's 1621 annotated version: two in the National Central Library of Taiwan and one in the Peking University Library. Ling's version is divided into fourteen fascicles instead of nine, and includes seventeen pieces not found in Hsü's 1590 version, but is otherwise the same.

11. Asakura Hisashi notes that in many ways it was the legend of Su Shih rather than the actual man that captured the imagination of these poet-monks. See *Zenrin no bungaku: Chūgoku bungaku juyō* (Zen literature: the influence of Chinese literature] (Osaka: Seibundō, 1985), pp. 457–530.

12. David Pollack, *Zen Poems of the Five Mountains* (New York: The Crossroad Publishing Company and Scholar Press, 1985), p. 155.

13. Chung Lai-yin, *Su Shih yü tao-chia, tao-chiao* [Su Shih and Taoist philosophy, Taoist religion] (Taipei: Taiwan hsüeh-sheng shu-chü, 1990), p. 45.

14. Quoted in Donald Gardner, *Chu Hsi: Learning to Be a Sage* (Berkeley: University of California Press, 1990), p. 12.

15. For a succinct overview of this period of Chinese history, see the revised edition of John K. Fairbank and Edwin O. Reischauer's classic *China: Tradition and Transformation* (New York: Houghton Mifflin, 1989), pp. 116–151.

16. For a discussion of these reforms, see James T. C. Liu's *Reform in Sung China: Wang An-shih (1021–1086) and His New Policies* (Cambridge: Harvard University Press, 1959), pp. 1–10.

17. Gardner, *Chu Hsi,* p. 62.

18. James T. C. Liu, *China Turning Inward: Intellectual-Political Changes in the Early Twelfth Century* (Cambridge: Published by the Council on East Asian Studies, Harvard University, and distributed by Harvard University Press, 1988), p. 37.

19. Ira E. Kasoff, *The Thought of Chang Tsai (1020–1077)* (Cambridge: Cambridge University Press, 1984), p. 17.

20. Ibid.

21. Ibid.

22. There are numerous excellent studies of the role of these men in the development of Neo-Confucianism, including Wm. T. de Bary and Irene Bloom, eds., *Principles and Practicality: Essays in Neo-Confucianism and Practical Learning* (New York: Columbia University Press, 1979); John King Fairbank, ed., *Chinese Thought and Institutions* (Chicago: Chicago University Press, 1957); David S. Nivison and Arthur F. Wright, eds., *Confucianism in Action* (Stanford: Stanford University Press, 1959); Arthur E. Wright, ed. *The Confucian Persuasion* (Stanford: Stanford University Press, 1960); and Arthur Wright and Denis Twitchett, eds., *Confucian Personalities* (Stanford: Stanford University Press, 1962). The influence of Buddhist ideas on Neo-Confucian thinkers has often been noted. Ch'eng Hao studied Ch'an Buddhism as a youth and was well read in Mahāyāna Buddhist sutras as was his brother Ch'eng I, who might have practiced Ch'an meditation as well. See Kenneth Ch'en, *Buddhism in China: A Historical Survey* (Princeton: Princeton University Press, 1964), pp. 396–397.

23. Quoted in A. C. Graham, *Two Chinese Philosophers* (London: Lund, Humphries, 1958), p. 84.

24. Ibid., p. 88. Also cited in Wm. Theodore de Bary, ed., *The Buddhist Tradition in India, China and Japan* (New York: Vintage Books edition, 1972), p. 243.

25. See Chu Hsi, *Chu-tzu yü-lei,* comp. Li Ching-te, ed. Lang Yeh, 1173 (Taipei: Shih-chieh reprint, 1960, 2 volumes), chüan 130, 16b–17a.

26. See Professor Abe's chapter on "Buddhism," in *Our Religions,* ed. Arvind Sharma (San Francisco: Harper, 1993).

27. Liu Nai-ch'ang, "Lun Fo-lao ssu-hsiang tui Su Shih wen-hsüeh kuan-hsi" [A discussion of the relationship between Buddhist/Taoist thought and Su Shih's writings], in *Su Shih wen-hsüeh lun-chi,* ed. Liu Nai-ch'ang (Chi-nan, Shantung: Chi lü shu-she, 1982), p. 86.

28. See Wang Shui-chao, "Lun Su Shih ts'ang-tso de fa-chan chieh-tuan" [A discussion of the stages of development of Su Shih's collected works], *She-hui k'o-hsüeh chan-hsien* 1984, no. 1, pp. 259–269. See also Ronald Egan's review of Michael Fuller's book, in *Harvard Journal of Asiatic Studies* 52:1 (June 1992), 317.

29. Chung Lai-yin in his book *Su Shih yü tao-chia, tao-chiao* examines the role of Taoism in the life and thought of Su Shih. Chung finds it necessary to deny repeatedly and sometimes vehemently that Buddhism had any significant influence on Su Shih's life and thought, not to mention his writings. In support of this, Chung Lai-yin points out that not only did Su Shih criticize the behavior of certain Buddhist followers, but he went so far as to change the sacred Buddhist texts to fit his own understanding and to practice Taoist breathing exercises in Buddhist temples. According to Chung, not once did Su express this kind of "disrespectful" attitude toward Taoist texts, practices, or priests. He uses this fact to substantiate his claim that Su used Buddhism exclusively as a means for facilitating his social exchange with Buddhists and that Su had no real interest in or respect for Buddhism as a way of life or as a school of thought. However, the jocular attitude and the mixing of Buddhist and Taoist allusions were characteristic of many poets, even the undoubtedly Buddhist-inclined Po Chü-i, as Burton Watson makes clear in his article "Buddhism in the Poetry of Po Chü-i." Chuang-tzu might well have been Su's favorite philosophical figure, and Su did engage in Taoist practices throughout his life. However, none of this means that his engagement with Buddhism was any less important to him.

2: BUDDHISM IN ELEVENTH-CENTURY CHINA

1. For a discussion of some of the reasons for this perception of post-T'ang decadence (which continues to this day), see Holmes Welch, *The Practice of Chinese Buddhism: 1900–1950* (Cambridge: Harvard Univer-

sity Press, 1968), pp. 395-407. See also T. Griffith Foulk, "Myth, Ritual, and Monastic Practice in Sung Ch'an Buddhism," pp. 147-151.

2. For accounts of this suppression, see Stanley Weinstein, *Buddhism under the T'ang* (Cambridge: Cambridge University Press, 1987), pp. 114-136; Kenneth Ch'en, *Buddhism in China,* p. 226; and E. O. Reischauer, *Ennin's Travels,* (New York: Ronald Press Company, 1955), pp. 223-224.

3. These figures are cited in Wang Chih-yüan, *Sung ch'u T'ien-t'ai Fo-hsüeh k'uei yao* [Aspects of T'ien-t'ai Buddhism in the early Sung] (Peking: Chung-kuo chien-she ch'u-pan-she, 1989), p. 7.

4. See Huang Min-chih, *Sung tai Fo-chiao she-hui ching-chi shih lun chi* [Collected studies on the socioeconomic history of Buddhism in the Sung] (Taipei: Taiwan hsüeh-sheng shu-chü, 1989), p. 327. This thoroughly researched book is an excellent source of information on the growth of Buddhist monasteries and monastics and their changing relationship with the court, the official class, and society as a whole.

5. Tantrism, or esoteric Buddhism, was introduced into China as early as the third century, although it was not established until the eighth century with the arrival of three important Indian Tantric masters, Subhakara-simha, Vajrabodhi, and Amoghavajra. Although Tantric practices were probably far more prevalent in China than is generally assumed, it would seem that by the Sung dynasty the cult had fallen into a serious decline, owing partly to the lack of charismatic teachers and partly to a general perception on the part of both Buddhists and Confucians that Tantric practices bordered too closely on immorality and superstition. See Kenneth Ch'en, *Buddhism in China,* pp. 325-337; Chou I-liang, "Tantrism in China," *Harvard Journal of Asiatic Studies* 8 (1945), pp. 241-332.

6. See Kenneth Ch'en, *Buddhism in China,* pp. 391-394.

7. See Henrik H. Sorenson, "The Life and Times of the Ch'an Master Yün-men Wen-yen," *Acta Orientalia* 49 (1988), pp. 105-106. See also Urf Erwin App, "Facets of the Life and Teachings of Ch'an Master Yunmen Wenyan (864-949)" (2 volumes) (Ph.D. dissertation, Temple University, 1989).

8. Sorenson, "Yün-men Wen-yen," p. 116.

9. Ibid., p. 123.

10. Yün-men Wen-yen was a man of great personal charisma, a charisma that apparently extended beyond his own lifetime. Bernard Faure quotes a document that records how, when Yün-men died, "his disciples received his 'whole body' and erected a stūpa; then they took the body out of his coffin and lacquered it. This was more than eight hundred years ago. During that time, the people, near and distant, officials and common folk alike, prayed to him for rain or for good weather, and he helped them silently and performed many miracles." In fact, Faure goes on to specu-

late, these supernatural powers must have helped insure the great popularity of his school during the Sung and afterward. Bernard Faure, *The Rhetoric of Immediacy: A Cultural Critique of Chan/Zen Buddhism* (Princeton, 1992), p. 155. See also Sorenson, "Yün-men Wen-yen," pp. 119–120.

11. Robert M. Gimello, "Mārga and Culture: Learning, Letters, and Liberation in Northern Sung Ch'an," p. 379.

12. See Su Hsün, "P'eng-chou Yüan-chüeh Ch'an yüan chi" [An Account of the Complete Illumination Ch'an Monastery of P'eng-chou," in *Chia-yu chi,* chüan 14 (*SPPY* edition). Also quoted in James T. C. Liu, *Ou-yang Hsiu: An Eleventh-Century Neo-Confucianist* (Stanford University Press, 1967), p. 166.

13. Quoted in *Tung-p'o i-shih,* ed. Shen Tsung-yüan (Shanghai Commercial Press, 1922), p. 44.

14. *FTTC,* in *T* 49:474c.

15. *FTLTTT,* in *T* 49:677a.

16. Gimello, "Mārga and Culture," p. 377.

17. Carl Bielefeldt, "Ch'an-lu Tsung-tse's *Tso-ch'an I* and the Secret of Zen Meditation," in *Traditions of Meditation in Chinese Buddhism,* ed. Peter N. Gregory, The Kuroda Institute Studies in East Asian Buddhism 4 (Honolulu: University of Hawaii Press, 1986), pp. 143–144.

18. "Shu Leng-chia ching hou" [Postface to the *Laṅkāvatāra Sūtra*], in *SSWC* 5:2085–2086.

19. "Yen-kuan ta-pei ko chi" [An account of the pavilion of the (Bodhisattva of) Great Compassion in Yen-kuan], in *SSWC* 2:386–388.

20. "Jih-yü" [The sun as simile], in *SSWC* 5:1980–1981. The translation is from Bol, *"This Culture of Ours,"* p. 275.

21. Gimello, "Mārga and Culture," p. 382.

22. Ibid.

23. Ibid. Su's comment is from his "Liu-i chü-shih chi-shu" [Preface to the collected works of Layman Liu-i (Ou-yang Hsiu)], in *SSWC* 1:315.

24. "Hsiao-chüan p'an-ju hsin-ching ts'an" [An appreciation of a small-seal (calligraphy) of the *Heart Sūtra*], in *SSWC* 2:618.

25. William R. LaFleur, *The Karma of Words: Buddhism and the Literary Arts in Medieval Japan* (Berkeley: University of California Press, 1983), p. 7.

26. Ibid., p. 8.

27. See his *I Kai* [Introduction to the arts] (Shanghai: Shanghai ku-chi ch'u-pan she, 1978), p. 66.

28. See Chou Yü-k'ai, "Wen-tzu Ch'an yü Sung-tai shih hsüeh" [Literary Ch'an and Sung dynasty poetics], in *Kuo-chi Sung-tai wen-hua yen-chiu t'ao-hui lun-wen-chi,* [An anthology of theses from the International Symposium on the Culture of the Sung Dynasty], ed. Sun Ch'in-shan,

et al. (Ch'eng-tu, Szechuan: Szechuan ta-hsüeh ch'u-pan-she, 1991), pp. 327–344.

29. Ibid., p. 337.

30. As the Ming dynasty Buddhist critic Ta-kuan Chen-k'o (1542–1603) notes, "The obstacles between form *(shih)* and principle *(li)* are unable to impede him." "Pa Su Chang kung chi" [A colophon for the works of Master Su], in *Tzu-po tsun-che ch'üan-chi* (The complete works of the Venerable Tzu-po), *HTC* 14:437a.

31. Paul L. Swanson, *Foundations of T'ien-t'ai Philosophy: The Flowering of the Two Truths Theory in Chinese Buddhism* (Berkeley, Calif.: Asian Humanities Press, 1989), p. 6.

32. Wang Chih-yüan, *Sung ch'u T'ien-t'ai Fo-hsüeh k'uei yao*, p. 27.

33. Peter N. Gregory, *Tsung-mi and the Sinification of Buddhism* (Princeton: Princeton University Press, 1991), p. 166.

34. Tomoaki Tsuchida, *Mind and Reality: A Study of the "Shoulengyanjing"* (Ph.D. dissertation, Harvard University, 1986), p. 23. I have modified his translation slightly.

35. Although there is a text in two chüan *(T* 642) translated by Kumārajiva titled *Śūraṃgama-samādhi-sūtra,* it is clear that the one Su Shih read was a later sutra in ten fascicles *(T* 945) of the same name that, although traditionally said to have been translated by Paramārtha in 705, is now generally considered to be of Chinese rather than Sanskrit origin. It became very popular after the mid-Tang (Po Chü-i was also very fond of it) mainly for the striking beauty of its prose and its wealth of imagery. During the Sung this sutra gradually became more closely associated with the Ch'an school, although the Hua-yen and T'ien-t'ai schools also had their own interpretations. It is sometimes translated into English as the *Great Heroic March Sūtra.*

36. Tsuchida, *Mind and Reality,* p. 153.

37. *FTTC,* in *T* 49:443c. It is also cited in Tsuchida, *Mind and Reality,* p. 8.

38. *SS,* in *T* 19:123c.

39. Tsuchida, *Mind and Reality,* p. 134.

40. Ibid., p. 135.

41. *SS,* in *T* 19:114a.

42. Tsuchida, *Mind and Reality,* p. 44.

43. Hatch, "Su Shih," p. 945.

44. Tsuchida, *Mind and Reality,* p. 49.

45. Wang Chih-yüan, *Sung ch'u T'ien-t'ai Fo-hsüeh k'uei yao,* p. 71.

46. "Chi Lung-ching Pien-ts'ai wen" [Eulogy for Pien-ts'ai of Lungching], in *SSWC* 5:1961.

47. Leo Tak-hung Chan, "Techniques of Persuasion: Proselytism and

Pure Land Buddhism in Sung China," *Chinese Culture* 32, no. 3 (September 1991), p. 26.

48. Not surprisingly, a number of Sung Ch'an teachers themselves objected to this characterization and tried to discredit the *Ching-t'u tz'u-pei chi.* See Huang Ch'ien-hua's discussion of this text in *Chung-kuo Fo-chiao,* [Chinese Buddhism], comp. Chinese Buddhist Association (Shanghai: Chih-shih Ch'u-pan-she, 1989), 4:20–21.

49. For more information on these societies, see Suzuki Chūsei, "Sōdai Bukkyō kessha no kenkyū" [Researches on the Buddhist associations of the Sung dynasty], *Shigaku zasshi* 52 (1941). See also Mochizuki Shinkō, *Shina Jōdo kyōrishi* [A history of Pure Land in China] (Kyoto: Hōzōkan, 1964), p. 393.

50. *Lo-pang wen-lei,* in *T* 47:187b.

51. Mochizuki Shinkō's *Shina Jōdo kyōrishi* provides a great number of examples of this particular expression of piety. See chapters 29–32.

52. Quoted in Lin Tzu-ch'ing, "Yüan-chao (1048–1116)," in *Chung-kuo Fo-chiao,* vol. 2, p. 254.

53. Robert M. Gimello, "Hua-yen," in *Encyclopedia of Religion,* ed. Mircea Eliade (New York: Macmillan Publishing Company, 1987), 6:488.

54. Gregory, *Tsung-mi and the Sinification of Buddhism,* pp. 6–7, note 8.

55. When in 1085 a Korean monk by the name of I-t'ien came to China to study the *Hua-yen ching,* he studied with Ching-yüan for three years. After returning home to Korea, he sent Ching-yüan three translations of this particular sutra written in gold, for which Ching-yüan built a special pavilion. See *FTLTTT,* in *T* 49:672b.

56. Gregory, *Tsung-mi and the Sinification of Buddhism,* p. 7.

57. D. T. Suzuki, quoted in Paul Williams, *Mahāyāna Buddhism: The Doctrinal Foundations* (London and New York: Routledge, 1989), p. 123.

58. Ch'ien Ch'ien-i, "Tu Su Chang-kung wen" [Reading the (prose) writings of Master Su], in *Ch'u-hsüeh chi,* chüan 83 (*SPTK* 88:878).

59. See *Tzu-po tsun-che ch'üan chi* [The complete works of Venerable Purple Cedar], in *HTC* 14:437a.

60. Translation by D. T. Suzuki, quoted in Paul Williams, *Mahāyāna Buddhism,* p. 124.

3: OF ARHATS AND ALTRUISTIC MONKS

1. In 1084 Su Shih visited his younger brother Su Ch'e, who at the time was living in exile in Yün-chou (Kao-an, Kiangsi province). Several days before Su's arrival, Su Ch'e's friend and teacher, the monk Yün-yen, dreamt that he, Su Ch'e, and another monk by the name of Ts'ung had gone to the outskirts of the city to meet Ch'an Master Wu-tzu Chieh.

Thinking the dream rather unusual, he was just describing it to Su Ch'e when Master Ts'ung arrived. As it turned out, the night before, Ts'ung had had the very same dream himself. Several days later, the three of them traveled to a temple located twelve *li* from the city to await Su Shih. They told Su of their shared dream, and Su in turn informed them that when he was eight or nine years old, he would often dream that he was a monk from Shan-yu. Moreover, he said, when his mother was pregnant with him, she dreamed that a monk who was blind in one eye arrived at her doorstep asking for lodging. Upon hearing this, Yün-yen exclaimed that Master Wu-tzu Chieh not only was from Shan-yu, but also was blind in one eye, just like the monk in Su's mother's dream. Wu-tzu Chieh had apparently spent his last years in Yün-chou, where he had passed away approximately fifty years previously. Since Su was forty-nine years old that year, the natural conclusion was that he was a reincarnation of Wu-tzu Chieh, a conclusion Su Shih had no intention of disclaiming! This account can be found in Hui-hung's *Leng-chai yeh-hua,* chüan 7.

2. Asakura Hisashi makes this point in an interesting study of imitations of Su Shih's poetry by Japanese Buddhist monks. He notes that for these monks, Su has become an idealized figure, his sanctity ensured by the fact that he was a reincarnation of Wu-tzu Chieh. See his book *Zenrin no bungaku: Chūgoku bungaku juyō* [Zen literature: the influence of Chinese literature] (Osaka: Seibundō, 1985), pp. 457–458.

3. *T* 47:275b.

4. This story appears in an anonymous hand-written text (undated, but probably printed in the early twentieth century) titled "San-shih-er fen yin-kuo" [Twenty-three cases of (karmic) cause and effect], which I found in the library of the Academia Sinica Institute of Ethnology in Taiwan. Bernard Faure also mentions this story in his *Rhetoric of Immediacy,* pp. 234–235.

5. "Shih-pa ta a-lo-han sung" [Hymn to the Eighteen Great Arhats], in *SSWC* 2:586–591.

6. As Donald K. Swearer notes, "The arhat, as one who has realized the summum bonum of the spiritual path, is worshipped on the popular level as a field of merit and source of magical, protective power. Some, such as Upagupta and Piṇḍola [Bhāradvāja], became in effect protective deities believed to have the power to prevent violence and illness. Offerings to their images or symbolic representations of their presence constitute cultic practice in both domestic and public rituals" (*Encyclopedia of Religion* 1:404). In China, the most famous of these arhats is Piṇḍola Bhāradvāja, the guardian of the monastery refectory known also for his healing powers. See John S. Strong, "The Legend of the Lion-Roarers: A Study of the Buddhist Arhat Piṇḍola Bhāradvāja," in *Numen* 26 (June 1979), pp. 50–97.

7. The Chinese title of this text is *Ta-a-lo-han-nan-t'i-mi-to-lo-so-shuo-fa-chu-chi* (Skt. *Nandimitrāvadāna; T* 2030), translated by Hsüan-tsang. It was said to have been set down by the Ceylonese Nandimitrā nearly eight hundred years after the Buddha's death. Traditionally, the group was made up of the sixteen major disciples of Sakyamuni Buddha, although later in China two additional figures were added, including sometimes Nandimitrā himself. The *lohan* described in this text soon became popular subjects for artists: an example is the T'ang poet and painter Wang Wei (701–761), who was known to have painted forty-eight pictures of the sixteen *lohan*. For a study of this cult in China and Japan, see Michihata Ryōshu, *Raken Shin-kōshi* [The Cult of the Arhats] (Tokyo: Daitō shuppansha, 1983). See also Faure, *Rhetoric of Immediacy,* pp. 266–272.

8. "Shih-pa ta a-lo-han sung," in *SSWC* 2:586–591.

9. See the entry on "The Sixteen Arhats," in G. P. Malalasekera, ed., *Encyclopedia of Buddhism,* vol. 2 (Ceylon: The Government Press, 1966), p. 49.

10. "Shih-pa ta a-lo-han sung," in *SSWC* 2:586–591.

11. Su's brother, Su Ch'e writes about his father's visit in a poem titled "Tseng Ching-fu Shun chang-lao" [Presented to Abbot Shun of Ching-fu], in *Luan-ch'eng chi,* chüan 11 *(SPPY).* By the time Su Shih visited Yüan-t'ung Monastery, almost forty years after his father's visit, Chu-no had passed away. However, Su took the opportunity to write out in his own hand the hymn, found in the *Vimalakīrti Sūtra,* with which the young Licchavi Ratnakara praises the Buddha after having, together with five hundred other youths, presented him with gifts of precious parasols. As it happened to be the anniversary of his father's death, Su presented the piece, along with a poem commemorating his visit, to the resident monk, a Master Ch'ien, in honor of Su Hsün's visits to this temple. *SSSC* 4:1211–1212. Master Ch'ien was delighted and revealed to Su Shih that the night before Su's arrival, he had had a vision of just such a precious parasol, which had appeared suddenly in the empty void and circled around him before disappearing. For a biography of Chu-no, see *CLSPC,* in *HTC* 137:171.

12. See *FTTC,* in *T* 49:474c. Ou-yang Hsiu, one of the most important political leaders and statesmen of the period, referred to Buddhism in his writings as the poison of the people and even went so far as to edit out any reference to Buddhism or Buddhist figures (for instance, there is no mention of the monk Hsüan-tsang's famous journey to India) in his *New T'ang History (Hsin T'ang shu).* However, he also recognized that the reason Buddhism was able to gain such a strong foothold in China was that a spiritual vacuum needed to be filled and that if Buddhism was to be properly refuted, Confucianism would have to get its own house in order. In his private life, Ou-yang often spent time with Buddhist monks, many of whom were well versed in the Confucian classics and men of great cultivation and

literary talent. For further discussion of the nature of Ou-yang's interest in Buddhism, see James T. C. Liu, *Ou-yang Hsiu,* pp. 159–172.

13. See "Pao-yüeh ta-shih t'a ming" [Inscription for the stupa of Eminent Master Pao-yüeh], in *SSWC* 2:467.

14. "Sheng-hsiang yüan ching-ts'ang chi" [An account of the sutra library of the Sheng-hsiang yüan], in *SSWC* 2:388.

15. "Chi-le yüan tsao liu p'u-sa chi" [An account of the making of the (statues of) six bodhisattvas for the Chi-le temple], in *Chia-yu chi,* chüan 14 (*SPPY* edition).

16. Hatch, "Su Shih," p. 905.

17. This area had long been vulnerable to nomadic excursions. In fact, in 1064, one of Su Shih's official duties was to oversee the drafting of soldiers to fight an incursion of Tangut horsemen. Fuller, *Road to East Slope,* p. 80.

18. "Wang Ta-nien ai-tse" [A eulogy for Wang Ta-nien], in *SSWC* 5: 1965–1967. I have been unable to find any further biographical information on Wang.

19. For the story of Su's rather difficult relationship with this man, see Lin Yutang, *The Gay Genius,* pp. 66–69.

20. This is included in the prefatory pieces in the Ming (1621) collection of Su's Buddhist-related poetry, *Tung-p'o Ch'an-hsi chi,* annotated by Ling Meng-ch'u.

21. "Wei-mo hsiang T'ang Yang Hui-chih su tsai T'ien-chu ssu" [The statue of Vimalakīrti by Yang Hui-chih of the T'ang at the T'ien-chu temple], in *SSSC* 1:110–111.

22. Fuller, *Road to East Slope,* p. 94.

23. Translation by A. C. Graham, *Chuang-tzu: The Inner Chapters* (London: George Allen and Unwin, 1981), p. 88. The Ch'ing critic Chi Yün (1724–1805) notes the agile use this poem makes of "the method of first obscuring and then revealing, so that [the poem] simply flows without being stiff or wooden" (see *SSSC* 1:110). Chi Yün is referring, I think, to the way Su combines textual allusions, metaphoric descriptions, personal expressions, philosophical abstractions, and touches of humor, moving from one to the next in a fairly spontaneous manner. This is very much characteristic of Su Shih's best poetry, somewhat reminiscent of the prose style of Chuang-tzu.

24. Graham, *Chuang-tzu: The Inner Chapters,* p. 97.

25. Ibid., p. 99.

26. "Shih K'o hua Wei-mo sung" [A hymn for the Shih K'o painting of Vimalakīrti], in *SSWC* 2:584–585.

27. Su Shih and his father, Su Hsün, were both very fond of the paintings of Wu Tao-tzu, and they made a special effort to see and, if possible,

collect anything they could find by this artist. Su wrote many poems describing these paintings. See H. C. Chang's "Su Tung-p'o's Poems on Wu Tao-tzu," *Tamkang Review* 1, no. 1 (1970), pp. 15–28.

28. This scene, popular with many T'ang and Sung painters, was based on the account of the Buddha's *parinirvāṇa* in the *Nirvāṇa Sūtra* (*T* 375). The *Wen chien hou lu* (chapter 28) describes Wu Tao-tzu's fresco as follows:

> At the K'ai-yuan temple in Feng-hsiang fu, on one of the inner walls of the great hall there is a painting by Wu Tao-tzu which [depicts] the important events of the Buddha's life: his birth, his cultivation of the Dharma, his preaching of the Dharma; and his final attainment of Nirvana. [In this painting we see] the Buddha in a great hall in the middle of the woods, with several thousands of people and tens of thousands of species of animals. It is the most beautiful and perfect work of all the ages. The monks assembled there are all weeping piteously, as if unable to control themselves. Even the birds of the air and the creatures of the ground seem to be crying out [in lamentation]. Only the Buddha himself is as placid as usual, with no trace of sorrow on his face. How could the painter have thus fathomed the mysteries of life and death? The answer was that he was inspired [enlightened?].

Cited and translated in Herbert Giles, *An Introduction to the History of Chinese Pictorial Art* (Shanghai, 1905), p. 45. The T'ang author Chang Yen-yüan, in a 742 description of this fresco, notes that "Feng-hsiang fu is now in the hands of our enemies, and its hamlets and buildings are but heaps of ruins; therefore I have made this record." Quoted in Arthur Waley, *An Introduction to the Study of Chinese Painting* (New York: Grove Press, 1958), p. 45.

29. "Chi so chien K'ai-yüan ssu Wu Tao-tzu hua Fo mieh t'u, i ta Tzu-yu, t'i hua Wen-shu, P'u-hsien" [An account of Wu Tao-tzu's painting of the Buddha's Parinirvana seen at the K'ai-yüan temple, written in response to Tzu-yu's inscription of a painting of Mañjuśrī and Samantabhadra], in *SSSC* 1:170–173. For another translation of this poem, see H. C. Chang, "Su Tung-po's Poems on Wu Tao-tzu," pp. 19–20.

30. See the commentary on the above poem in *SSSC* 1:170. I am unable to locate the original source.

31. However, it would seem that the credit for these luminous images must go to Wu Tao-tzu himself, who was known for his skill at painting aureoles. Giles records a story of how one day when Wu was painting an aureole around a Buddhist figure, "all the people of Chang'an, young and old, scholars and laborers alike, gathered around the picture. . . . The

aureole was produced by a few rapid strokes, which seemed as if driven by a whirlwind, and everybody declared that his hand must have been guided by a god." See Giles, *Chinese Pictorial Art,* p. 46.

32. "Wang Wei Wu Tao-tzu hua" [The paintings of Wang Wei (and) Wu Tao-tzu], in *SSSC* 1:108–110. For another translation of this poem, see H. C. Chang's "Su Tung-p'o's Poems on Wu Tao-tzu" (pp. 16–17). There is also a description of the painting in the *Wen chien hou lu,* translated by Herbert Giles in *Chinese Pictorial Art,* p. 50.

33. Su's Ch'ing dynasty commentator Wang Wen-kao notes that in this regard, Su Shih was very much a man of his time: "Although [Wu Tao-tzu] was a 'Divine Painter' *(hua sheng),* his 'tone' did not coincide with that of the [Sung] literati. Wang Wei was not a 'Divine Painter,' but his 'tone' did coincide with that of the literati." Quoted in Liu I-sheng, ed., *Su Shih shih-hsüan* [Selected poems of Su Shih] (Hong Kong: San-lien shu-tien, 1986), p. 8.

34. K. Ruthven, *Critical Assumptions* (Cambridge: Cambridge University Press, 1979), p. 92.

35. Michael Fuller discusses Su's different uses of the idea of *li* in *The Road to East Slope,* pp. 82–91.

36. For a biography of Huai-lien, see *CLSPC,* in *HTC* 137:257–258, and *FTLTTT,* in *HTC* 49:665b/c.

37. See "Yü Ta-chüeh Ch'an-shih" [To Ch'an Master Ta-chüeh], in *SSWC* 5:1879–1880.

38. "Ch'en-k'uei ko p'ei" [Stele (inscription) for the Ch'en-k'uei Pavilion], in *SSWC* 2:501–502.

39. See "Ssu p'u-sa ko chi" [Account of the pavilion of the four bodhisattvas], in *SSWC* 2:385–386.

40. Hatch, "Su Shih," p. 905.

41. "P'u Hsiang yü Ch'ang-an Ch'en Han-ch'ing chia, chien Wu Tao-tzu hua Fo, t'sui-lan k'o-hsi. Ch'i hou shih yü nien, fu chien chih yü Hsien-yu Tzu-ling chia, tse i chuang-bei wan-hao. Tzu-ling i chien i, tso shih hsieh chih" [When I was staying at the home of Ch'en Han-ch'ing in Ch'ang-an, I saw a painting of the Buddha by Wu Tao-tzu, which unfortunately was tattered and torn. Over ten years later, [when] I again saw it at the home of Hsien-yu Tzu-ling, it had been mounted and completely repaired. Tzu-ling gave it to me, [and] I wrote this poem to thank him]. See *SSSC* 3:829–831.

4: In Buddha Country

1. Hatch, "Su Shih," p. 939.

2. I have relied on the generally reliable Wang Wen-kao for all of these allusions. See *SSSC* 2:347–350.

3. Literally, the breath of clams from the sea, a prescientific explanation of the peculiar phenomenon caused by light.

4. An allusion to *Chuang-tzu:* "The mountain trees do themselves harm; the grease in the torch burns itself up" (Burton Watson, trans., *The Complete Works of Chuang-tzu* [New York: Columbia University Press, 1968], pp. 66–67). The idea is that because the wood of the mountain trees is valuable, they get chopped down, and because the grease can be used for light, it is burned up.

5. "Yu Ching-shan" [An excursion to Ching-shan], in *SSSC* 2:247–250.

6. "Kuo Kuang-ai ssu, chien San-hsüeh Yen shih, kuan Yang Hui-chih su Pao-shan, Chu Yao hua Wen-shu, P'u-hsien" [Passing by the Kuang-ai temple, I met with Master Yen San-hsüeh (and) saw Yang Hui-chih's sculpture of Eagle Peak and Chu Yao's painting of Mañjuśrī and Samantabhadra], in *SSSC* 2:459–461.

7. "I hsüeh-hsiao kung chu chuang" [Memorial regarding the selection of officials by means of examination], in *SSWC* 2:725.

8. "Hai-yüeh Pien-kung chen-ts'an" [A true appreciation of Master Hai-yüeh Pien], in *SSWC* 2:638.

9. See *FTTC,* in *T* 49:214a–215b, for a biography of Fan-chen.

10. "Shih jih su Shui-lu ssu chi Pei-shan Ch'ing-shun seng erh shou" [Two poems (composed) this day while lodging at the Shui-lu ssu and sent to Ch'ing-shun of North Mountain], in *SSSC* 2:390–391.

11. See "Ch'ien-t'ang Ch'in shang-jen shih-chi shu" [A preface to the poetry collection of the eminent (monk) Ch'in of Ch'ien-t'ang], in *SSWC* 6:321–322.

12. "Tseng Hui-ch'in ch'u pa seng chih" [Presented to Hui-chin (on the occasion of) his recent retirement from monastic (administrative) duties], in *SSSC* 2:576–577. "The Drunken Old Man" was a sobriquet used by Ou-yang Hsiu.

13. Quoted in Yu Hsin-li, *Su Tung-p'o ti wen-hsüeh li-lun* (Taipei: Hsüeh-sheng shu-chü, 1980), p. 47

14. Quoted in Ronald C. Egan, *The Literary Works of Ou-yang Hsiu (1007–72)* (Cambridge University Press, 1984), p. 95.

15. "K'o-chiu Ch'ing-shun" [K'o-chiu and Ch'ing-shun], in *SSWC* 6: 2302.

16. "Hsiu-chou Pao-pen Ch'an-yüan hsiang seng Wen chang-lao fang-chang"[Head Priest Abbot Wen, a Szechuanese monk at the Pao-pen Ch'an cloister in Hsiu-chou], in *SSSC* 2:412.

17. "Liu-kuan t'ang tsan" [An appreciation of Six-Meditation Hall], *SSWC* 2:607–608.

18. Toshihiko Izutsu, *Toward a Philosophy of Zen Buddhism* (Boulder: Prajna Press, 1982), p. 100.

19. For an account of Pien-ts'ai's life see *FTLTTT,* in *T* 49:675b/c.

20. "No chai chi" [Account of the Slow Tongue Studio], in *SSWC* 6: 2418–2419.

21. A. C. Graham, *Chuang-tzu: The Inner Chapters,* p. 49.

22. "Chi Lung-ching Pien-ts'ai wen" [A Eulogy for Pien-ts'ai of Lung-ching], in *SSWC* 5:1961.

23. The "White-footed Monk" was the name given to Master Yün-shih, a disciple of Kumārajīva. Legend had it that this monk's feet not only were whiter than his face, but they never got dirty even when he walked through the mud. Later the appellation was sometimes used to refer to monks in general.

24. "Tseng Shang T'ien-chu Pien-ts'ai shih" [Presented to Master Pien-ts'ai of Upper T'ien-chu], in *SSSC* 2:464. The reference in the next to the last line is to an early Sung monk from the K'ao Pao ssu in K'ai-feng who, because he excelled at reciting the *Lotus Sūtra,* was called Lotus Sūtra Chang. He pretended to be crazy but was apparently able to predict the future with remarkable accuracy (see *CLSPC,* in *T* 137:259–260.) The last line refers to an eccentric monk from Su-chou who was fond of frying live carp, which he would eat before they were fully cooked.

25. Su relates these happenings in "No chai chi," *SSWC* 6:2418–2419.

26. The great Ch'an master Lin-chi speaks of "the true man of no fixed position who, from his forehead, sends out the light that shakes the world." Quoted in Lu K'uan-yü (Charles Luk), trans., *The Śūrangama Sūtra (Leng Yen Ching)* (London: Rider and Co., 1966), pp. 12–13, note 1. The *FTLTTT* biography of Pien-ts'ai also notes that often when the monk was deep in solitary meditation, he would emit a light that would fill the room and could be seen by others.

27. The Buddha's teaching is often described as a rain cloud refreshing both the parched earth and "dried-out beings" and causing all life to prosper and flourish. See chapter 5 of the *Lotus Sūtra* (Leon Hurvitz, trans., *Scripture of the Lotus Blossom of the Fine Dharma* [Columbia, 1976], pp. 104–109).

28. Chi K'ang of the Chin dynasty would often train under a large tree. One day Chung Hui came to investigate his activities, but Chi K'ang, knowing his intentions were not good ones, paid no attention to him and continued with his training exercises. After a long time, as Chung Hui was about to leave, Chi K'ang asked him mockingly: "What did you hear that impelled you to come here? What did you see that now impels you to leave?" Su is trying to fit this story into the context of a Ch'an koan that might be used by a Buddhist master who understands the relativity of coming and going.

29. The *anāgāmin (pu-lai),* or the nonreturning arhat, refers to someone who has reached the stage of spiritual cultivation where he or she no longer will be reborn in this world, but will continue to advance toward nirvana from one of the other Buddhist heavens. The reference to "nondwelling" can also be found, among other places, in the *Diamond Sūtra:* "Whoso-

ever says that the Tathagata goes or comes, stands, sits or lies down, he does not understand the meaning of my teaching. And why? 'Tathāgata' is called one who has not gone anywhere, nor come from anywhere. Therefore he is called 'the Tathāgata, the Arhat, the fully Enlightened One' " (Edward Conze, trans., *Buddhist Wisdom Books: The Diamond Sutra and the Heart Sutra* [London: Allen and Unwin, 1958], p. 64). Also, "Subhuti, this son of good family, who is the foremost of those who dwell in Peace, does not dwell anywhere; that is why he is called 'a dweller in Peace, a dweller in Peace' " (p. 44).

30. There were apparently two kinds of arbutus berry that grew in the Hang-chou area, the red and the white. The local people called the white one "holy monk arbutus." This poem is titled "Wen Pien-ts'ai fa-shih fu kuei Shang T'ien-chu, i shih hsi-wen" [Hearing that Dharma Master Pien-ts'ai has returned agin to Upper T'ien-chu, [I] inquire [after him] with a playful poem] (*SSSC* 3:824).

31. Fuller, *Road to East Slope,* p. 171.

32. This idea also meshed with the ideas of Confucian literati such as Ou-yang Hsiu, who in reference to the art of calligraphy spoke of the art of *lodging,* rather than fixing oneself on objects, in order to have the freedom to create spontaneously.

33. In this place there is also a stupa, built in 837, that was said to contain the relics of Bodhidharma, the first patriarch of Ch'an Buddhism.

34. "Hu-pao ch'uan" [Tiger Run Spring], in *SSSC* 2:476.

35. "Shu Chiao shan Lun chang-lao pi" [Written on Abbot Lun's wall at Mt. Chiao], in *SSSC* 2:551.

36. Fuller, *Road to East Slope,* p. 170.

37. "Hai-yüeh Pien-kung chen-tsan" [A sincere encomium for Hai-yüeh Pien-kung], in *SSWC* 2:638.

38. Ibid.

39. An allusion to the Indian monk Tao-sheng (355–434), who used to preach in the Kao-tso ssu, located outside the south gate of the Chin-ling (present-day Nanking) city walls. It was said that when the monk began to preach, even the ghosts and gods would stop to listen and the dharma hall would be filled with light.

40. An allusion to T'ang poet Po Chü-i's (Le-t'ien) preference for Pure Land Buddhism over Taoist practices.

41. "Tiao T'ien-chu Hai-yüeh Pien shih" [A poem of mourning for Hai-yüeh Pien of T'ien-chu], in *SSSC* 2:479–480.

42. Robert A. F. Thurman, trans., *The Holy Teaching of Vimalakīrti* (University Park: Pennsylvania State University Press, 1976), p. 22.

43. "Kuo Yung-le Wen chang-lao i tsui" [Passing by Yung-le, Abbot Wen had already passed away], in *SSSC* 2:566–568.

44. "Ch'ü-nien ch'iu, yü yu Pao-shan shang fang, ju i hsiao yüan, mo-

jan wu jen. Yu i seng, yin chi ti t'ou tu-shu. Yü chih yü. Mo-jan pu shen tui. Wen ch'i lin chih seng, yüeh: Ts'e yün-che-li yeh, pu ch'u shih-wu nien i. Chin nien liu yüeh, tzu Ch'ang, Jun huan, fu chih ch'i shih, tse ssu tsang shu yüeh i. Tso shih t'i ch'i pi" [Last autumn, I happened to make an excursion to the upper reaches of Pao Mountain. I went inside a small monastery, which was quiet and empty but for a monk, his head bent over his table reading. I addressed a few words to him, but he was silent and did not respond. I asked a nearby monk [about him], and he said: "That is Ācārya Yün. He has not been out for fifteen years." In the sixth month of the present year, when I was returning from Ch'ang[-chou] and Jun [-chou], I again stopped by his quarters, but he had already been dead and buried for several months. I wrote this poem and inscribed it on his wall]. *SSSC* 2:575–576.

45. "Shu Nan-hua chang-lao Chung-pien shih i-shih" [An account of the remains of Master Chung-pien, abbot of Nan-hua], in *SSWC* 5:2053. Hui-hung's account in *CLSPC* (*HTC* 137:273–274) also dwells at some length on the wonderful relics that appeared in Ch'i-sung's cremated remains as proof of his high spiritual attainments. See also Faure, *Rhetoric of Immediacy*, p. 139.

46. *SS*, in *T* 19:110c.

47. There are several biographies of Ch'i-sung. In English, there is Jan Yün-hua's biography "Ch'i-sung," in *Sung Biographies* 1:185–194. See also Koichi Shinohara, "Buddhism and Confucianism in Ch'i-sung's Essay on Teaching *(Yüan-tao), Journal of Chinese Philosophy* 9, no. 4 (1982), pp. 401–422, and Huang Chi-chiang, "Experiment in Syncretism: Ch'i-sung (1007–1072) and Eleventh-Century Buddhism" (Ph.D. dissertation, University of Arizona, 1986).

48. Jan Yün-hua, "Ch'i-sung," p. 185.

49. See Mochizuki Shinkō, *Shina Jōdo kyōrishi*, p. 393.

50. "A-mi-t'o-fo sung" [Hymn to Amitabha], in *SSWC* 2:585.

51. *SS*, 114a.

52. Fuller, *Road to East Slope*, p. 161.

53. "Tzu P'u-chao yu erh yen" [An excursion from P'u-chao [Temple] to the two hermitages], in *SSSC* 2:434.

54. Fuller, *Road to East Slope*, p. 161.

5: In a Wilderness of Mulberry and Hemp

1. Hatch, "Su Shih," p. 930.

2. Li I-ping, *Su Tung-p'o chüan* [Biography of Su Tung-p'o] (Hongkong: Lien-ching ch'u-pan shih-yeh kung-ssu, n.d.), 1:329.

3. "Chao-jan t'ai chi" [Account of the Pavilion of Transcendence], in *SSWC* 2:351–352. Michael Fuller translates the entire account in his *Road to East Slope*, pp. 210–212. See also Hatch, "Su Shih," p. 946.

4. *SS,* in *T* 19:111c.

5. "Sung ch'un" [Seeing off spring], in *SSSC* 2:828.

6. Gregory, *Tsung-mi,* p. 7. For translations of this text, see Thomas Cleary, *Entry into the Inconceivable* (Honolulu: University of Hawaii Press, 1983), pp. 69–124, and Robert Gimello, "Chih-yen (602–668) and the Foundations of Hua-yen Buddhism" (Ph.D. dissertation, Columbia University, 1976), pp. 454–512. See also Garma C. C. Chang, *The Buddhist Teaching of Totality* (University Park: Pennsylvania State University Press, 1971), pp. 208–223.

7. Gregory, *Tsung-mi,* p. 7.

8. See Ch'ien Ch'ien-i, *"Shou Leng-yen ching* ho lun," in *HTC* 18: 103–105.

9. According to the *Śūraṃgama Sūtra,* Avalokiteśvara achieved *samādhi* by means of meditation on the organ of hearing. As the bodhisattva himself relates in the sutra:

> At first by directing the organ of hearing into the stream of meditation, this organ was detached from its object, and by wiping out [the concept of] both sound and stream-entry, both disturbance and stillness became clearly non-existent. Thus advancing step by step both hearing and its object ceased completely, but I did not stop where they ended. When the awareness of this state and this state itself were realized as non-existent, both subject and object merged into the void, the awareness of which became all-embracing. With further elimination of the void and its object both creation and annihilation vanished, giving way to the state of Nirvana which then manifested. (Lu K'uan-yü, trans., *Śūrangama Sūtra,* p. 135)

10. "Ch'eng-tu Ta-pei ko chi" [An account of the Pavilion of Great Compassion in Ch'eng-tu], in *SSWC* 2:394–396.

11. *SS,* in *T* 19:129c.

12. Ibid.

13. "Ch'eng-tu Ta-pei ko chi," *SSWC* 2:294.

14. *SS,* in *T* 19:130a–131c.

15. Quoted in Ch'ien Ch'ien-i, *"Leng-yen ching* shu-chüeh meng-ch'ao," in *HTC* 21:767.

16. Quoted in *Tung-p'o i-shih,* ed. Shen Tsung-yüan, p. 44.

17. Ibid.

18. "Ts'an-liao-tzu chen-tsan" [A sincere encomium for Master Ts'an-liao], in *SSWC* 2:639.

19. This refers to China's first "real" poet, Ch'ü Yüan, the fourth century B.C. author of the *Li Sao.* The term was later used to refer generically to all poets.

20. According to the *Vimalakīrti Sūtra,* one of the prerequisites of the bodhisattva is that he is willing to "give up body and life in order to uphold the holy Dharma; never being satisfied with the roots of virtue already accumulated; taking pleasure in skillful dedication, having no laziness in seeking the Dharma; being without selfish reticence in teaching the Dharma" (Thurman, *Holy Teaching of Vimalakīrti,* p. 88).

21. The term "silken words" refers in Buddhism to profane or, more specifically, sexual talk. The literati used it to refer simply to poems having to do with love and romantic themes.

22. The Mani refers to a precious jewel, most often the pearl, which in its luminosity, purity, and perfection is symbolic of the Buddha and his teaching. In the *Nirvāṇa Sūtra* it is said that when the Mani Pearl is thrown into turbid water, the water will become purified.

23. "Tz'u-yün Seng Tao-ch'ien chien ts'eng" [Following the rhymes of (a poem) sent to me by the monk Tao-ch'ien], in *SSSC* 3:879–882.

24. Philip B. Yampolsky, trans., *The Platform Sutra of the Sixth Patriarch* (New York: Columbia University Press, 1967), p. 129.

25. An allusion to the story of a certain Chao Shih-hsiung of the Sui dynasty, who retired to Mount Lo-fu to live. One day as he was resting under some pine trees, he met a beautiful woman, wearing only the lightest of makeup. They drank together and Chao fell into a deep sleep. When he woke he found himself lying under a large plum tree with only a kingfisher feather to remind him of the joys of the previous evening.

26. "Tsai ho Ch'ien shih" [Again harmonizing with (a poem by) Master Chien], in *SSSC* 4:1185–1186.

27. "Chu Shou-ch'ang Liang Wu ch'an ts'an chieh" [*Gāthā* on Chu Shou-ch'ang's appreciation of the *Confessions of (Emperor) Wu of Liang*], in *SSWC* 2:643.

28. "Blow on a flute and you get a nice shrill note; but blow on the ring of your sword hilt and all you get is a feeble wheeze" (Burton Watson, trans., *The Complete Works of Chuang Tzu,* [Columbia, 1968], p. 285).

29. "Sung Ts'an-liao shih" [Seeing off Master Ts'an-liao], in *SSSC* 2: 905–907.

30. Han Yü, "Sung Kao-hsien shang-jen hsü," in *Ch'ing-ting chuang T'ang wen* (Taipei: Hua-lien ch'u-pan-she, 1965 reprint of 1814 ed.), 555: 196–201. Quoted and translated in Ronald C. Egan, *The Literary Works of Ou-yang Hsiu,* p. 97.

31. Ibid.

32. Quoted in Bush, *Literati and the Art of Painting,* p. 50.

33. Ronald C. Egan, "Ou-yang Hsiu and Su Shih on Calligraphy," *Harvard Journal of Asiatic Studies* 29, no. 2 (December 1989), p. 408.

34. Ibid.

35. Richard John Lynn, "The Sudden and the Gradual in Chinese Poetry: An Examination of the Ch'an Poetry Analogy," in *Sudden and Gradual: Approaches to Enlightenment in Chinese Thought,* ed. Peter N. Gregory, Kuroda Institute Studies in East Asian Buddhism 5 (Honolulu: University of Hawaii Press, 1987), pp. 385–386.

36. "Hsiao-chüan p'an-ju hsin-ching ts'an" [An encomium for a copy of the *Heart Sūtra* done in small seal script], in *SSWC* 2:618.

37. For a biography of Fo-yin, see *CLSPC,* in *HTC* 137:279–280.

38. See W. L. Idema, "Poet Versus Minister and Monk," *T'oung Pao* 73 (1987): 209–216, for a discussion of the dramatic works built around these two characters. For a selection of the many witty exchanges between Su Shih and Fo-yin, see Iriya Yoshitaka, "Tōba mu," *Shinagaku* 12 (1947), pp. 347–352.

39. A copy of this text, which scholars date to no later than 1202, is preserved in the Naikaku bunko in Japan. See Chang Cheng-lang, "Wen ta lu yü shuo ts'an-ch'ing," *Kuo-li Chung-yang yen-chiu-yüan li-shih yü-yen yen-chiu-so chi-k'an* 17 (1984), pp. 1–2.

40. See *HTC* 129:791.

41. Master Red Pine is one of the first historical references to magician-ascetics who were able not only to prolong their lives, but also to fly, some to P'eng-lai, the Island of the Immortals. He appears in the *Ch'u-tz'u* [Songs of the south], composed between the third century B.C. and the second century A.D., and is referred to numerous times in the *Pao p'u-tzu* [The Master who embraces simplicity] by Ko Hung (283–343).

42. Legend had it that the island of P'eng-lai, home of the immortals, was separated from the mainland by the thirty-thousand-*li*-long River Jo, making it impossible for anyone but the winged immortals to go there.

43. Some of the first Buddhist monks who arrived in China from Central Asia had blue or green eyes. Since then, this association has remained. (Bodhidharma was sometimes called the blue-eyed foreign monk.) Here Su is referring to Fo-yin.

44. Here Su is comparing Fo-yin to Kumarajiva, who was said to have recited a thousand *gāthās* every single day.

45. The noble youth Sudhana, hero of the *Avataṃsaka Sūtra,* travels in search of enlightenment and visits many teachers. One of the first of these is the monk Sagaramegha (Ch. Te-yün).

46. "Chin shan miao kao t'ai" [The Mt. Sumeru pavilion of Mt. Chin], in *SSSC* 5:1368. The way of immortality refers to the Taoist path, whereas the way of deathlessness refers to the Buddhist path.

47. "Ta Li Tuan-shu shu" [Written in reply to Li Tuan-shu], in *SSWC* 5:1432–1433.

48. "Ta Ch'in T'a-hsü shu" [Written in reply to Ch'in T'a-hsü], in *SSWC* 4:1536.

49. Ch'ien Ch'ien-i, "Tu Su Chang-kung wen" [Reading the writings of Master Su], in *Ch'u-hsüeh chi,* chüan 83 (*SPTK* 88:878).

50. "Ta Pi Chung-chu shu" [Letter written in reply to Secretary Pi], in *SSWC* 4:1671.

51. As Murck puts it: "Tightly reasoned philosophical structures in Su Shih's opinion misrepresent the nature of the Confucian Way, and mislead those who want to follow it. In his own terms, then, Su's reading of the *Chung yung* offers an alternative to what he conceived of as overly dry intellectualism." See his "Su Shih's Reading of the *Chung yung,*" in *Theories of the Arts in China,* ed. Murck and Bush (Princeton: Princeton University Press, 1983), p. 285.

6: AN ANT ON A MILLSTONE

1. According to the *T'ien wen chih* of the *Chin shu,* the edges of the heavens turn to the left like a millstone. The sun and the moon go to the right but also follow the leftward movement of the heavens; therefore, the sun and the moon in fact travel east, and the heavens pull them down into the west. It is like an ant on top of a grinding stone: the stone turns to the left and the ant goes to the right. The stone is fast and the ant is slow; therefore, it has no choice but to go backward following the leftward movement of the stone. For a discussion of these ideas, see Ho Peng-yoke, *Astronomical chapters of the Chin Shu* (Paris: Mouton, 1966).

2. See Liu I-ch'ing, *A New Account of Tales of the World (Shih shuo hsin yü),* trans. Richard Mather (Minneapolis: University of Minnesota Press, 1976), p. 424. "Huan Hsüan was once playing "sequences" (a word game) . . . with Yin Chung-k'an, and they . . . did sequences on the word 'danger.' Huan Hsüan began: Poised on a spear point, rice is washed, and on a sword point steamed."

3. Tu Hsi of the Chin dynasty often admonished and reprimanded the heir-apparent, who finally became piqued and had needles put into the rug Tu usually sat on.

4. "Ch'ien ju Lin-kao t'ing" [Moving to Lin-kao Pavilion], in *SSSC* 4: 1053-1054.

5. See *SS,* in *T* 19:120a, for a scriptural account of how these four wheels were created and how they ensure the continuity of the physical universe.

6. See, for example, Stanley M. Ginsberg's study of these four years of exile, "Reconciliation and Alienation of a Chinese Poet."

7. "Huang-chou An-kuo ssu chi" [An account of the An-kuo ssu of Huang-chou], in *SSWC* 2:391-392. Translated in Andrew March, "Landscape in the Thought of Su Shih," p. 106 (also quoted in Hatch, "Su Shih," pp. 950-951).

8. "Tz'u-yün Tzu-yu 'Yü' pa" [Following the rhymes of Tzu-yu's "Bathing"], in *SSSC* 7:2302–2303.

9. "Ch'i-t'ing," in *SSSC* 4:1203–1209.

10. Ibid.

11. Ibid.

12. "Ying meng lo-han chi" [An account of a dream-manifestation of a *lohan*], in *SSWC* 2:394.

13. Hatch, "Su Shih," p. 934.

14. Sangharakshita summarizes this vision as follows:

> To Sudhana's wondering gaze, the interior of the Tower reveals itself as being as wide as the sky. Besides being all paved with precious stones, it contains countless palaces, porches, windows and other features, besides a corresponding quantity of flowers, wreaths, incense-burners, golden flakes, gem-thrones, and tapestries. There are also innumerable figures wrought of gold and jewels. Countless beautiful birds sing melodiously, while throughout the infinity of the Tower are disposed infinitudes of lotus-flowers in full bloom, rows of trees, and great mani-gems emitting rays of light. Moreover within the tower there are hundreds of thousands of towers, each one as exquisitely adorned as the main tower and as wide as the sky, and each one, while preserving its individual existence, at the same time offering no obstruction to all the rest.

Sangharakshita, *The Eternal Legacy* (London: Tharpa Publications, 1985), pp. 229–230.

15. "Sheng-hsiang yüan ching-tsang chi" [Account of the sutra library of the Sheng-hsiang yüan], in *SSWC* 2:388–389.

16. See "Tung-p'o tsang-chi," in Hui-hung's *Leng-chai yeh-yü* (chüan 5), where he writes:

> When Wang [An-shih] was at Chung Mountain, he had a guest who had come from Huang-chou. Wang asked him: "What wonderful poems has Tung-p'o produced lately?" The guest said: "While Tung-p'o was spending the night at Ling-kao, after waking from an intoxicated dream, he got up and composed the more than thousand lines of [this piece] without stopping to make corrections except for one or two characters. I happen to have a copy in my boat." Wang then quickly went to the boat, and when he arrived the moon had risen over in the southeast, and the shadows of the trees were on the ground. Wang unrolled and read the scroll beneath the eaves, and the pleasure he felt could be seen in his face. And he said, "Tzu-chan is a dragon among men!"

17. *SS,* in *T* 19:115a/b.
18. Ibid.
19. Ibid., 19:126b.
20. A good example, one Su Shih probably was familiar with, can be found in the *Ching-te ch'uan-teng lu* under the entry for Master Pen Ching (d. 761):

> To look at life is like being in a dream;
> It is really noisy being in the dream.
> Everything stops when the dreamer suddenly awakens,
> And in the same way as a dreamer awakes,
> The wise understand how to wake from the dream.
> The deluded believe in the dream and are disturbed
> That understanding and dreaming seem to be two aspects.
> When once the truth is comprehended,
> there is no other comprehension.

See Sohaku Ogata, trans., *The Transmission of the Lamp: Early Masters* (Wakefield, N.H.: Longwood Academic, 1990), p. 176.
21. Toshihiko Izutsu, *Toward a Philosophy of Zen Buddhism,* p. 99.
22. Ibid., p. 101.
23. Tsuchida, *Mind and Reality,* p. 147.
24. "Lun 'Hsiu-yang tieh' chi Tzu-yu" [A discussion of the "Hsiu-yang tieh" sent to Tzu-yu], in *Tung-p'o chih-lin,* chüan 2. See also Lin Yutang, *The Gay Genius,* p. 239.
25. Tsuchida, *Mind and Reality,* p. 154.
26. Yampolsky, *Platform Sutra,* p. 114. The version Su read would not have been exactly the same as the Tunhuang manuscript on which most English translations, including Yampolsky's, are based (*T* 2008). However, he is responding to basically the same ideas.
27. Ibid., p. 115.
28. Ibid., p. 116.
29. Ibid., p. 141.
30. Ibid., p. 181.
31. Ibid., p. 142.
32. "Lun Liu-tzu t'an ching" [A discussion of the *Platform Sutra of the Sixth Patriarch*], in *SSWC* 5:2082–2083.
33. In a dialogue with Ananda, the Buddha says:

> Ananda, if it is called not seeing when there is no light, [a person] should not see darkness. If he does, this is because there is no light; how then can there be no seeing? Ananda, in the dark, if this is

called not seeing solely because he does not see the light, then when there is light, if he does not see darkness, this is again called not seeing; thus there would be no seeing in both cases. But in these two states which replace each other, the nature of your seeing does not cease for an instant.

See Lu K'uan-yü, trans., *The Śūrangama Sūtra,* pp. 46–47.

34. Yampolsky, *Platform Sutra,* p. 142.

35. "Lun Liu-tzu t'an ching," in *SSWC* 5:2082–2083.

36. Yampolsky, *Platform Sutra,* p. 178.

37. Ibid., p. 142.

38. Ibid.

39. "Lun Liu-tzu t'an ching," in *SSWC* 5:2082–2083.

40. Ch'ien Ch'ien-i, "Tu Su Chang-kung wen" [Reading the writings of Master Su], in *Ch'u-hsüeh chi,* chüan 83 (*SPTK* 88:878).

41. The five *kleśa*s, or hindrances to liberation, include desire, ill will, sloth and torpor, restlessness, and doubt.

42. "Yü ch'en kuan sung" [Hymn of the fish-bone cap], in *SSWC* 2:593.

43. "Ti-yü pien hsiang chieh" [*Gāthā* of the "Transformation painting of the (Buddhist) hells"], in *SSWC* 2:644.

44. "Pa Wu Tao-tzu ti-yü" [A colophon about Wu Tao-tzu's hells], in *SSWC* 5:2212.

45. Hui-hung, *Shih-men wen-tzu Ch'an* (*SPTK* 320:1).

46. Thomas Cleary, trans., *The Flower Ornament Scripture: A Translation of the Avatamsaka Sutra* (Boulder: Shambhala, 1986), vol. 1.

47. For biographies of Ch'ang-ts'ung, see *CLSPC,* in *T* 137:268–269, and *FTLTTT,* in *T* 49:674a/b.

48. See Gregory, *Tsung-mi,* pp. 306–307.

49. See Ch'ien Ch'ien-i, *Ta-Fo ting shou Leng-yen ching shu chüeh men-ch'ao,* in *HTC* 21:769.

50. "Tung-lin ti i tai Kuang-hui Ch'an-shih chen-tsan" [A sincere encomium for the first-generation Ch'an master of Kuang-hui (temple) at Tung-lin], in *SSWC* 2:623.

51. Dōgen Zenji, *Shōbōgenzō* [The Eye and treasury of the true law], vol. 1, trans. Kosen Nishiyama and John Stevens (Tokyo: Daihokkaikaku, 1973), p. 92.

52. "Tseng Tung-lin Ts'ung chang-lao" [Presented to Abbot Ts'ung of Tung-lin], in *SSSC* 4:1218–1219.

53. Thomas Cleary, trans., *Entry into the Realm of Reality: The Text* (Boston: Shambhala Press, 1989), p. 166.

54. Dōgen, *Shōbōgenzō* 1:92.

55. Ibid.

56. This anecdote is quoted in Jung Hsi, "Su Tung-p'o tu-tzu li te Ch'an tsung ku hsün" [Bones of the Ch'an sect in the belly of Su Tung-p'o] *Jen sheng,* no. 18 (March 1954), pp. 15–16.

57. Ken Wilber, *Eye to Eye* (New York: Anchor Book, 1983), p. 156.

58. Ibid.

59. "T'i Hsi-lin pi" [Written on the wall at Hsi-lin Temple], in *SSSC* 4:1219.

60. See the commentary to the above poem in *SSSC* 4:1219.

61. A. C. Graham, trans., *Chuang-tzu: The Inner Chapters,* p. 89.

62. An allusion to Chuang-tzu's "External Things" chapter:

> All things that have consciousness depend upon breath. But if they do not get their fill of breath, it is not the fault of Heaven. Heaven opens up the passages and supplies them day and night without stop. But man on the contrary blocks up the holes. The cavity of the body is a many-storied vault, the mind has its Heavenly wanderings. But if the chambers are not large and roomy, then the wives and sisters will fall to quarreling. If the mind does not have its Heavenly wanderings, then the six apertures of sensation will defeat each other. (Watson, trans., *The Complete Works of Chuang-tzu,* pp. 300–301.)

63. The reference to the gossamer thread of life is from the *Tao-te-ching:* "Lingering like gossamer, it has only a hint of existence / and yet when you draw upon it it is inexhaustible" (quoted in A. C. Graham, *Chuang-tzu,* p. 161).

64. "Sung Ch'ien tao-shih kuei Lu-shan" [Seeing off Taoist Master Ch'ien on his return to Mt. Lu], in *SSSC* 5:1597–1598.

65. Hatch, "Su Shih," p. 935.

7: A THOUSAND KALPAS IN THE PALM OF HIS HAND

1. Literally, the Duke of Yang. Legend has it that the duke of the ancient state of Yang became a water god after he died from drowning. The P'eng-lai pavilion was located in the mountains on the northern coast of Shantung. It had been built on the ruins of a shrine to the Sea God. In another poem written the same year, called "Hai shih," or "Mirage at Sea," Su describes a mirage that sometimes appeared off the coast and was said to be a vision of the Sea God's palace.

2. In a poem written in 1071 on the occasion of an excursion to Mt. Chin, Su describes how on dark nights one could sometimes see a flickering flamelike object that would move about marshes like a man holding a candle. The Chinese called this phenomenon, akin to what we know as the will-o'-the-wisp, the "dark fire," or *yin huo.*

3. "Our universe" is Jambudvipa, the southern of the four continents that, according to early Indian Buddhist cosmology, comprise all of the world inhabited by human beings. It is located south of Mt. Meru and derives its name from the fact that it was said to be shaped like a triangle resembling the triangular leaves of the Jambu trees. The *Śūraṃgama Sūtra* contains the following:

> Perfect and clear by nature is the Bodhi ocean,
> Pure and faultless Bodhi is in essence wonderful.
> Its fundamental brightness shone, so by chance creating
> An object which then obscured its radiant nature.
> Thus in delusion there appeared one-sided emptiness
> In which an imaginary world arbitrarily was built.
> Steadying itself, the thinking process made the continents
> While the (illusory) being became a living being.
> The voidness so created within Bodhi
> Is but a bubble in the ocean.
> Worldly realms, countless as the dust, arose
> In this (relative) emptiness.
> When the bubble bursts, the void's unreality
> Is exposed: how much more so is that of the three realms?

Lu K'uan-yü, trans., *Śūrangama Sūtra,* p. 143.

4. "Wen-teng P'eng-lai ko hsia, shih pi ch'ien chang, wei hai lang so chan, shih yu ts'ui lieh, t'ao-sa sui chiu, chieh yüan shu k'o-ai, tu jen wei ts'e t'an-tzu huo yeh. Ch'u shu pai chang, i yang shih ch'an-p'u, ch'ieh tso shih i Ch'ui-tz'u t'ang lao-jen" (Below the Peng-lai pavilion in Wen-teng there is a thousand-*chang*-high rock cliff, pieces of which sometimes break off from the force of the waves hitting against it. [These pieces] have been worn down over a long period of time and become round and smooth and attractive. The natives call this [place] the "Pellet Whirlpool." I took several hundred pebbles in order to make beds for my calamus plants; I also composed a poem to send to the Old Man of Ch'ui-tz'u Hall). *SSSC* 5: 1651–1652.

5. Hsi-ho is the Apollo of Chinese myth, who pulls the chariot of the sun and is thus symbolic of time.

6. "Ho Chiang Fa-yün" [Accompanying Transport Minister Chiang], in *SSSC* 5:1432.

7. Thurman, *The Holy Teaching of Vimalakīrti,* p. 94.

8. Izutsu, *Toward a Philosophy,* p. 43.

9. *SS,* in *T* 19:119. This is an idea that is found over and over in Hua-yen Buddhism with its philosophy of totality and interpenetration. In his history of Chinese philosophy, Jen Chi-yü points out how the Hua-yen mas-

ters sought to upset conventional distinctions between the one and the many so as to demonstrate their total interdependence. He quotes from various Buddhist commentaries and then goes on to conclude that

> Those who believe in non-definite forms say that because what is small is not definitely [unchangeably] small, therefore it can contain what is large; The large, because it is not unchangeably large, can contain the small. . . . The large is the small, the small is the large. The small lack definite characteristics, therefore it can circulate naturally throughout the ten regions [of the universe]; the large does not have a definite shape, therefore it can illuminate the world over the karmic ages. Thus, one can know that the small is in fact large: Mount Sumeru is contained within a mustard seed; and the large is in fact small: the waters of the ocean can be contained within the palm of the hand.

Jen Chi-yün, *Chung-kuo che-hsüeh shih* (Peking: Jen-min ch'u-pan-she, 1964), 3:63.

10. "Shu Leng-chia ching hou" [A postscript to the *Laṅkāvatāra Sūtra*], in *SSWC* 5:2085–2086.

11. For this and the previous quote, see ibid., p. 2085. In another account it is said that Chang recognized the script as being his own and that he had been a monk scribe in the library of the Lang-yeh monastery in Hsü-chou who had passed away before completing his copy. See Hui-hung, *Leng-chai yeh-hua* (Peking: Chung-hua shu-chü, 1988), 7.3b.

12. "Shu Leng-chia ching hou," in *SSWC* 5:2085. I have here used (with certain modifications) D. T. Suzuki's translation of this passage in *Studies in the Lankavatara Sutra* (London: George Routledge and Sons, 1932), p. 58.

13. Ibid., p. 96.

14. Although the origins of the *shui-lu chai* are not altogether clear, the ceremony seems to be a combination of Tantric rituals for the dead with a rite traditionally attributed to Emperor Wu of Liang. Tradition has it that this emperor was told in a dream of the intolerable sufferings of all the creatures in the six samsaric realms and urged to offer a ceremony of this kind for the relief of their souls. The first *shui-lu chai* seems to have taken place at Mt. Chin Temple around 505 or 508. It was occasionally performed during the T'ang as well, but enjoyed a minor revival during the Northern Sung. In 1084, several years before Su's return to Hang-chou, his friend Fo-yin Liao-yüan had personally conducted a large-scale *shui-lu* ceremony at Mt. Chin sponsored by a group of sea merchants. In 1093, when Su was serving as magistrate of Ting-chou in Hupei province, he would himself sponsor a *shui-lu* ceremony on behalf of his departed second wife,

Wang Fu-chih. For a description of this ceremony and its history, see the entry by Lin Tzu-ch'ing in *Chung-kuo Fo-chiao* 2:383–387.

15. "Pien-ts'ai lao-shih t'ui-chü Lung-ching, pu fu ch'u-ju. Yü wang chien chih. Ch'ang ch'u chih Feng-hsüan ling. Tso-yu ching yüeh: 'Yüan kung fu kuo Hu-hsi i.' Pien-ts'ai hsiao yüeh: 'Tu Tzu-mei pu yün hu: "Yü tzu ch'eng er lao, lai wang i feng-liu." ' Yin tso t'ing ling shang, ming yüeh Kuo-hsi, i yüeh erh lao, ch'in tz'u Pien-ts'ai yün fu shih i shou" [Once Master Pien-ts'ai retired to Lung-ching, he never left it. Once when I was there on a visit, we (traveled) all the way to Feng-huang Peak. Startled, I looked around and said: "Master Yüan has once again crossed the Dragon Stream!" Pien-ts'ai laughed and said: "Did not Tu Tzu-mei (Tu Fu) say: 'I will grow old together with you, coming and going we will be as carefree as the wind?' " And so we built a pavilion on top of the peak, which we called "Crossing the Stream" or (simply) "The Two Oldsters." Respectfully, I composed a poem to harmonize with the rhymes of (a poem by) Pien-ts'ai]. *SSSC* 5:1714–1716.

16. "Kuei-shan Pien-ts'ai shih" [Master Pien-ts'ai of Mt. Kuei], in *SSSC* 4:1295–1296.

17. Graham, *Chuang-tzu*, p. 95.

18. Quoted in the notes to "Shu Pien-ts'ai ts'e-yün Ts'an-liao shih" [A calligraphy of Pien-ts'ai's (poem) following the rhymes of (a Poem by Ts'an-liao), in *SSWC* 5:2144.

19. Ibid.

20. See "T'ang Hu-chou Chu-shan Chiao-jan chüan" [Biography of T'ang dynasty Chu-shan Chiao-jan of Hu-chou], in *Tōdai no shijin: Sono denki* [The Biographies of the monk-poets of the T'ang dynasty], edited by Ogawa Tamaki (Tokyo: Taishūkan shoten, 1975), pp. 625–635.

21. The *Shan-hai ching* [Classic of mountains and seas] speaks of a bird with a human tongue—obviously a parrot—that lived on Mt. Huang and spoke like a child, that is, naturally and spontaneously. This line may mean that the monk speaks (and writes) with spiritual spontaneity, but it may simply mean that, like a child, Chung-shu loves to eat sweet things. See, for example, the *Ssu-shih-er chang ching* [Sutra of forty sections]: "Sex and money are like a sword coated with honey; If a child licks it, there is the danger of cutting his tongue." *T* 784:723.

22. The antidote prescribed by the doctor for the poison administered by his jealous wife was honey. Although Chung-shu never again ate meat, he apparently retained his love of honey. There is a story that one day Su and some friends visited Chung-shu and were served a meal all of which was cooked with honey. Su was the only one who was able to eat everything, and so was the only one who left the table satisfied.

23. "An-chou lao-jen shih mi ko" [Song of the honey-eating old man from An-chou], in *SSSC* 5:1707–1708.

24. For biographical information on this monk, see *CLSPC*, in *HTC* 137:278–279; and *FTLTTT*, in *T* 49:679b/c–680a.

25. "Sung Hsiao-pen Ch'an-shih fu Fa-yün" [Sending off Ch'an Master Hsiao-pen to Fa-yün], in *SSSC* 6:1757.

26. The Triloka, the three worlds of sensuous desire (kāmaloka), form (rūpaloka), and the formless world of pure spirit (arūpaloka).

27. "Kuan-t'ai" [Meditation tower], in *SSSC* 5:1688.

28. *SS,* in T 19:127.

29. These refer to some of the cosmological ideas of Su's day. One of these held that heaven was like an egg and the earth was the yolk in the center of the egg. Outside this "egg" was a body of water on which both earth and heaven floated.

30. See Chuang-tzu's "Autumn Floods": "Compare the area within the four seas with all that is between heaven and earth—is it not like one little anthill in a vast marsh? Compare the Middle Kingdom with the area within the four seas—is it not like one tiny grain in a great storehouse? . . . What the Five Emperors passed along, what the Three Kings fought over, what the benevolent man grieves about, what the responsible man labors over— all is not more than this!" (Watson, trans., *The Complete Works of Chuang-tzu,* p. 176).

31. National Teacher Wu-yeh of Fen-chou once said: "Look at those men of the past who attained the Way: after doing so, they lived in thatched huts or stone rooms, and breaking off the shackles around their feet, they used them to cook their rice." Here Su seems to be referring to the ability of Abbot Yüeh to attain a state of inner freedom despite, or rather because of, his rigorous spiritual discipline. This story is from the *Ching-te ch'uan-teng lu,* although I have been unable to track down the exact location.

32. *Wei-na* is the Chinese transliteration of *karmadana,* or the duty distributor, the second highest position (after that of the abbot) in the monastery.

33. "Tseng Yüeh chang-lao" [Presented to Abbot Yüeh], in *SSSC* 6: 1802–1803. "Thereupon, the Buddha said to the Licchavi Vimalakīrti, 'Noble son, when you would see the Tathāgata, how do you view him?' Thus addressed, the Licchavi Vimalakīrti said to the Buddha, "Lord, when I would see the Tathāgata, I view him by not seeing any Tathāgata. Why? I see him as not born from the past, not passing on to the future, and not abiding in the present time." (Thurman, trans., *The Holy Teaching of Vimalakīrti,* p. 91).

34. *SS,* in *T* 19:111.

35. "Shui-lu fa-hsiang tsan" [An encomium for the dharma images (of the) land and water (ritual)], in *SSWC* 2:631–635.

36. Ibid., p. 631.

37. "Chieh sha" [Renouncing killing], in *Tung-p'o chih-lin/Ch'ou ch'ih pi-chi* (Su-chou: Hua-tung Shih-fan ta-hsüeh ch'u-pan-she, 1983), pp. 226–227.

38. Junjirō Takakusu, *The Essentials of Buddhist Philosophy,* edited by W. T. Chan and Charles A. Moore (Honolulu: University of Hawaii, 1947), p. 137.

39. *SS, T* 19:145.

40. "Shu *Chin-kuang-ming ching* hou," in *SSWC* 5:2086–2087.

41. Sangharakshita, *Eternal Legacy,* p. 248. There are several translations of this text, including *The Sutra of Golden Light,* trans. by R. E. Emmerick (London, 1970).

42. "Shu *Chin-kuang-ming ching* hou," in *SSWC* 5:2086–2087.

43. "Pa Wang-shih *Hua-yen ching* chüeh" [A colophon for Master Wang's commentary on the *Avataṃsaka Sūtra*] in *SSWC* 5:2060.

44. "Shu Chin-kuang-ming ching hou," in *SSWC* 5:2087.

45. "Tseng Ch'ing-liang ssu Ho Chang-lao" [Presented to Abbot Ho of Ching-liang ssu], in *SSSC* 6:2031–2032.

46. "Nan-hua ssu" [Nan-hua temple], in *SSSC* 6:2061–2062.

47. Vincent Yang, *Nature and Self: A Study of the Poetry of Su Dongpo with Comparisons to the Poetry of William Wordsworth* (New York: Peter Lang, 1989), p. 168.

8: Like a Withered Tree

1. "Kuo Ta-yü ling" [Passing over Ta-yü Peak], in *SSSC* 6:2056–2057.

2. See Chung Lai-yin, *Su Shih yü tao-chia, tao-chiao,* p. 157.

3. "Ch'ien chü" [Moving house], in *SSSC* 7:2194–2196.

4. A. C. Graham, trans., *Chuang-tzu,* p. 43.

5. *SS,* in *T* 19:127.

6. The T'ang dynasty essayist and poet Liu Ts'ung-yüan spent his last years in the south as an official of Liu-chou. He was so highly regarded that he was called Liu Liu-chou. In a stele written by Han Yü at the Lo-ch'ih temple of Liu-chou, Han Yü records how a local temple was made into a shrine in honor of Liu Ts'ung-yüan and how the local farmers would bring red lichee as offerings.

7. See James R. Ware, *Alchemy, Medicine and Religion in the China of* A.D. *320: The Nei P'ien of Ko Hung* (Pao-p'u tzu) (Cambridge, Mass: The M.I.T. Press, 1966), p. 47.

8. "Chi yu Sung-feng t'ing" [An account of an excursion to Pine Wind Pavilion], in *SSWC* 5:2271. See also Andrew March's translation in "Self

and Landscape in Su Shih," *Journal of the American Oriental Society* 86, no. 3 (1966), p. 379.

9. Chü Meng was a Han dynasty knight-errant from Loyang who was known not only for his valor, but also for his fondness for gambling.

10. Grdhrakuta, or Eagle Peak, where the Buddha is said to have often preached. It is also the imaginary setting for the preaching of the *Lotus Sūtra,* which is also known as the *Eagle Peak Gāthā.* Here Su is saying that Wu has made a vow to retire to a life of spiritual cultivation and seclusion.

11. "Wen Ch'ao-yang Wu Tzu-yeh ch'u chia" [Hearing that Wu Tzu-yeh of Ch'ao-yang has "left home"], in *SSSC* 8:2554-2555.

12. "Wen Yang-sheng" [Asking about "nourishing life"], in *SSSW* 5: 1982-1983.

13. "Meng chai ming," in *SSWC* 2:575-576.

14. In the Han dynasty poet Ssu-ma Hsiang-ju's famous *fu* (prose-poem) titled "Sir Fantasy," one of the narrators boasts that of the state of Ch'u's seven marshes or lowlands, the smallest of them, called Cloud-Dreams (Yün-meng), is nine hundred *li* square, and in the center there is a mountain "which winds and twists upward, rearing its lofty crags on high, covered with jagged jutting peaks, that blot out the sun and moon and entangle them in their folds." See Burton Watson, *Chinese Rhyme-Prose* (New York: Columbia University Press, 1971), p. 31.

15. "Wu Tzu-yeh chiang ch'u-chia tseng i shan shan chen-p'ing" [Presented to Wu Tzu-yeh on the occasion of his setting forth into the homeless life along with a folding pillow screen painted with a mountain landscape], in *SSSC* 6:1974-1975. This same image also appears in the opening couplets of an inscription Su wrote on a fresco said to have been painted by a monk from Szechuan on a temple wall in Hui-chou. The painting depicts an intoxicated monk with his face lifted toward the heavens.

> Staring straight up into the Beginningless
> His breath spits out rainbows;
> The Five Lakes and the Three Islands
> All exist within his breast.

See "Hui-chou Ling-hui yüan, pi chien hua i yang mien hsiang t'ien seng, yün shih Shu seng Ying-lien so-tso, t'i shih yü ch'i hsia" [On the walls of the Ling-hui yüan in Hui-chou is a painting of an intoxicated monk with his face lifted toward the sky; it is said to be the work of a monk from Shu, Ting-lien, [so] I inscribed a poem beneath it]. *SSSC* 6:2558-2559.

16. "Tseng T'an-hsiu" [Presented to T'an-hsiu], in *SSSC* 7:2190.

17. "Tz'u-yün Ting-hui Ch'in chang-lao chien chi pa shou" [Following the rhymes of eight poems sent to me by Abbot Ch'in of Ting-hui], in *SSSC* 7:2114-2118.

18. Su was not overly fond of Chia Tao's poetry, once commenting that it was too "bony." See "Shou-ch'in" [Shou-ch'in], in *SSWC* 6:2301.

19. In another poem written in Hai-nan, Su describes a five-feather oriole he saw there. This bird has often been associated with Mt. Lo-fu.

20. There is a reference in the *Shen hsien chuan* [Biographies of the Immortals], a collection of biographies of eighty-four Taoist masters, traditionally ascribed to Ko Hung, to a man who one day saw two fine-looking dogs chasing each other into a grove of aspens. Wondering at this, he dug up the trees and found that their roots were in the shape of dogs.

21. *SS,* in *T* 19:125.

22. See *Analects* 2:2. "The Master said, 'In the Book of Poetry are three hundred pieces, but the design of them all may be embraced in one sentence: "Having no depraved thoughts" ' " (James Legge, *The Four Books,* [New York: Paragon Book Reprint Corp., 1966], p. 135).

23. "Ssu wu hsieh chai ming" [An Inscription for the studio of "Having No Depraved Thoughts"], in *SSWC* 2:575–576.

24. "Hui-chou ch'ien Ch'ao-yün shu" [A sacrificial prayer (written) for Ch'ao-yün in Hui-chou], in *SSWC* 5:1909–1910.

25. Twenty *li* northeast of Hui-chou was Pai-shui (White Water) Mountain, which contained a Buddha's Footprint Peak and the Buddha's Footprint Monastery. Next to the waterfall were several tens of very large footsteps, which local legend attributed to the Buddha. Su may well have had this location in mind when he wrote this piece.

26. "Hui-chou ch'ien Ch'ao-yün shu," in *SSWC* 5:1909–1910.

27. See chapter 1 of Tairyō Makita's *Chūgoku kinsei Bukkyō shi kenkyū* [Researches in the history of Modern Chinese Buddhism] (Kyoto: Heirakuji shoten, 1957) for discussion of the cult of Sangha during the Sung dynasty.

28. "Seng-chia tsan" [An encomium for Seng-chia], in *SSWC* 2:619, and "Ssu-chou Seng-chia t'a" [The pagoda of Seng-chia in Ssu-chou], in *SSSC* 1:289.

29. See *FTTC,* in *T* 49:369b/c.

30. "Tz'u-yün tseng Ch'ing-liang chang-lao" [Following the rhymes (of an Old Poem) and presented to the abbot of Ch'ing-liang], in *SSSC* 7:2456.

31. "Yü Wang Hsiang shu" [Letter to Wang Hsiang], in *SSWC* 4:1422–1423.

32. Chapter 16 of the *Tao-te-ching:* "Returning to one's roots is known as stillness" see D. C. Lau, trans., *Mencius* (New York: Penguin Books, 1970) p. 72.

33. From the *Vimalakīrti Sūtra:* "To say, 'This is impure' and 'This is immaculate' makes for duality. One who, attaining equanimity, forms no conception of impurity or immaculateness, yet is not utterly without con-

ception, has equanimity without any attainment of equanimity—he enters
the absence of conceptual knots. Thus, he enters into nonduality" (Thurman, trans., *The Holy Teaching of Vimalakīrti,* p. 74).

34. The master (Yang Shan Hui-chi, 814–890) asked Hsiang-yen, "What
have you seen recently, brother monk?" Hsiang-yen replied, "I cannot tell
you." But he made a *gāthā:*

> My poverty of last year was not real poverty.
> This year it is want indeed.
> In last year's poverty there was room for a piercing
>   gimlet,
> In this year's poverty even the gimlet is no more.

The master said, "You have the Ch'an of the Tathagatas, but you do not
have the Ch'an of the Patriarchs." See Chang Chungyuan, trans., *Original
Teachings of Ch'an Buddhism* (New York: Grove Press, 1982), p. 215.

35. "Tz'u-yün Tzu-yu yü pa" [Following the rhymes of Tzu-yu's "Bathing"], in *SSSC* 7:2302–2303.

36. Heinrich Dumoulin, S.J., *The Development of Chinese Zen after the
Sixth Patriarch in the Light of Mumonkon,* trans. Ruth Fuller Sasaki (New
York: First Zen Institute of America, 1953), p. 18.

37. "Tzu Nan-hai kuei kuo, kuo Ch'ing-yüan hsia Pao-lin ssu, ching
ts'an Ch'an-yüeh so hua shih-pa ta lo-han" [On (my) return from the
southern sea, I passed by the Pao-lin temple by the Ch'ing-yüan Gorges,
where I reverentially (composed) this appreciation of the eighteen great
arhats], in *SSWC* 2:626–630. For further discussion of these particular
arhats, see the article by Lo Hsiang-lin, "Wang T'ang Kuan-hsiu hui shih-
liu lo-han ying-chen hsiang shih k'o shu cheng" [A report on the stone
carvings of the sixteen great worthy *lohan* painted by Kuan-hsiu of the late
T'ang], in *Hsüeh-shu chi-k'an* 6, no. 7, pp. 1–9.

38. "Chuang-pei lo-han ch'ien Ou-yang fu shu" [The mounting of (a
painting) of *lohan* presented in memory of the (departed) wife of Ou-yang
(Hsiu)], in *SSWC* 5:1909.

39. In China, Piṇḍola Bhāradvāja is perhaps the most famous of the
arhats. He was said to have suffered long in hell with nothing to eat but
bricks and stones; hence his gaunt and haggard appearance. He is also
the guardian of monastery refectories. An anonymous text titled "The Piṇḍola Ritual" *(Ch'ing Pin-t'ou-lü fa),* translated into Chinese in 457,
has this sage man urging the wealthy to provide help to the poor and
aged.

40. "Nan-hua chang-lao t'i-ming chi" [An account of an inscription
written for the abbot of Nan-hua], in *SSWC* 2:393–394.

41. This is an allusion to a passage in the *Lotus Sūtra:*

There are even children who in play
Gather sand and make it into Buddha-stupas.
Persons like these
Have all achieved the Buddha Path.

Hurvitz, trans., *Scripture of the Lotus Blossom of the Fine Dharma,* pp. 38–41.

42. "Nan-hua Chang-lao t'i-ming chi," in *SSWC* 2:393–394.

43. Although there is no specific reference in the text to Vimalakīrti, I take the phrase "do not dare to ask after [his] illness" *(pu jen wen chi)* to be an allusion to the *Vimalakīrti Sūtra.* The great layman-sage Vimalakīrti is master of the use of *upāya,* or skillful means, to teach the Buddhist dharma. In the sutra he feigns a serious illness, and when people (and bodhisattvas) come to inquire after his health, he then engages them in a discussion of various Buddhist doctrinal points, in particular the meaning of emptiness, or *śūnyatā.* Vimalakīrti's understanding is so profound that, one by one, the great bodhisattvas find themselves unable to match that understanding.

44. Wing-tsit Chan, *A Source Book in Chinese Philosophy* (Princeton, N.J.: Princeton University Press, 1963), p. 95. As Tu Wei-ming points out, the *Chung yung* had by the early Sung acquired a reputation as a major classic, and many of the major figures of this period, such as Ssu-ma Kuang (1019–1086), wrote commentaries on it. There were also a number of Buddhist commentaries on this text, including one by Chih-yuan (967–1022), who called himself Master Chung-yung, and Ch'i-sung (1007–1072), a friend of Su Shih's. See Tu Wei-ming, *Centrality and Commonality: An Essay on Confucian Religiousness* (Albany, N.Y.: State University of New York Press, 1989), p. 14.

45. Translated by Wing-tsit Chan, in *A Source Book in Chinese Philosophy,* p. 100.

46. Tu Wei-ming, *Centrality and Commonality,* pp. 31–32.

47. Literally, "boring holes and climbing over walls." See Mencius VIII:B, 31. D. C. Lau's translation of the Mencius passage Su is paraphrasing is as follows:

Mencius said, "For every man there are things he cannot bear. To extend this to what he can bear is benevolence. For every man there are things he is not willing to do. To extend this to what he is willing to do is rightness. If a man can extend to the full his natural aversion to harming others, then there will be an overabundance of benevolence. If a man can extend his unwillingness to suffer the actual humiliation of being addressed as 'thou' and 'thee,' then wherever he goes he will not do anything that is not right.

"To speak to a Gentleman who cannot be spoken to is to use speech as a bait; on the other hand, not to speak to one who could be spoken to is to use silence as a bait. In either case, the action is of the same kind as that of boring holes and climbing over walls."

Mencius, p. 200.

48. "Nan-hua Chang-lao Yi-ming chi," *SSWC* 2:393.

49. Ibid.

50. *SSSC* 2:5861.

51. "Shu tseng Shao tao-shih" [Written and presented to Taoist Shao], in *SSWC* 5:2083.

52. "Shu jih ch'ien, meng i seng ch'u erh ching ch'iu shih, seng i ching chih jih chung, ch'i ying shen i, ch'i i ju pa-chiao, ch'i i ju lien-hua, meng chung yü tso shih." *SSSC* 8:2532–2533.

53. *SS,* in T 19:112b.

54. A kalpa is the period of time between the creation and recreation of a world or universe. A complete period is divided into four kalpas relating to formation, existence, destruction, and nonexistence. Each of these four kalpas is itself divided into twenty small kalpas. Each *mahākalpa,* or complete period, consists of eighty small kalpas.

55. "Ch'i shu-chu tseng Nan Ch'an Shih lao" [Requesting Buddhist rosary beads: presented to Abbot Shih of Nan Ch'an], in *SSSC* 7:2432–2433.

56. This according to Wang Wen-kao; see the commentary on *SSWC* 5:2083. I have been unable to locate the original source.

57. "Shu tseng Shao tao-shih," in *SSWC* 5:2083.

58. See Junjirō Takakusu, *Essentials of Buddhist Philosophy,* pp. 157–159, for a discussion of Tathāgata and Patriarchal meditation.

59. See the commentary in *SSWC* 5:2083. I have been unable to locate the original source.

60. "Tseng Ch'ien-chou shu-shih Hsieh Chin-ch'en" [Presented to the Ch'ien-chou diviner Hsieh Chin-ch'en], in *SSSC* 7:2430.

61. "San hsing hsing" [Song of three stars], in *Ch'üan t'ang shih,* (Peking: Chung-hua shu-chü, 1960), chüan 339 (vol. 10, p. 3798).

62. *T* 19:131.

63. "Ta Ching-shan Lin chang-lao" [Reply to Abbot Lin of Mt. Ching], in *SSSC* 7:2439.

64. See Hui-hung, *Shih-men t'i-pa* 2:20.

65. *HTC* 109:407.

9: EPILOGUE

1. Hatch, "Su Shih," p. 901.

2. Ibid.

3. Bol, *"This Culture of Ours,"* p. 258.

4. Ibid., p. 282.

5. Ibid., p. 266.

6. Ibid.

7. Ibid., p. 291.

8. "Su-chou ch'ing T'ung chang-lao shu" [A memorial prayer (written in) Su-chou for Abbot T'ung], in *SSWC* 5:1905.

9. Bol, *"This Culture of Ours,"* pp. 284–285.

10. Ibid., p. 274.

11. Ibid., pp. 274–275.

12. Ibid., p. 275.

13. "Wu-ming ho-shang sung Kuan-yin chieh" [A *gāthā* on a hymn to Kuan-yin by the monk Wu-ming], in *SSWC* 2:642.

14. Bol, *"This Culture of Ours,"* p. 274.

15. Ibid.

16. "Tsai ho Chien shih," in *SSSC* 4:1185.

17. "Sung Ts'an-liao shih," in *SSSC* 2:908.

18. "Sung Ch'ien-t'ang seng Ssu-ts'ung kuei Ku-shan hsü" [A preface (written on the occasion of) sending off the monk Ssu-ts'ung on his return to Mt. Ku], in *SSWC* 1:325–336. Translation by Peter Bol, in ibid., p. 296, modified.

19. Ibid.

20. Ibid., p. 298.

21. "Kuei-shan Pien-ts'ai shih," in *SSSC* 4:1296.

22. Yoshitaka Iriya, "Chinese Poetry and Zen," *The Eastern Buddhist,* n.s. 6, no. 1 (May 1973), p. 59.

23. "Hsi shu" [Written in jest], in *SSSC* 8:2552.

24. Bol, *"This Culture of Ours,"* p. 274.

SELECT BIBLIOGRAPHY

Abe, Masao. "Buddhism." In *Our Religions,* ed. Arvind Sharma, pp. 71–137. San Francisco: Harper, 1993.

Andō Tomonobu. "O An-seki to bukkyō: Shōzan inseiki o chūshin to shite"[Wang An-shih and Buddhism, with a focus on his retirement at Chung-shan]. *Tōhō shūkyō* 28 (1966), pp. 20–34.

App, Urf Erwin. "Facets of the Life and Teachings of Ch'an Master Yun-men Wenyen (864–949)." Ph.D. diss., Temple University, 1989.

Asakura Hisashi. *Zenrin no bungaku: Chūgoku bungaku juyō* [Zen literature: the influence of Chinese literature] (Osaka: Seibundō, 1985).

Bielefeldt, Carl. "Ch'an-lu Tsung-tse's *Tso-ch'an I* and the Secret of Zen Meditation." In *Traditions of Meditation in Chinese Buddhism,* ed. Peter N. Gregory, pp. 143–144. The Kuroda Institute Studies in East Asian Buddhism 4. Honolulu: University of Hawaii Press, 1986.

———. *Dōgen's Manuals of Zen Meditation.* Berkeley: University of California Press, 1988.

Bol, Peter. *"This Culture of Ours": Intellectual Transitions in T'ang and Sung China.* Stanford: Stanford University Press, 1992.

Bush, Susan. *The Literati and the Art of Painting: Su Shih (1036–1101) to Tung Chi-chang (1555–1636).* Cambridge, Mass.: Harvard University Press, 1971.

Chan, Leo Tak-hung. "Techniques of Persuasion: Proselytism and Pure Land Buddhism in Sung China." *Chinese Culture* 32, no. 3 (September 1991), pp. 21–36.

Chan, Wing-tsit. "The Evolution of the Neo-Confucian Concept of *Li* as Principle." *Tsing Hua Journal of Chinese Studies,* n.s. 4, no. 2 (February 1964), pp. 123–148.

———. *A Source Book in Chinese Philosophy.* Princeton, N.J.: Princeton University Press, 1963.

Chang, Carson. *The Development of Neo-Confucian Thought.* New Haven: College and University Press, 1963.

Chang Chien. "Su Shih wen-hsüeh p'i-p'ing yen-chiu" [Study of Su Shih's literary criticism]. In *Sung Chin ssu-chia wen-hsüeh p'i-p'ing yen-chiu*

[Studies in the literary criticism of four figures of the Sung and Chin], 2:116. Taipei: Liao-ching ch'u-pan, 1975.

Chang Chungyuan, trans. *Original Teachings of Ch'an Buddhism*. New York: Grove Press, 1982.

Chang, Garma C. C. *The Buddhist Teaching of Totality*. University Park: Pennsylvania State University Press, 1971.

Chang, H. C. "Su Tung-p'o's Poems on Wu Tao-tzu." *Tamkang Review* 1, no. 1 (1970), pp. 15–28.

Cheang, Alice Wen-chuen. "The Way and the Self in the Poetry of Su Shih (1037–1101)." Ph.D. diss., Harvard University, 1971.

Ch'en Erh-t'ung. *Su Shih shih hsüan* [Selected poems of Su Shih]. Peking: Jen-min wen-hsüeh ch'u-pan-she, 1957.

———. *Su Tung-p'o shih tz'u hsüan* [Selection of Su Tung-p'o's poems and lyrics]. Wen-hsüeh hsiao ts'ung-shu 123. Peking: Jen-min wen-hsüeh ch'u-pan-she, 1960.

Ch'en, Kenneth. *Buddhism in China: A Historical Survey*. Princeton University Press, 1964.

Chi Yün. *Su Wen-chung Kung shih chi*. Taipei: Hung-yeh, 1969; reprint of 1917 reprint of the 1836 edition.

Chikusa Masaaki. "So Shoku to Bukkyō" [Su Shih and Buddhism]. *Tōhō gakuhō*, no. 36 (October 1964), pp. 457–480.

———. *So Tōba* (Su Tung-p'o). Tokyo: Jimbutsu ōraisha, 1967.

———. "Ssu-ma Kuang Wang An-shih yü Fo-chiao" [Ssu-ma Kuang and Wang An-shih and Buddhism]. In *Chi-nien Ssu-ma Kuang Wang An-shih shih-shih chiu-pai chou-nien hsüeh-shu yen-t'ao-hui lun-wen chi* [Collected articles from the scholarly symposium commemorating the nine-hundredth anniversary of the deaths of Ssu-ma Kuang and Wang An-shih]. Taipei: Wen shih che, 1986.

Chou I-kan, "Pei Sung ti Ch'an tsung yü wen-hsüeh" [Northern Sung Ch'an sect and literature]. *Wen-hsüeh i-ch'an* no. 3, 1983, pp. 44–50.

Chou Yü-k'ai, "Wen-tzu Ch'an yü Sung-tai shih hsüeh" [Literary Ch'an and Sung dynasty poetics]. In *Kuo-chi Sung-tai wen-hua yen-chiu t'ao-hui lun-wen-chi* [An anthology of theses from the International Symposium on the Culture of the Sung Dynasty], ed. Sun Ch'in-shan et al. Ch'eng-tu, Szechuan: Szechuan ta-hsüeh ch'u-pan-she, 1991.

Chu Hsi, *Chu-tzu yü-lei,* Comp. by Li Ching-te, ed. by Lang Yeh, 1173 (Taipei: Shih-chieh reprint, 1960, 2 volumes).

Chung-kuo Fo-chiao [Chinese Buddhism]. Compiled by the Chinese Buddhist Association. 4 volumes. Shanghai: Chih-shih ch'u-pan-she, 1989 edition.

Chung Lai-yin. *Su Shih yü Tao-chia, Tao-chiao* [Su Shih and Taoist philosophy, Taoist religion]. Taipei: Taiwan hsüeh-sheng shu-chü, 1990.

Clark, Cyril Drummond Le Gros. *The Prose-Poetry of Su T'ung-p'o.* 2d ed. New York: Paragon Book Reprint Corp., 1964.

———. *Selections from the Works of Su Tung-p'o.* London: Jonathan Cape, 1931.

Cleary, Thomas. *Entry into the Inconceivable: An Introduction to Hua-yen Buddhism.* Honolulu: University of Hawaii Press, 1983.

———, trans. *Entry into the Realm of Reality: The Text.* Boston: Shambhala Press, 1989.

———, trans. *The Flower Ornament Scripture: A Translation of the Avatamsaka Sutra.* Boulder: Shambhala Press, 1986.

Conze, Edward., trans. *Buddhist Wisdom Books: The Diamond Sutra and the Heart Sutra.* London: Allen and Unwin, 1958.

Cook, Francis H. *Hua-yen Buddhism: The Jewel Net of Indra.* University Park: Pennsylvania State University Press, 1977.

De Bary, Wm. Theodore, ed. *The Buddhist Tradition in India, China and Japan.* New York: Vintage Books, 1972.

De Bary, Wm. T., and Irene Bloom, eds. *Principles and Practicality: Essays in Neo-Confucianism and Practical Learning.* New York: Columbia University Press, 1979.

Dōgen Zenji. *Shōbōgenzō* [The eye and treasury of the true law], vol. 1. Trans. Kosen Nishiyama and John Stevens. Tokyo: Daihokkaikaku, 1973.

Dumoulin, Heinrich. *The Development of Chinese Zen after the Sixth Patriarch in the Light of Mumonkan.* Trans. Ruth Fuller Sasaki. New York: First Zen Institute of America, 1953.

Egan, Ronald E. *The Literary Works of Ou-yang Hsiu (1007-72).* Cambridge University Press, 1984.

———. "Looking on Curiously: Poet-Monks' Perceptions of Literati Culture." Unpublished paper, 1992.

———. "Ou-yang Hsiu and Su Shih on Calligraphy." *Harvard Journal of Asiatic Studies* 49, no. 2 (1989), pp. 365–420.

———. "Poems on Paintings: Su Shih and Huang T'ing-chien." *Harvard Journal of Asiatic Studies* 43, no. 2 (1983), pp. 413–451.

———. Review of Michael Fuller's *Road to East Slope. Harvard Journal of Asiatic Studies* 52:1 (June 1992), p. 317.

———. *Word, Image and Deed in the Life of Su Shi. Harvard Yenching Institute Monograph Series,* no. 39. Cambridge: 1994.

Eliade, Mircea, editor-in-chief. *The Encyclopedia of Religion.* 16 volumes. New York: Macmillan and Free Press, 1987.

Faure, Bernard. *Chan Insights and Oversights: An Epistemological Critique of the Chan Tradition.* Princeton: Princeton University Press, 1993.

————. *The Rhetoric of Immediacy: A Cultural Critique of Chan/Zen Buddhism.* Princeton: Princeton University Press, 1992.

Feng Ying-liu, comp. *Su Wen-chung Kung shih ho chu.* Printed in 1793.

Foulk, T. Griffith. "Myth, Ritual and Monastic Practice in Sung Ch'an Buddhism." In *Religion and Society in T'ang and Sung China,* ed. Patricia Buckley Ebrey and Peter N. Gregory, pp. 147–208. Honolulu: University of Hawaii Press, 1993.

Franke, Herbert, ed. *Sung Biographies* Wiesbaden: Franz Steiner Verlag, 1976.

Freeman, Michael D. "Loyang and the Opposition to Wang An-shih: The Rise of Confucian Conservatism, 1068–1086." Ph.D. dissertation, Yale University, 1973.

Fuller, Michael. *The Road to East Slope: The Development of Su Shi's Poetic Voice.* Stanford: Stanford University, 1990.

Gardner, Daniel K. *Chu Hsi: Learning to Be a Sage.* Berkeley: University of California Press, 1990.

Giles, Herbert. *An Introduction to the History of Chinese Pictorial Art.* Shanghai, 1905.

Gimello, Robert M. "Ch'an Buddhism, Learning and Letters during the Northern Sung: The Case of Chüeh-fan Hui-hung (1071–1128)." Unpublished paper.

————. "Chih-yen (602–668) and the Foundations of Hua-yen Buddhism." Ph.D. dissertation, Columbia University, 1976.

————. "Mārga and Culture: Learning, Letters, and Liberation in Northern Sung Ch'an." In *Paths to Liberation: the Mārga and Its Transformations in Buddhist Thought,* ed. Robert E. Buswell, Jr., and Robert M. Gimello. Honolulu: University of Hawaii Press, 1992.

Ginsberg, Stanley M. "Alienation and Reconciliation of a Chinese Poet: The Huang-chou Exile of Su Shih." Ph.D. dissertation, University of Wisconsin, 1974.

Girardot, Norman J. "Chinese Religion and Western Scholarship." In *China and Christianity: Historical and Future Encounters,* ed. James D. Whitehead, Yu-ming Shaw, and Norman J. Girardot. Notre Dame: University of Notre Dame Press, 1979.

Graham, A. C. *Chuang-tzu: The Inner Chapters.* London: George Allen & Unwin, 1981.

————. *Two Chinese Philosophers.* London: Lund, Humphries, 1958.

Gregory, Peter N. *Tsung-mi and the Sinification of Buddhism.* Princeton: Princeton University Press, 1991.

Hatch, George. "Su Hsün." In *Sung Biographies,* ed. Herbert Franke, pp. 885–900. Wiesbaden: Franz Steiner Verlag, 1976.

————. "Su Shih." In *Sung Biographies,* ed. Herbert Franke, pp. 900–968. Wiesbaden: Franz Steiner Verlag, 1976.

————. "The Thought of Su Hsün (1009–1066): An Essay on the Social Meaning of Intellectual Pluralism in Northern Sung." Ph.D. dissertation, University of Washington, 1978.

Hervouet, Yves, ed. *A Sung Bibliography.* Hong Kong: The Chinese University Press, 1978.

Ho Peng-yoke. *Astronomical Chapters of the Chin shu.* Paris: Mouton, 1966.

Hu Yün-i. *Sung shih yen-chiu* [Research on Sung poetry]. Hong Kong: Commercial Press, 1959.

Huang, Chi-chiang. "Experiment in Syncretism: Ch'i-sung (1007–1072) and Eleventh-Century Buddhism." Ph.D. dissertation, University of Arizona, 1986.

Huang Min-chih. *Sung tai Fo-chiao she-hui ching-chi shih lun-chi* [Collected studies on the socioeconomic history of Buddhism in the Sung]. Taipei: Taiwan hsüeh-sheng shu-chü, 1989.

Hui-hung. *Leng-chai yeh-hua* [Evening discourses from a cold studio]. Peking: Chung-hua shu-chü, 1988.

————. *Shih men wen-tzu Ch'an* [Stone Gate's literary Ch'an]. *Ssu-pu ts'ung-k'an,* 56.

Hung Po-chao. "Su Shih yü Hui shih ssu-hsiang t'an-hsi" [A discussion of Su Shih's thought during the Hui (Chou) period]. In *Lun Su Shih Ling-nan shih chi ch'i-t'a* [Talks on Su Shih's Ling-nan poetry and other (topics)]. Kuangtung: Kuang-tung jen-min ch'u-pan-she, 1986.

Hurvitz, Leon, trans. *Scripture of the Lotus Blossom of the Fine Dharma.* New York: Columbia University Press, 1976.

Idema, W. L. "Poet Versus Minister and Monk." *T'oung Pao* 73 (1987), pp. 209–216.

Iriya, Yoshitaka. "Chinese Poetry and Zen." *The Eastern Buddhist* 6, no. 1 (May 1973), pp. 54–67.

————. "Tōba mu." *Shinagaku* 12 (1947), pp. 347–352.

Izutsu, Toshihiko. *Toward a Philosophy of Zen Buddhism.* Boulder: Prajna Press, 1982.

Jan Yün-hua. "Ch'i-sung." In *Sung Biographies,* ed. Herbert Franke, pp. 185–194. Wiesbaden: Franz Steiner Verlag, 1976.

Jen Chi-yün. *Chung-kuo che-hsüeh shih.* Peking: Jen-min ch'u-pan-she, 1964.

Kasoff, Ira E. *The Thought of Chang Tsai (1020–1077).* Cambridge: Cambridge University Press, 1984.

Kondō Mitsuo. *So Tōba* [Su Tung-p'o]. *Kanshi taikei,* vol. 17. Tokyo: Shūeisha, 1964.

Kuo P'eng, *Sung Yüan Fo-chiao* [Sung-Yuan Buddhism]. Fukien: Jen-min ch'u-pan-she, 1981.

LaFleur, William R. *The Karma of Words: Buddhism and the Literary Arts in Medieval Japan.* Berkeley: University of California Press, 1983.

Lau, D. C. *Mencius.* New York: Penguin, 1970.

Legge, James, trans. *The Four Books.* New York: Paragon Reprint Corp., 1966.

Levering, Miriam. "Ch'an Enlightenment for Laymen: Ta-hui and the New Religious Culture of the Sung." Ph.D. dissertation, Harvard University, 1978.

Li I-ping, *Su Tung-p'o hsin chuan* [A new biography of Su Tung-p'o]. 2 volumes. Hong Kong: Lien-ching ch'u-pan shih-yeh kung-ssu, 1981.

Lin K'o-t'ang. *Sung ju yü Fo-hsueh* [Sung Confucians and Buddhism]. Taipei: Shang-wu, 1966 reprint of 1928 publication.

Lin Yutang. *The Gay Genius.* New York: John Day, 1947.

Liu Hsin-ju (Xinru). "Buddhist Institutions in the Lower Yangtze Region during the Sung Dynasty." *Bulletin of Sung Yüan Studies* 21 (1989).

Liu I-ch'ing. *A New Account of Tales of the World* [Shih Shuo hsin yü]. Trans. Richard Mather. Minneapolis: University of Minnesota Press, 1976.

Liu I-sheng, ed. *Su Shih shih-hsüan* [Selected poems of Su Shih]. Hong Kong: San-lien shu-tien, 1986.

Liu, James J. Y. *Chinese Theories of Literature.* Chicago: University of Chicago Press, 1959.

———. *Lyricists of the Northern Sung.* (Princeton, N.J.: Princeton University Press, 1974).

———. Review of Burton Watson's *Poetry of Su Tung-p'o. Tsing Hua Journal of Chinese Studies,* new series no. 1 (August 1968).

Liu, James T. C. *China Turning Inward: Intellectual-Political Changes in the Early Twelfth Century.* Cambridge: Published by the Council on East Asian Studies, Harvard University, and distributed by Harvard University Press, 1988.

———. *Ou-yang Hsiu: An Eleventh-Century Neo-Confucian.* Stanford: Stanford University Press, 1967.

———. *Reform in Sung China: Wang An-shih (1021–1086) and His New Policies.* Cambridge: Harvard University Press, 1959.

Liu Nai-ch'ang. *Su Shih hsüan chi* [A selected anthology of Su Shih]. Chi-nan, Shantung: Ch'i-Lü shu-she, 1980.

———, ed. *Su Shih wen-hsüeh lun-chi* [Collected studies on Su Shih's writings]. Chi-nan, Shantung: Ch'i-Lü shu-she, 1982.

Liu Tsai-hsi. *I Kai* [Introduction to the arts]. Shanghai: Shanghai ku-chi ch'u-pan she, 1978.

Lo Hsiang-lin. "Wang T'ang Kuan-hsiu hui shih-liu lo-han ying-chen hsiang shih k'o shu cheng" [A report on the stone carvings of the sixteen great worthy *lohan* painted by Kuan-hsiu of the late T'ang]. *Hsüeh-shu chi-kan* 6, no. 7, pp. 1–9.

Lo Ken-tzu. *Liang Sung wen-hsüeh p'i-p'ing shih* [The history of literary criticism during the two Sungs]. Taipei, 1968.

Lu K'uan-yü (Charles Luk), trans. *The Śūrangama Sūtra (Leng Yen Ching)*. London: Rider and Co., 1966.

Lynn, Richard John. "The Sudden and the Gradual in Chinese Poetry: An Examination of the Ch'an Poetry Analogy." In *Sudden and Gradual: Approaches to Enlightenment in Chinese Thought,* ed. Peter N. Gregory. Kuroda Institute Studies in East Asian Buddhism 5. Honolulu: University of Hawaii Press, 1987.

Makita Tairyō. *Chūgoku kinsei Bukkyōshi kenkyū* [Researches in the history of modern Chinese Buddhism]. Kyoto: Heirakuji shoten, 1957.

Malalasekera, G. P. ed. *Encyclopedia of Buddhism,* vol. 2. (Ceylon: The Government Press, 1966).

March, Andrew L. "Landscape in the Thought of Su Shih." Ph.D. diss., University of Washington, 1964.

———. "Self and Landscape in Su Shih." *Journal of the American Oriental Society* 86, no. 3 (1966), pp. 377–396.

Mochizuki Shinkō. *Shina Jōdo kyōrishi* [A History of Pure Land in China]. Kyoto: Hōzōkan, 1964.

Murck, Christian. "Su Shih's Reading of the *Chung yung*." In *Theories of the Arts in China* ed. Christian Murck and Susan Bush. Princeton: Princeton University Press, 1983.

Nivison, David S. and Arthur F. Wright, eds. *Confucianism in Action.* Stanford: Stanford University Press, 1959.

Ogata, Sohaku, trans. *The Transmission of the Lamp: Early Masters.* Wakefield, N.H.: Longwood Academic, 1990.

Ogawa Tamaki. *So Shoku* [Su Shih]. 2 volumes. *Chūgoku shijin senshū,* 2d series, vols. 5–6. Tokyo: Iwanami, 1973.

———. *Tōdai no shijin sono denki* [Biographies of poets of the T'ang dynasty]. Tokyo: Taishūkan shoten, 1975.

Ogawa Tamaki and Yamamoto Kazuyoshi, trans. *So Tōba shishū* [The collected poetry of Su Tung-p'o]. Tokyo: Chikuma shobō, 1983–.

———. *So Tōba shū* [Su Tung-p'o's collected works]. *Chūgoku bunmei sen,* vol. 2. Tokyo: Asahi Shinbunsha, 1972.

Pollack, David. *Zen Poems of the Five Mountains.* New York: The Crossroad Publishing Company and Scholar Press, 1985.

Ruthuen, K. *Critical Assumptions.* Cambridge: Cambridge University Press, 1979.

Sangharakshita. *The Eternal Legacy.* London: Tharpa Publications, 1985.

Shen Tsung-yüan, ed. *Tung-p'o i-shih* [Anecdotes concerning Tung-p'o]. Shanghai: Commercial Press, 1922.

Shinohara Koichi. "Buddhism and Confucianism in Ch'i-sung's 'Essay on Teaching' [*yüan tao*]." *Journal of Chinese Philosophy* 9, no. 4 (1982), pp. 401–422.

Smith, Kidder, Jr.; Peter K. Bol; Joseph A. Adler; and Don Wyatt. *Sung Dynasty Uses of the I Ching.* Princeton: Princeton University Press, 1990.

So Tōba shishū [The collected poetry of Su Tung-p'o]. Annotated and translated by Iwamizu Kentoku, Venerable Seitan, and Kubo Tenzui. *Zokkoku yaku kanban taisei* series. 6 volumes. Tokyo: Kokumin bunko kankōkai, 1936 reprint of 1931 publication.

Sorenson, Henrik H. "The Life and Times of the Ch'an Master Yün-men Wen-yen." *Acta Orientalia* 49 (1988).

Strong, John S. "The Legend of the Lion-Roarers: A Study of the Buddhist Arhat Piṇḍola Bhāradvāja." *Numen* 26 (June 1979), pp. 50–97.

Su Shih. *Chiao-cheng Ching-chin Tung-p'o wen-chi shih-lüeh* [Annotated selections of Su Shih's prose]. Edited by Lang Yeh. Peking: Wen-hsüeh ku-chi, 1957.

―――. *Su Shih hsüan-chi* [Selected works of Su Shih]. Compiled and edited by Wang Shui-chao. Shanghai: Shanghai ku-chi, 1984.

―――. *Su Shih Ling-nan shih-wen hsüan-chu* [An annotated anthology of Su Shih's Ling-nan poetry and prose]. Annotated by Fan Hui-ling and Chu I-hui, Hai-nan shih-fan hsüeh-yüan ku-chi yen-chiu shih. Peking: Pei-ching shih-fan ta-hsüeh ch'u-pan-she, 1990.

―――. *Su Shih lun wen-i* [Su Shih on literature and art]. Compiled by Yen Chung-ch'i Peking: Pei-ching ch'u-pan-she, 1985.

Su Shih hsüan-chi [A selected anthology of Su Shih]. Edited and annotated by Wang Shui-chao. Shanghai: Ku-chi ch'u-pan-she, 1984.

Su Shih yen-chiu chuan-k'an [A special issue on Su Shih research]. *Ssu-ch'uan ta-hsüeh hsüeh-pao ts'ung-k'an* 6 (1980).

Su Tung-p'o i-shih hui-pien [Collected anecdotes about Su Shih]. Compiled by Yen Chung-ch'i. Hunan: Yüeh-lu shu-she, 1984.

Suzuki Chusei, "Sōdai Bukkyō kessha no kenkyū" [Researches on the Buddhist associations of the Sung dynasty]. *Shigaku zasshi* 52 (1941).

Suzuki, D. T. *Studies in the Lankavatara Sutra.* London: George Routledge and Sons, 1932.

Swanson, Paul L. *Foundations of T'ien-t'ai Philosophy: The Flowering of the Two Truths Theory in Chinese Buddhism* (Berkeley, California: Asian Humanities Press, 1989.

Takakusu, Junjirō. *The Essentials of Buddhist Philosophy.* Edited by W. T. Chan and Charles A. Moore. Honolulu: University of Hawaii, 1947.

Tao Yüan. *Ching-te ch'uan-teng lu* [The record of the transmission of the lamp published in the Ching-te era]. 30 chüan. (Completed in 1004). *T* 51:196–467.

Thurman, Robert A. F., trans. *The Holy Teaching of Vimalakīrti.* University Park and London: Pennsylvania State University Press, 1976.

Tomlonovic, Kathleen M. "Poetry of Exile and Return: A Study of Su Shih (1037–1101)." Ph.D. diss., University of Washington, 1989.

Ts'an-ning. *Sung kao seng chuan* [Sung biographies of eminent monks]. 3 volumes. Peking: Chung-hua shu-chü, 1987 reprint.

Ts'ao Shu-min. "Su Tung-p'o yü Tao Fo chih kuan-hsi" [The relationship between Su Tung-p'o and Taoism and Buddhism]. In *Kuo-li Chung-li t'u-shu-kuan kuan-k'an,* 3, nos. 3 and 4 (October 1970), pp. 34–55.

Tseng Tsao-chuang. *Su Shih p'ing-chuan* [Critical biography of Su Shih]. Ch'eng-tu: Ssu-ch'uan jen-min ch'u-pan-she, 1981.

———, ed. *San Su wen-i ssu-hsiang* [The literary thought of the three Su's]. Ch'eng-tu: Ssu-ch'uan wen-i ch'u-pan-she, 1985.

Tsuchida, Tomoaki. *Mind and Reality: A Study of the "Shoulengyanjing."* Ph.D. dissertation, Harvard University, 1986.

Tu Sung-po. *Ch'an yü shih* [Chan and poetry]. Taipei: Hung-tao wen-hua, 1970.

Tu, Wei-ming. *Centrality and Commonality: An Essay on Confucian Religiousness.* Albany, N.Y.: State University of New York Press, 1989.

Tung-p'o yen-chiu lun-ts'ung [Studies of Su Tung-p'o]. Third collection in the series *Su Shih yen-chiu lun-wen chi* [Collected articles on Su Shih]. Ch'eng-tu: Ssu-ch'uan wen-i, 1986.

Waley, Arthur. *An Introduction to the History of Chinese Painting.* New York: Grove Press, 1958.

Wang Chih-yüan. *Sung ch'u T'ien-t'ai Fo-hsüeh k'uei yao* [Aspects of T'ien-t'ai Buddhism in the early Sung]. Peking: Chung-kuo chien-she ch'u-pan-she, 1989.

Ware, James R. *Alchemy, Medicine and Religion in the China of* A.D. *320: The Nei P'ien of Ko Hung.* Cambridge, Mass.: The M.I.T. Press, 1966.

Watson, Burton. "Buddhism in the Poetry of Po Chü-i." *Eastern Buddhist,* new series vol. 21, no. 1 (Spring 1988).

———. *Chinese Rhyme-Prose.* New York: Columbia University Press, 1971.

————, trans. *The Complete Works of Chuang Tzu*. New York: Columbia University Press, 1968.

————, trans. *Su Tung-p'o: Selections from a Sung Dynasty Poet*. New York: Columbia University Press, 1965.

Weinstein, Stanley. *Buddhism under the T'ang*. Cambridge: Cambridge University Press, 1987.

Welch, Holmes. *The Practice of Chinese Buddhism: 1900–1950*. Cambridge: Harvard University Press, 1968.

Williams, Paul. *Mahāyāna Buddhism: The Doctrinal Foundations*. London and New York: Routledge, 1989.

Wu Lu-shan et al., eds. *Su Shih shih hsüan chu* [An annotated anthology of the poetry of Su Shih]. Tientsin, Shantung: Pai-hua wen-i ch'u-pan-she, 1982.

Yampolsky, Philip, trans. *The Platform Sutra of the Sixth Patriarch*. New York: Columbia University Press, 1967.

Yang, Vincent. *Nature and Self: A Study of the Poetry of Su Dongpo with Comparisons to the Poetry of William Wordsworth*. New York: Peter Lang, 1989.

Yoshikawa Kōjirō. *An Introduction to Sung Poetry*. Translated by Burton Watson. Cambridge: Harvard University Press, 1967.

————. "So Tōba no bungaku to Bukkyō" [Su T'ung-po's writings and Buddhism]. In *Tsukamoto hakushi shōju kinen Bukkyō shigaku ronshū*, pp. 939–950. Kyoto: Research Institute for Humanistic Studies, 1961.

Yu Hsin-li. *Su Tung-p'o te wen-hsüeh li-lun* [The literary theories of Su Tung-p'o]. Taipei: Hsüeh-sheng shu-chü, 1981.

GLOSSARY

An-kuo ssu	安國寺	ch'i Fo	欺佛
chai	齋	Chi Hsien	季鹹
Chang An-tao	張安道	chi-lin	麒麟
Chang Fang-p'ing	張方平	Chi Yün	紀昀
Chang Hsüan	張宣	Chia Tao	賈島
Chang Nan-pen	張南本	Chia-yu ssu	嘉佑寺
Chang Shang-ying	張商英	Chiang-hu feng-yüeh	江湖風月
Chang-shui Huai-yüan	長水懷遠	chiao	教
Chang Tsai	張載	Chiao-jan	皎然
Ch'ang-ts'ung	常聰	chieh	戒
Chao-jan t'ai	超然台	ch'ieh	切
Ch'en Chi-ch'ang	陳季常	chich-fa	捷法
Ch'en Chi-ju	陳繼儒	Ch'ien Ch'ien-i	錢謙益
Ch'en Han-ch'ing	陳漢卿	chien-hsing	見性
chen-hsin	真心	Chih-i	智顗
chen-k'ung kuan-fa	真空觀法	Chih-li	知禮
Ch'en Kung-pi	陳公弼	*Ch'ih-pi fu*	赤壁賦
Ch'en Shu-ku	陳述古	Chih-yüan	智圓
Ch'eng Hao	程顥	*Chin-kang k'o-i*	金剛科儀
Ch'eng I	程頤	*pao-chüan*	寶卷
Ch'eng-kuan	澄觀	Ch'in Kuan	秦觀
Ch'eng-t'ien ssu	承天寺	*Chin-kuang-ming ching*	金光明經
Cheng Yin	鄭隱	chin-shih	進士
ch'i	氣	ch'ing	輕
chi-feng	機鋒	ch'ing	清

241

Ching-hsing she	淨行社	Fan-chen	梵臻
Ch'ing-liang ssu	清涼寺	Fan Chung-yen	範仲淹
Ch'ing-shun	清順	fang-shih	方士
Ching-te ch'uan-teng lu	景德傳燈錄	Feng Meng-chen	馮夢真
Ching-t'u tz'u-pei chi	淨土慈悲集	Fo	佛
Ching-yin Ch'an ssu	淨因禪寺	Fo-kuo	佛國
Ching-yüan	淨源	*Fo-tsu t'ung-chi*	佛祖統紀
chou-pien han-jung kuan	周遍含融觀	Fo-t'u-teng	佛圖澄
		Fo-yin Liao-yüan	佛印了元
Chou Tun-i	周敦頤	Hai-yüeh Hui-pien	海月惠辯
chu	住	Han Ch'i	韓琦
Chu Hsi	朱熹	Han-lin	翰林
Chü Meng	劇孟	Han Shan	寒山
Ch'u-ming	楚明	Han T'ui-chih	韓退之
ch'u shih	出世	Han Yü	韓愈
ch'u shih-chien fa	出世間法	Hsiang-fu ssu	祥符寺
Chu Shou-ch'ang	朱壽昌	Hsiang-lin Ch'eng-yüan	香林澄遠
Chu Yao	朱瑤	Hsiao-pen	小本
Ch'u Yuan	屈原	Hsieh Chin-ch'en	謝晉臣
Chuang-tzu	莊子	Hsieh Ling-yün	謝靈運
Chüeh-fan Hui-hung	覺範惠洪	hsin-ching	心精
ch'un	純	hsing	興
Chung Lai-yin	鍾來因	Hsing-k'ung	性空
Chung-shu	仲殊	Hsü Chang-ju	徐長孺
Chung yung	中庸	Hsüan-tsang	玄奘
Fa-chieh kuan-men	法界觀門	Hsüeh-feng I-ts'un	雪峰義存
Fa-tsang	法藏	Hsüeh-tou Chung-hsien	雪竇重顯
Fa-yen	法眼	*Hua-yen ching*	華嚴經
Fa-yen Wen-i	法眼文益	Huan-chung	寰中
Fa-yün Fa-hsiu	法雲法秀	Huang-lung	黃龍
Fa-yün Shan-pen	法雲善本	Huang-lung Hui-nan	黃龍慧南
Fa-yün ssu	法雲寺	Huang T'ing-chien	黃庭堅
Fan Chen (Ching-jen)	範鎮 (景仁)	*Huang-t'ing ching*	黃庭經

hui	慧	Kuo-i Fa-ch'in	國一法欽
Hui-ch'in	慧勤	Lao-tzu	老子
Hui-jih	慧日	*Leng-yen ching*	楞嚴經
Hui-lin Tsung-pen	慧林宗本	li	理
Hui-neng	慧能	li (calligraphy)	隸
Hui-ssu	慧思	Li I-p'ing	李一平
Hui-yin ssu	慧因寺	Li K'ang-nien	李康年
Hui-yüan	慧遠	Li Kou	李購
i	意	Li Kung-lin	李公麟
i-hsin	一心	*Li Sao*	離騷
I-hsüan	義玄	li-shih wu-ai kuan	理事無礙觀
I-t'ien	義天	Li Yüan	李源
Jen-yüeh	仁岳	Liang-chieh	良價
Ju-lai tsang	如來藏	Liao-hsing	了性
ju shih	入世	Lin-chi	臨濟
K'ai-hsien Ch'ih-tao	開先遲道	Ling Meng-ch'u	凌蒙初
K'ai-yüan ssu	開元寺	Liu Ching-ch'en	劉景臣
Kao Hsien	高閑	Liu Hsi-tsai	劉臨載
K'o-chiu	可久	Liu Nai-ch'ang	劉乃昌
Ko Hung	葛洪	Liu Ts'ung-yüan	柳宗元
K'o-ming	可明	Liu Yen	劉燮
kuan	觀	*Lo-pang wen-lei*	樂邦文類
Kuan-hsiu (Ch'an-yüeh)	貫休（禪月）	Lo Yüeh	樓鑰
Kuan-shi-yin	觀世音	*lohan*	羅漢
Kuan-ting	灌頂	Lu Shu-sheng	陸樹聲
Kuan-yin	觀音	*Lung-shu tseng-kuang*	龍舒增廣
Kuang-ai ssu	廣愛寺	*Ching-t'u wen*	淨土文
k'uang-yen i-yü	狂言逸語	Lung-t'an Huai-cheng	籠潭懷證
Kuei-feng Tsung-mi	圭峰宗密	Ma-tsu Tao-i	馬祖道一
Kuei-shan Ling-yu	溈山靈佑	Mei Yao-ch'en	梅堯臣
Kuei-yang	偽仰	miao-miao wen-hsin	妙妙聞心
k'ung	空	Ming-chiao Ch'i-sung	明教契嵩
kung-an	公案	Ming-chih	明智

Ming-hsing	明性	Shou-ch'in	守欽
Mo-ho chih-kuan	摩訶止觀	*Shou leng-yen ching*	首楞嚴經
Mu-chou Ch'en-tsun-su	睦州陳尊宿	*ho-lun*	合論
Nan-hua (ching)	南華(經)	Shou-sheng ssu	受生寺
Nan-hua ssu	南華寺	shui ching	水鏡
nei-tan	内丹	shui-lu chai	水陸齋
nien	念	shui-lu tao-ch'ang	水陸道場
Nien-fo pai-wen	念佛百問	shun	順
nung ch'iao ch'eng cho	弄巧成拙	*Ssu-fen lü*	四分律
Ou-yang Hsiu	歐陽修	Ssu-ma Kuang	司馬光
Pai-chang	百丈	Su Ch'e	蘇轍
Pao-chüeh	寶覺	Su Hsün	蘇洵
Pao-p'u-tzu	抱樸子	Su Kuo	蘇過
Pao-yüeh chi	寶月集	Su Shih	蘇軾
Pi-yen lu	碧巖錄	Su Tung-p'o	蘇東坡
Pien-ts'ai Yüan-ching	辯才元淨	Sun Chih-wei	孫知微
p'ing-tan	平淡	Ta-chüeh Huai-lien	大覺懷璉
Po Chü-i	白居易	Ta-kuan Chen-k'o	達觀真可
pu-chu	不住	*Ta-sheng ch'i-hsin lun*	大乘起信論
pu wang sheng	不往生	T'an-chao	曇照
san-hsüeh	三學	T'an-luan	曇鸞
shan-chia	山家	T'ang Wen-hsien	湯文獻
Shan-tao	善導	*tao*	道
shan-wai	山外	Tao-ch'ien	道潛
Shan-yu	陝右	Tao-cho	道綽
she-sheng ch'u-sheng	捨生處生	Tao-hsüan	道宣
sheng	生	*tao-hsüeh*	道學
Sheng-ch'ang	省常	*Tao-te-ching*	道德經
shi	事	Tao-yüan	道元
shih-chien fa	世間法	T'ao Yüan-ming	陶淵明
Shih K'o	石恪	T'ien-chu ssu	天竺寺
Shih-p'ing	詩評	T'ien-t'ai	天台
shih-shih wu-ai	事事無礙	ting	定

Ts'an-liao	參寥	Wang Wen-tu	王文度
Ts'an-ning	贊寧	wang-yen	忘言
Ts'ao-tung	曹洞	Wei-chien	惟簡
Tsun-shih	遵式	Wei-lin	維琳
Tsung Ching	宗鏡	wen	文
Tsung-hsiao	宗曉	*wen-hsüeh*	文學
Tu Shun	杜順	*wen-tzu Ch'an*	文字禪
tun	敦	Wen-ya Wei-qing	文雅惟慶
Tung Chung-shu	董仲舒	Wen Yen-po	文彥博
Tung-lin Ch'ang-tsung	東林常總	wu	無
Tung-p'o Ch'an-hsi chi	東坡禪喜集	wu	悟
Tung-p'o chü-shih	東坡居士	Wu-ch'ing	悟清
Fo-yin ch'an yü-lu	佛印禪語	Wu-en	晤恩
wen-ta	錄問答	Wu Fu-ku	吳復古
Tung-p'o jou	東坡肉	wu-hsiang	無想
Tung-shan Hsiao-ts'ung	洞山曉聰	wu-hsin	無心
Tzu-hsüan	子璿	Wu-k'ai	悟開
tzu-jan	自然	Wu Tao-tzu	吳道子
Tz'u-min	慈愍	wu-tso	無作
Tzu-ssu	子思	Wu-tzu Chieh	五租戒
wai-tan	外丹	Wu Tzu-yeh	吳子野
Wang An-shih	王安石	wu-wei	無爲
Wang Chao-yün	王朝雲	wu-yen	無言
Wang Fu	王弗	Yang Hui-chih	楊惠之
Wang Heng	王珩	Yang Shih	楊時
wang-hsin	妄心	Yeh Meng-te	葉夢德
Wang Jih-hsiu	王日休	Yen Chün-p'ing	嚴君平
Wang Ta-nien	王大年	Yen-tzu	顏子
Wang Tan	王旦	yin huo	陰火
Wang T'an-chih	王坦之	yu	有
Wang Tzu-jung	王子榮	Yu Hsin-li	游信利
Wang Wei	王維	yü-lu	語錄
Wang Wen-kao	王文高	Yüan-chao	元照

yüan chüeh	圓覺	Yüan-wu K'o-ch'in	圓悟克勤
Yüan-chüeh ching	圓覺經	yüeh-fu	樂府
Yüan-jen lun	原人論	Yün-men	雲門
Yüan-tse	圓澤	Yün-men Wen-yen	雲門文偃
Yüan-t'ung Chu-no	圓通居訥	Yung-ming Yen-shou	永明延壽

INDEX

247

ABOUT THE AUTHOR

BEATA GRANT received her Ph.D. in Chinese literature from Stanford University and is currently teaching Chinese language, literature, and religion at Washington University in St. Louis. In addition to her work on Su Shih, she has published on the subject of women in Chinese religious literature. She is presently working on the topic of women's religious experience in Late Imperial China.

Production Notes

Composition and paging were done on the
Quadex Composing System and typesetting
on the Compugraphic 8400 by the design
and production staff of University of
Hawaii Press.

The text typeface is Times Roman and
the display typeface is Optima.

Offset presswork and binding were done by
The Maple-Vail Book Manufacturing Group.
Text paper is Glatfelter Offset Vellum,
basis 50.